Understanding Karl Rahner
Volume 2

The Mystery of Man and the Foundations of a Theological System

Understanding Karl Rahner
Volume 2

George Vass

IN MEMORY OF
REV. DANIEL E. FINN

Christian Classics
Westminster
and
Sheed & Ward
London

ISBN 0-87061-116-X
ISBN 0-7220-9322-5

Nihil obstat Charles Acton, S.T.L., Censor
Imprimatur +David Konstant, Bishop in Central London, Westminster,
5 March 1985

First published in 1985 by:

Sheed & Ward Ltd
2 Creechurch Lane   *and*
London, EC3A 5AQ

Christian Classics Inc
P.O. Box 30
Westminster, MD 21157

Filmset by Witwell Ltd, Liverpool.
Printed and bound in Great Britain by A. Wheaton & Co. Ltd, Exeter.

Contents

vi

Introduction

Rahner never produced an all-embracing system of Christian beliefs. Hence it is not easy to indicate the kernel of his work on which a coherent system of Christian doctrines could be built up. Nonetheless, any student of his writings will suspect that there *is* such a kernel to his thought. Now this could mean a matrix constantly present at every crucial point of his writing; it could mean a strategy or choice of method; or it could mean a central tenet or doctrine to which every particular subject in hand is referred. We shall endeavour to identify this kernel under each of these three aspects.

This attempt leads us into the scope of this present volume. Our question is not primarly concerned with theories of science (*Wissensnschaftstheorien*) as applicable to Rahner's theological writings.[1] To ask about the scientific status of positions and statements would inevitably lead us away from our secondary purpose which is still, to a certain extent, a comprehensive presentation of our author. Our aim lies in between a critical analysis and a straightforward (almost lexicographical) presentation of Rahner's thought.[2]

I shall call this latter – intermediary – aspect the search for a *systematic truth (Systemwahrheit)*.[3] By this I mean that truth-value which accrues to any single statement on account of its position within a more or less closed system. It will be presupposed that no single statement stands on its own: it is a part of a group of statements. As Newman affirmed in his essay on the development of doctrine, one accepts the whole body of ecclesiastical dogmas or none at all.[4] What he supposed was not only the inner coherence of these christian doctrines, but also their dynamic unfolding nature – the 'Idea' of Christianity. Now this dynamic and unfolding nature of truth can also be applied to the thought of a systematic theologian, like Rahner. The coherence of doctrines (for the time being abstracting from their truth-claim) can, on an objective level, easily be shown. Yet they are built on the decision of the theologian: which of the manifold aspects he takes as the cornerstone of his theology, from where he would set off in thinking out Christianity. Thus it must have been an agonising question for Schleiermacher, the father of modern systematic theology, whether he would deal first with Christ, the redeemer, or with God, the creator.[5] And when Karl Barth turned the tables on his life-long 'enemy-friend', Schleiermacher, in starting his *Church Dogmatics* with the doctrine of the Word of God, disguised as the trinitarian position of Christianity, we have to do with a free decision of a systematician.[6] No doubt Barth's decision was motivated by the thrust of his whole theological thought in reacting against protestant liberalism. But this motivation would not be understandable had it not come from a certain matrix of thought about encountering the christian message, in which he must have perceived the possibilities of thinking and writing about it. So the searcher for a systematic truth first and foremost assesses the theologian himself before proceeding to weigh up the scientific value of his statements or presenting in detail his various positions. The theologian is a free agent who, because aware of his possibilities as a theologian, decides or chooses the strategy according to which he is going to proceed, and as a result of his commitment to this latter, moulds his own explicit positions.

All this is, I believe, applicable to Rahner as a systematic theologian. In order to establish the core of his theology we must first ask ourselves what is the central tenet which rules his thought. This will inevitably lead us to work out how everything else is related to this central point. Considering the way theological topics are related to this central tenet will, secondly, yield two important insights: we shall be able, on the one hand, to assess his strategy in choosing the explicit method which pervades his theological writings and, on the other, to uncover those subsidiary principles by means of which he strives to arrive at a coherent system in presenting Christianity. Thirdly, only at the end of our considerations shall we be in a position to spot that personal motivating force, the matrix out of which his thinking at every point of the system is moulded. Both the central doctrine and the matrix of thought are constantly present when the theologian applies his method to any theological subject-matter: the first as point of reference and the other as the basic inspiration. Although the strategy and the explicit method are not deducible from either of these, their conscious choice may or may not influence the very content of what the central doctrine purports to assert and how the matrix of thought lets itself be defined. In Rahner's case, it will be up to us to judge whether his methodological choice dictates the central doctrine and yields the matrix of his underlying thought, or whether it is the other way round, the preferred strategy being dictated by the personal inspiration and its objective counterpart, the central doctrine. In the first case, the methodological tail might wag the theological content, and in the other *vice versa*. In the first case it is very likely that an a priori choice of strategy and method will be unamenable to theological content and in the second we are likely to witness the unfolding of a theological system which, though the logical coherence may be impaired, will reflect a more genuine understanding of Christianity by a theological thinker.

For those who are acquainted with Schleiermacher's and Barth's theological edifices, our abstract introduction will not be amiss, nor will mention of that problem which is going to plague us in the discussion of Rahner's fundamental theology. Schleiermacher's *The Christian Faith*[7] is an apt example of a most coherent system where the methodological choice predetermines the unfolding presentation of Christianity. This method assumes that theology can only coherently speak of subject matters which are somehow present in man's consciousness. The analysis of consciousness will be his selected method, from which starting point, the feeling of absolute dependence, *alias* God-consciousness, is the only available entry to theology. It is in accordance with this that the rest of Christian doctrines will be unfolded or truncated to the very end of the system, causing a late interpreter, Brunner, to point to Schleiermacher's basic, and for him inadmissible, mysticism as the matrix of his thought.[8] *Mutatis mutandis*, the same could be said of the *Systematic Theology* of his twentieth century follower, Tillich.[9] At the other end of the scale, Barth's monumental *Church Dogmatics* could be understood in an opposite way. Its central doctrine, the Word of the Trinitarian God, is the point of reference for any theological discourse, and this is ultimately motivated by his deep seated conviction of man's incapacity to speak about God, unless God speaks of himself. In relating other doctrines of Christianity to this basic tenet, Barth will apply different methods which, though impairing the lucidity and logical sequence of his system, make his *Church Dogmatics* a genuine witness to Christianity as presented in a modern world. Our question is, which one of these two roughly sketched ways will Rahner's own theological thought follow?

In anticipation we can say that Rahner's central theological tenet seems to be connected with something already known from his philosophical theology: God the Mystery.[10] It was the point of arrival of his ontoligico-metaphysical thought and one of its basic implications will be the point of departure in founding theology. If God is the absolute Mystery, so is man a mystery to himself. Thus the mystery of man, being the central doctrine of his theology, will yield on the one hand a strategy verbalized in an explicit methodology and, on the other, a subsidiary principle which allows him consequently to build up a kind of anthropologically orientated theological system. At the beginning of his career as a theologian this principle will be sighted and named as the *supernatural existential*, whereas the former will be summed up later under the title of anthropological conversion (*die anthropologische Wende*) of theology. The combination of this strategy, dangerously similar to that followed in philosophy, will be expressed as the method of transcendental theology or – hermeneutics – whilst the central doctrine, God the mystery, will allow him to deal within the confines of propaedeutics with such basic Christian tenets as grace and man's coming to faith. Is the invention of the Supernatural Existential the dictate of a formerly implicit strategy then explicit methodology, or is it the other way round, that this subsidary principle is the basis of his method in theology? This question has yet to be answered. However, whatever our answer, at the end of our work it will be shown that the constant matrix of Rahner's developing thought apparently remains the same. In anticipation of what we shall expound in subsequent volumes, we can name it: the experience of grace, the mediated immediacy of

God to every individual throughout history.

In this present volume, however, we shall have to restrict ourselves to topics preliminary to the explicit and categorial teaching of Christianity: Rahner's fundamental theology is but an access to fully-fledged Christian faith. Yet it anticipates strictly revealed tenets and does not confine itself to reasoned apologetics arguing the obligation of man to accept the mysteries of revelation. These doctrines are formally present in our minds without strict material and dogmatic content: they affect human consciousness, since they draw upon the simple everyday experience of being human and, as such, being called to the vision of God.

In what follows, we shall forgo the chronological presentation of Rahner's ideas and start with what we believe to be his central doctrine, insofar as it is implied in his whole theological strategy and suggests his explicit method (1). Only after this shall we point out with Rahner why man, as he lives in his concrete history, is a mystery to himself (2). In order to explain the origin or eventually the consequence of this strategy, we shall discuss an all important insight which, though subject to subsequent development, will serve him as a subsidiary principle at the threshold of technical theology: the Supernatural Existential (3). With the help of these premises, we shall then turn to their application, apparently anticipated from doctrinal yet dealt within fundamental theology: to grace (4) and to man's coming-to-faith (5). Man is a mystery to himself because he is called to salvation. But this call is more than an offer, in a way it is already at work within him, whether he knows it or not. To what man is called is here only indicated, as in his philosophical theology, by the blanket term of 'the vision', yet it will be unpacked in the pattern of christian doctrines coming to us through God's revelation alone. This will be the topic of our subsequent volumes.

The reader will find that in trying to work out what we have called the systematic truth in Rahner's writings, the present author seems, as compared with the first volume of this series, to be more critically distancing himself from the system he is discussing. This is intentional, not, however, to oppose Rahner's fundamental theology as a whole, but rather to establish a friendly dialogue in order to extract a counter-position which, we believe, will make both Rahner's and our own theology more understandable. A more or less coherent system of thought (such as Rahner's) can only be assessed, improved upon or even bypassed from the standpoint of an, at least, slightly divergent system. This precisely is our goal.

Table of Abbreviations

Inspiration	*Inspiration in the Bible*, London and New York 1961 (ET of *Ueber die Scriftsinspiration*, Freiburg-im-Breisgau 1958)
'Integration'	*'Revelation, B: Theological Integration', *SM* V, 348–55 and 358f
Investigations	*Theological Investigations*, 20 vols., London, Baltimore and New York, 1961ff (ET of *Schriften*)
IPQ	*International Philosophical Quarterly*
ITQ	*Irish Theological Quarterly*, Dublin 1951ff (n.s.)
'Justification'	*'Questions of Controversial Theology on Justification', *Investigations* IV, 189–225
'Kerygma'	'Kerygma und Dogma' *MS* I, 622–703
LTK	*Lexikon für Theologie und Kirche*, 10 vols, ed. J. Höfer K. Rahner, Freiburg-im-Breisgau 1957–65^2
'Methodology'	*'Reflections on Methodology in Theology', *Investigations* XI, 68–114
MS	*Mysterium Salutis*, 5 vols., ed. Foirer, Löhrer et al., Einsiedeln 1965ff
MSR	*Mélanges scientifiques et religieux*,
'Mystery'	*'Mystery', *SM* IV, 133–6
'Nature'	*'Nature and Grace', *Investigations* IV, 165–88
NRT	*Nouvelle revue théologique*, Tournai-Louvain 1879ff
NS	*New Scholasticism*
'Order'	*'Order, III: Supernatural Order', *SM* IV, 297–300
Orient	*Orientierung*
PhJb	*Philosophische Jahrbuch*
PJ	*Philosophical Journal*
PL	*Patrologiae cursus completus, series Latina*, ed. J.P. Migne, Paris 1844ff
'Potentia'	*'Potentia Oboedientialis', *SM* V, 65f
Problem	*Das Problem der Hominisation*, Freiburg-im-Bresigau 1961 (ET: *Hominisation*)
'Problems'	*'Reflections on the Problems Involved in Devising a Short Formula of the Faith', *Investigations* XI, 230–44
PT	*Philosophy Today*

RAM	*Revue d'ascétique et de mystère*, Toulouse 1920ff
'Relationship'	*'Concerning the Relationship between Nature and Grace', Investigations* I, 296–317
Revelation	**Revelation and Tradition*, London and New York 1966 (ET of *Offenbarung und Ueberlieferung*)
RGG	*Religion in Geschichte und Gegenwart*, ed. K. Galling, Tübingen 1956³ff
RSR	*Recherches de science religieuse*, Paris 1910ff
SCG	St Thomas Aquinas, *Summa contra gentiles*
Schol	*Scholastik*, Freiburg-im-Breisgau 1926ff
Schriften	**Schriften für Theologie*,20 vols.,Einsiedeln 19 ff (ET: *Investigations*)
'Sin of Adam'	**'Sin of Adam', Investigations* XI, 247–62
SM	*Sacramentum Mundi*
Spirit	**Spirit in the World*, London and New York 1968 (ET of *Geist²*)
ST	St Thomas Aquinas, *Summa theologiae*
SZ	*Stimmen der Zeit*, Freiburg-im-Breisgau 1871ff
TG	*Theologie und Glaube*, Paderborn 1909ff
Thom	*The Thomist*, Washington (D.C.) 1939ff
Tht	*Thought*
Todes	**Zur Theologie des Todes*, Freiburg-im-Breisgau 1958 (ET: *Death*)
TQ	*Theologische Quartalschrift*, Tübingen 1819ff
TR	*Theologische Rundschau*, Tübingen 1897ff
'Transcendental'	**'Transcendental Theology', SM* VI, 287–9
TS	*Theological Studies*, Baltimore 1940ff
TT	*Tijdschrift voor Theologie*, Nijmegen 1961ff
'Uncreated'	'Some Implications of the Scholastic Concept of Uncreated Grace', *Investigations* I, 315–46
Visions	**Visions and Prophecies*, London and New York 1963 (ET of *Visionen und Prophezeihungen*, Freiburg-im-Breisgau 1960)
WW	*Wissenschaft und Weisheit*, Düsseldorf 1934ff
ZFPT	*Zeitschrift für freiburger Philosophie und Theologie*
ZKT	*Zeitschrift für katholische Theologie*, Innsbruck 1877ff
ZPT	*Zeitschrift für Philosophie und Theologie*

*An asterisk denotes an article or book by Karl Rahner himself. Note that, for quicker and easier reference by the reader, abbreviations for his works take the form of single key words, whereas standard acronymic abbreviations have been adopted for all periodicals and works by other authors (or works by Karl Rahner in association with other authors).

Understanding Karl Rahner
Volume 2

Chapter 1

The Mystery of Man

Main literature
'Anthropology' (*Investigations* IX, 28–45 = *Schriften* VIII, 43–65);
'Methodology' (*Investigations* XI, 68–114 = *Schriften* IX, 89–126);
'Transcendental', *SM* VI, 287–9

Rahner's theology of God's word rebounds on man himself. In the stage preparatory to the encounter with the word, man, transcendentally of course, discovers in himself a hardly definable potency for God (*potentia oboedientialis*), as well as an a priori obligation to listen to God's historical word. Thus not only is God *the* Mystery to which all aspects of human life are attuned, but also man, in facing the Mystery of God's self-communication, is a mystery to himself. To put it in other words: Rahner's theology is built upon the mystery (now with a lower-case initial) of man.

Fischer, in his eminent study, selects this view as the key to Rahner's whole theological thought.[1] He is correct. At the very heart of Rahner's writings there is the tacit assumption of man's incomprehensibility. That God in himself is the Mystery who communicates himself in words and deeds was registered as a turning point in Rahner's advance from a philosophical to a theological viewpoint. Undoubtedly, the substitution of God the Mystery for the philosophical IPSUM ESSE has been subservient to a mystagogical motive. Yet the real motive in the change of terminology is a conversion to man, *eine anthropologische Wende*, which turns our attention from God, from his existence and historical words and deeds, from his self-communication in history, to man as he concretely experiences himself in his own incomprehensibility.

1

This thought-pattern also underlies his spiritual writing. 'I am as I am', he writes in a retreat given to priests, 'inescapably the known-unknown, as the being-present-to-itself and as that which is in control of itself'. The reader acquainted with his philosophy will recognise the *Bei-sich-sein* of the early books now transposed to another context. In almost the next sentence Rahner goes on to say, 'if man is really referred to God he can never "become clear" to himself.' We can hear the intimation of man's incomprehensibility. Indeed, his rhetorical exclamation, 'How incomprehensible it really is!', is followed by a warning to the effect that man must never make himself comfortable in the comprehensibility of his own existence. This would lead us to suspect that his retreatants were being confronted with God the Mystery. Yet, as he says, when we 'blissfully' accept this incomprehensible Mystery of God we pronounce our 'yes' not only to it, but to ourselves: 'then we have said "yes" to the incomprehensibility *of our own existence*'.[2]

Man is therefore a mystery because he is essentially related to the ever greater Mystery which is God in his self-communication by means of his word. Man is also a mystery because God's call has entered the very structure of his created being, and has radically relativised his knowledge of himself. He can find his own self in what is strictly speaking not his own. This is why man's own self-disclosure has to be the half-way house on his way towards disclosure of God and his concrete word.

In the following section we propose to discuss the significance of this *anthropological conversion*: Does it mean a change in the subject-matter of theology from God to man (1), or is it rather only a *methodological device* which can give a coherent structure to the whole of theology (2)? Our comments and questions (3) will appreciate this method in its basic trend, yet they will try to improve upon its underlying pattern and propose a slightly divergent approach to theology.

1.1 The Anthropological Conversion

It is in a programmatic lecture delivered in 1966 in a theological symposium at St Xavier College, Chicago, and published in the form of an article in the following year, that Rahner explains his own mode of theologizing. 'Theology and Anthropology' appears in the important eighth volume of the *Schriften* and is translated in the ninth of *Investigations*. It is explicit about that turning-point in theology which hitherto implicitly characterized Rahner's whole strategy in his approach to the mystery of God and the mysteries of Christian faith. Theology also as strict dogmatics is based on an anthropology of a transcendental type:

> Therefore, he writes, if one wishes to pursue dogmatics as transcendental anthropology it means that whenever one is confronted with an object of dogma, one inquires as to the conditions necessary for it to be known by the theological subject, ascertaining that the *a priori* conditions for knowledge of the object are satisfied, and showing that they imply and express something about the object, the mode, methods and limits of knowing it.[3]

In other words, any theological investigation implicitly enhances man's knowledge of himself: theology is basically anthropology. This is what is called, the 'anthropological conversion', the *anthropologische Wende*.

We are going to consider this position by restricting ourselves to the presentation of the above mentioned article. It is a position adequately prepared by his earlier views and repeatedly expanded in his later writings.[4] The article, as indicated, proposes a programme vaguely similar to Bultmann's theology in Continental Protestant circles. Rahner is aware of his kinship with Bultmann: he assumed, at that time, that Bultmann's theology was prevailing over Barth's positivism of revelation. He opts for the truth-element contained in the theological liberalism and rationalism of European Protestant theology.[5] This is, of course, not a wholesale adaptation of Bultmann's method. Rahner has his own *praesupposita* alien to Protestant liberalism. Yet the result, if not the same, will be similar to this school of thought. Just as this latter, Rahner will aim at pointing out the *antecedent correspondence* between what man is and what is going to happen to him in the process of his salvation.[6] The vehicle of this discovery is man's self-experience, qualified now explicitly as transcendental experience – or the experience of grace.

In order to argue the necessity of this anthropological conversion Rahner will reassume his philosophical insights, on the one hand, and anticipate the way he is going to deal with special theological topics, on the other. The first, philosophical, purview is, of course, what we have already labelled 'transcendentalism'. The human subject in his indefatigable questioning preapprehends the *totality* of the real and the totality of available truth. Man's subjectivity is regarded as an empty mould for any truth to be encountered. In the moment of encounter with God's truth the a posteriori and in itself undeducible element will be experienced as corresponding to those a priori expectations which man always had. This meta-experience (i.e. an experience of an experienced correspondence) will be relevant for both the subject's self-knowledge and the truth of God offered by the encounter. Thus even in encounter with most obstruse subjects of theology (such as the doctrine on the angels of the trinitarian speculations) man's, as it were, a priori apparatus is activated in order to see, if not the clear and explicit truth in these fields, then their anthropological *significance*. The human a priori, thanks to man's transcendental orientation, enters into a mutual interaction with the a posteriori content of revelation. Without the a priori – the *de facto* encountered would remain insignificant, mythical and irrelevant, whereas the a posteriori as it were, clinches the transcendental self-understanding of man (which is of course a priori). As we shall presently see, man needs e.g., actual confrontation with the living person of Jesus the Christ, but (as we suspect) Rahner is more in need of an antecedent *idea* of 'the absolute saviour' in order to interpret his encounter with the living Jesus. The first is a posteriori, the second is a priori – and their correspondence is the understanding of faith, the verification of its intelligibility and/or of its human significance. Briefly, the vehicle of a reasonable theology is this transcendental meta-experience.

To go in detail into Rahner's argumentation in establishing the necessity of this anthropological conversion would mean to repeat material already discussed. All that is necessary is a brief summary of the presuppositions of his transcendental meta-experience to remind us again of the thought-pattern of his world view. The anthropological conversion in theology is postulated, first, on the ground of ultimate convertibility between philosophy and theology.[7] 'A really *theological* question can only be put ... if it is understood as being simultaneously a philosophical one'.[8] Since Rahner's kind of philosophy is supposed to affirm the limitless totality of being, it is concerned both with the human subject and the objects to be known, including theological objects. Theology is at the same time anthropology and *vice versa*. The totality in question (according to Rahner, preapprehended as positive and existent by the human mind) has its term of orientation in what we might call God and all that we can know about God, including his self-revelation: it is relevant both for the subject knowing and the theological object known. This means that man in knowing more about God knows more about himself and *vice versa*. Man, in knowing himself, knows at least the inner structure and limits of God's self-revelation. We saw this previously: the fact that revelation is possible makes man by necessity the hearer of the divine word. The fact, however, that man is a possible hearing subject of the word is regarded as 'the inner motive and precondition of the existence of revelation'.[9] The structures of this latter match the structures of human subjectivity. Since, however, revelation has to do with human salvation, that which is revealed in an a posteriori encounter only has significance if it, by necessity, fulfils and accomplishes man's transcendental thrust: 'Only those things can belong to man's salvation which, when lacking, injure man's being and wholeness'.[10] Any question of revealed theology is bound to imply man's concrete nature, in so far as this nature is susceptible to the 'saving' influence of a theological object, and any such 'saving' theological object is only significant if it discloses the *saving receptivity* of man for it. In one sentence, whereas the subject lays down the conditions of the significance of the revealed object, this latter 'also to some extent lays down the conditions of the subject's receptivity.'[11]

It is here that Rahner, by way of an illustration, reveals the underlying pattern of his anthropological conversion. His appeal is to the event of human love in its concrete occurrence. The implications of this example will be relevant for the rest of Rahner's theology as well as for our confrontations with it. I shall be quoting the text presently.

What Rahner intends to illustrate with the example of human encounter in love is that the saving content of revelation, although it occurs in concrete history, although it is a free and *a posteriori* event, is not arbitrary in its nature. Is means a 'must' for man, 'otherwise [man] could eschew salvation, without thereby being in danger of losing it.'[11] It is free — therefore not *deducible* from man's transcendental subjectivity — yet, at the same time, necessary, because once *reduced* to man as a transcendental subject it is no longer a matter of free choice. In order to understand this free necessity Rahner proffers his analogy:

> A comparison may clarify what is meant: the concrete beloved person who is the object of my love and in whom it [this love] is realised (and without whom it does not exist) cannot be deduced *a priori* from human possibilities, but is rather a historical occurrence, an indissoluble fact which has to be accepted. *But in spite of this* such love for this concrete person can only be understood when one comprehends man as the being who must of necessity fulfil himself in love in order to be true to his nature. Even the most unpredictable concrete love, occurring in history, must therefore be understood transcendentally in this way in order that it may be what it should be.[12]

The example illustrates the posteriori and not deducible occurrence of this concrete love for this concrete person and exemplifies in what way this particular occurrence reveals the universal and a priori obligation impinging on human nature. To be fulfilled by love is man's transcendental necessity: the contingent should be *reduced* to this necessity in order that it may be what it should be. If we transfer the message of this human encounter to man's possible encounter with the words of and the Word of God, it will follow that not precisely the concrete encounter saves man but the love that may be engendered by it. This love, in its turn, *must* be accepted by man in order to fulfil his nature destined to love in general. To ask more pointedly: Is the historical Christ the saving event, or is it not rather man's acceptance of the necessity of loving the concretely encountered Saviour? Revelation *in concreto* is only the condition of possibility for transcendental love to be 'consummated in salvation or the loss of it.'

Leaving aside for the moment the ambivalence of this example, Rahner's next step is predictable: the condition of possibility for the transcendental fulfilment of this love is the divine Mystery in its self-communication. And since the person who allows love to be engendered in him is present to the lover in his immediacy, so is God present to man in the form of grace. Grace must therefore belong at least to the core of salvation/revelation reality.[13] It is part and parcel, if not of man's static, then of his dynamic transcendental nature which is, or is going to be, in encounter with God's self-communication. But if this self-communication is a concrete and free historical offer, indeed a history of grace or man's 'engracement', it must be understood as Christ's grace. For in Christ the historical engracement of humanity has achieved its irreversible apogee and therefore the mystery of incarnation is implied in the mystery of grace, indwelling transcendentally orientated mankind. Now the incarnation, as experienced in grace implies the mystery of the triune God, so that the

> most objective reality of salvation is at the same time necessarily the most subjective: the direct relationship of the subject with God through God himself.[14]

In other words, transcendental experience is the experience of grace implying the very core of salvation: our faith in the Trinity and in the Incarnation. This trancendental experience is both anthropological and theological. On this ground the anthropological conversion (at least for modern man) is a necessity. From this it is hoped that man can be led to see what is meant by the various mysteries of Christian faith: if these are in the above suggested way reduced to a transcendental experience, 'he will appreciate that Christianity is connected with his understanding of himself.'[15]

A daring programme for theology, one might say. A strategy which is more or less explicitated in Rahner's own theological *methodology*. The very heart of Rahner's method is termed a transcendental theology.

1.2 The Three Aspects of Rahner's Explicit Methodology
In the sixties there was a considerable interest in Roman Catholic circles of the Anglo-Saxon world in method or methods in

theology. At that time Lonergan's comprehensive book on *Method in Theology* was only a promise, although its central chapter ' functional specialities' was already published and duly critizised by Rahner.[16] About this time Rahner was asked for his own contribution to the question of method, which then appeared in the ninth volume of his *Schriften* and was translated in the eleventh volume of *Investigations* under the title of 'Reflections on Methodology in Theology'. In dealing with God the Mystery in our first volume we have already referred to this lecture. In it he does not intend to give, like Lonergan, a comprehensive methodology, yet one cannot avoid the impression that the article is a true mirror of his own theological activity before and, I dare say, after 1969. It is, in my opinion, a methodical projection of Rahner's anthropological conversion for the whole programme of his theology.

What appears to be new in this article is the first aspect of theological method later to be developed in his *Grundkurs*. It consists in, what Rahner calls 'indirect methods' for entering theology in our present day situation of pluralism. He starts indeed with an existential analysis of the Catholic theologian for whom the method of neo-Scholasticism has ceased to exist,[17] and who is overwhelmed by the *data* of a great variety philosophical and theological approaches in interpreting Christianity. The theologian cannot master all the aspects of the methods of knowing: he lives, as he puts it, in a situation of *gnoseological concupiscence.*[18]

This expression, to my knowledge, is new in Rahner's vocabulary. It may have been inspired by his developing view of an all-embracing pluralism with which the one creed of the Church is faced.[19] The theologian inevitably finds himself in dialogue with these various branches of scholarship. Indeed, in a later article he tells us what he explicitly means by this new-fangled term:

> I mean the fact that in human awareness there is a pluralism between the various branches of knowledge such that we never can achieve a full or comprehensive view of them all together, and that they can never be integrated in a unified system by man in a way which makes them fully controlable or comprehensible to him.[20]

In other words, the danger of all scientific disciplines, including that of theology, is somewhat similar to what was characterised by concupiscence in the situation of the individual who is not capable of grasping himself as one and whole and yet attempts 'to grasp to himself this idea ... of radically systematizing his own existence with all its impulses and instincts'. In the same way any scientific branch can set itself up as an absolute value and suppose 'that the key it carries within itself will fit every door'.[21] Though theology, like other sciences, ought to be aware of this danger, its temptation has always been to claim the last word.

With regard to this 'concupiscent' situation Rahner now suggests by-passing the plurality of material insights as gained by other branches of knowledge and searching for methods of justifying the given faith in all honesty by taking one of these areas for conscious reflection. The proviso is, of course, that the thus developed justification of faith should not be put up as claiming any permanent or universal validity. The theologian must be aware and must beware of that *hybris* which endangers him in his gnoseologically concupiscent situation.

At the time of first reading this essay the present author was, like others no doubt, puzzled by this methodological suggestion. He understood the drift of Rahner's thought by the given examples: one can in all honesty develop a conviction in a particular matter (e.g. assent to the existence of God, to the claims of the Roman Catholic Church, etc.) without being able to grasp the intricacy of views as propsed about the same. Yet the full meaning has become clear after perusal of the *Grundkurs*. Here, of course, the plurality out of which an indirect method leads, is the one within theology itself. The particular and exact methods of theology in its various branches can be by-passed by a pre-scientific run-through of its whole field in order to arrive at an intellectually honest acceptance of the faith.

It must be theoretically possible to ground faith in a way which is antecedent to the legitimate tasks and methods of contemporary disciplines in theology.[22]

It is here that Rahner appeals to Newman's illative sense, where decision is asked not as regards a variety of particular subject-matters, but on a global level. There is a convergence of probabilities, a certainty leading to honest and responsible assent before the actual totality of faith is worked out. This is the method proper to the 'first level of reflection'; a basic trust in the self-authentication of faith.[23]

It is in this sense that Rahner will appeal in 'Methodology' to his own experience as a theologian: his task was a very personal reflection upon the faith of ' a Church which is actually using this faith as the basis of its activities.'[24] He stood in a critical dialogue with it, he risked the censure of his Church, because his most subjective convictions (yes, the 'insuperable subjectivity' of faith) must correspond ultimately to the most objective forms and expressions of faith as proposed by this Church. This correspondence, of course, is a matter 'only attainable in that love which is most all-embracing and free'.[25] And which is at the same time an act of hope (that can) only prove to be justified by its own results.[26] It is hence that Rahner can express his mistrust of reducing theology to an all embracing methodology. Theology is not only its own hermeneutics in which the knife is sharpened before cutting the meat. The subject matter of theology should be not faith and its theological explanation by a methodical way, but the very object aimed at: surrender to the object of faith. This is the ultimate task of all theology. We might say: the proof of the pudding is in the eating.

The existential-practical approach to faith, in spite of all its mistrust of a set methodology, seems all the same to contain a definite strategy in theology. As Eicher remarks in a short article, published in the same year as the *Grundkurs*, the indirect methods (on the first level of reflection in *Foundations*) correspond to the transcendental approach, whereas the direct methods (being the second level of reflection in *Foundations*) correspond to the categorial approach in Rahner's theology. In other words, here too, the transcendental-categorial scheme underpins his thinking.[27] The one is pre-scientific and avoids speaking of any particular subject matter in order to embrace the totality of faith, whilst the other investigates particular objects and occurrences. The two approaches are self-involving: the one conditions the other. Yet one wonders if this opinion is altogether correct. On the one hand, there emerges the question why Rahner in 'Methodology' deals with transcendental theology as another aspect of theological methodology. He obviously distinguishes the indirect methods of the first level of reflection from the method of transcendental theology. On the other hand, even in this practical entry to theology, Rahner reckons with the meta-experience of 'the most subjective convictions' corresponding to 'the most objective truth' of the Christian faith. This experience is the basis of transcendental method applied even in theology: it *does* have, as we shall see, a concrete reality within man's consciousness to be laid bare in self-reflection. Hence, it seems to me, that the difference between the two aspects, indirect and transcendental, is that the second opts explicitly for a certain kind of philosophy to perform the task of self-reflection. This, rather cautious, adoption is argued in the second part of 'Methodology'.

From 1969 there is nothing particularly new in his present-ation of transcendental method in theology, except that in his contribution to Volume VI of *Sacramentum Mundi*, 287ff ('Transcendental') a caution concerning this approach now prevails. This caution is felt when Rahner tries to define transcendental *philosophy* as the basis of this theological method – in most generic terms: 'Transcendental theology is that theology which uses transcendental philosophy as its method'.[29]

However, by the use of this philosophy he does not mean one particular tradition as beginning from Descartes through Kant up to the existentialists, but rather a universal mode of questioning, present even before the invention of transcendental reflection. In this generic sense all rational inquiry is of a transcendental kind (including, of course, that of Aquinas). This cautious and, indeed, pre-scientific use of transcendental philosophy within theology does not impede him from taking over its basic tenet already known: the structures of the knowing subject are the same as that of the known object.[30] But here again, there is another note of caution: the structures of subjectivity correspond to their object as an empty question corresonds to its answer; furthermore these structures are not inborn to the subject but given to it. Thus man 'experiences the act of self-realisation of his own transcendentality *as communicated to him* through the *a posteriori* experience of the object which of itself manifests itself to him or refuses to manifest itself to him.[31] The knowing subject is not the master of the object to be known, the a priori is, in a sense, subject to the a posteriori, the transcendental to the categorial.

The second cannot and must not be deduced from the first (this is all the more true in the matter of historicity and of freedom where the human subject anticipates creatively that which is yet to come!).

Yet, in spite of all this caution, Rahner makes transcendental philosophy a necessary constituent of a theology to be based on faith. Though the priori and the anticipative element in man's knowing and free action does not dominate the concrete occurrence of objects and events; though it is somehow determined by the a posteriori – the question itself is an (existent) reality

> which is prior to every kind of knowledge which introduces material divisions of the subject matter into particular departments as the prior condition making this possible.[32]

In other words, the a priori in man is all the same a reality (*Wirklichkeitsbereich*) on an equal footing with the a posteriori to be encountered. From this follows that reflective awareness of human subjectivity is the precondition of all knowing – even that of faith. The transcendental method in theology inquires precisely into this a priori subjectivity of man. This means that , because of this philosophical element involved in the very heart of theology, man's access to faith (yes, to the creeds of Christianity!), man's approach to his own future, cannot be understood without reflection upon his subjectivity. Briefly Rahner's position in the use of transcendental theology is most dialectical. It is evident that theology *must* be transcendental theology, yet this not the whole of theology. On the one hand transcendental theology is a necessity for a theological activity 'in order to make the knowledge of a specific reality possible,' yet on the other,

> it is always true that in practice and in concrete it only becomes possible at that stage at which the object involved has already come to be known.[33]

In applying this method to theology, Rahner goes even further: the a priori in the subject believing is the presence of God's word; God has his 'existence' in man's own conscious thought;[34] this presence is, of course God's free self- communication, etc. It does not really matter if pre-cartesian theology was not aware of *this* implicit transcendentality; it does not matter that such a transcendental-theological disclosure is *de facto* possible only after the object of faith has been revealed and been communicated to the believing subject – it still holds true

> that the acceptance of the realities of salvation through the word of revelation *ab externo* [and] takes place in the power of the saving reality itself as communicated to the a priori transcendental subjectivity of man.[35]

With all this, we are treading on the well known ground of Rahner's fundamental theology. His recurring question is how something external can become intrinsically (*innerlich*) understandable; how the factual (*das Zufällige*) can become necessary and hence obligatory for man; how man in his singularity can be related to the totality, to the whole of existence.[36] Rahner's task is similar to the encyclopedic programme of German Idealism, i.e., of a philosophy the transcendental claims of which Rahner now welds with his own theology. He does so, indeed, with a caution: transcendental philosophy as employed in theology must limit itself — it cannot explain or deduce everything by necessity — its *pièce de résistance* is history, the facticity of human life, the nature of dialogue, of language and of man's 'hermeneutical experience'.

> Without this self-restriction philosophy would fall into the error of *hybris* and the crudity of claiming to solve all things in terms of reflective thought.[37]

So is Rahner's philosophical self warned by the theologian. Yet the question is whether or not in this very cautious handling of transcendental philosophy, the ambitious claims of this latter would not come in again by the backdoor. For fundamental theology in the very act of reminding the trancendental philosopher of concrete history ('which is not susceptible of analysis by reflective thought')[38] still has to point out the perceptible structure in history in its being either a saving history (*Heilsgeschichte*) or the history of perdition (*Unheilsgeschichte*). With the perception of this structure of history itself the basic thrust of transcendental philosophy, albeit on a different level, has reared its head in theology. It is here that Rahner assumes, on the analogy of transcendental philosophy, that this free and now historical self-communication of God affects human subjectivity. As we shall see presently, human subjectivity which is affected by God's self -communication is something permanent in the very structure of man, a gift of God embracing human nature, a 'transcendental state in which man is constituted'.[39]

A self-reflective analysis of this grace-like state of man still belongs to the transcendental aspect of theological method. It is however, in itself, insufficient and needs to be extended by the next aspect of Rahner's methodology.

This aspect is called by Rahner *reductio ad mysterium*:

> every theological statement is only truly and authentically such at the point at which man willingly suffers it to extend beyond his comprehension into the silent mystery of God.[40]

Although we are already acquainted with his philosophical approach to God the Mystery, here it becomes a theological awareness and, for Rahner, fulfils two methodological purposes. The first refers to the content of faith, to the *fides quae*. As we shall see, the concept of Mystery will help to organize the various doctrines of Christianity whilst the second function is concerned, technically speaking, with the subjective appropriation, the *fides qua*, of these mysteries and of the one Mystery of God itself. For the mystery with which theology deals is God's self-bestowal, in so far as God himself becomes the specification of the creature. Thus the Mystery, to which all theological statements are to be 'surrendered' is not only God himself , but the very mystery of man who experiences how he gradually is taken up in the historical process of God's self-communication. In this sense man's historical subjectivity and the awareness of the same is central to the subject matter of theology. Indeed, it is theology's ultimate and ineffable experience. A theology true to its name does not abide with conceptual formulations, but in silent contemplation, in a *theologia meditativa*, tries also to embrace the mystery of man to whom God's self-communication was imparted. Thus not only the *fides quae* must come to terms with

God as the Mystery, but also the *fides qua*. For this, 'true theology should offer a direction'. It should constitute a *mystagogia* leading to the experience of grace.[41]

It is here that the spiritual and quasi-mystical trait of Rahner's theology triumphs over and above the more reasoning elements. It is here that theology instead of remaining a rational discipline becomes a true mystagogy for the man of prayer. The secret, however, of how Rahner is able to arrive at this approach to the whole of theology is his anthropological conversion. Man, and not only God, is at the centre, because he is a mystery to himself: 'man is therefore mystery in his essence, his nature', writes Rahner in meditating upon the Incarnation.[42] This means that man cannot be defined, because by his very nature he is referred to the incomprehensible God:

> our whole existence is the acceptance or rejection of the mystery we are, as we find our poverty referred to the Mystery of the fullness. [Indeed] the pre-existent object of our acceptance or refusal of the decision which is the deed of our lives concerns the mystery which we are. And this mystery is our nature, because the transcendence which we are and which we accomplish brings our existence and God's existence together; and both as the mystery [accepted in love.][43]

This, in brief, is Rahner's methodological project.

1.3   *Comments and Questions*

By starting the presentation of Rahner's fundamental theology with the theme of anthropological conversion and his explicit methodology, we may have prejudiced the attentive reader. In fact, we have anticipated an apparent latecomer in his development as a theologian. For, chronologically speaking, Rahner's first achievement was not in the field of theological methodology, but on the level of explaining the human subject who is not only called listen to God's self-communicating word but, in a sense yet to be seen, is moved in his interior being to accept it. One could discuss whether or not this basically anthropological insight in his early theology projected itself to an explicit *anthropologische Wende* and to the threefold method in theology.

In our opinion, this is not the case. The anthropological conversion took place at the peak of his philosophy of religion where, a theologian at heart, he was in search of an apt philosophy. He found it in God the Mystery that implies its human counterpart, and with this hypothesis he instinctively developed a strategy to be applied to theological topics. The result was his fundamental theology and the threefold method to be explained later in life. Nonetheless, in turning from philosophical to theological thought, he needed to point to an experience which would distinguish one from the other. This, though alluded to in abstract philosophical terms in *Hearers of the Word*, is the experience of love. Love, however, is no longer explained in the analysis of man's ontological set-up, but in the reality of concrete encounter. It all depends how this experience is seen and presented while the theologian in full swing, as he was in 1966. ('Anthropology') and 1969 ('Methodology'), verbalizes his own way of theological thinking.

We can, therefore, safely take the experience of man's encounter with the loved person as the underlying pattern of Rahner's anthropological conversion. This is neither new in theology, nor reserved to one school of thought. Whilst renouncing the reference to parallel uses in illustrating theology with the parable of human love, old and new, the present author is at one with Rahner on this point. In order to see how far this agreement goes, we shall first examine the way in which Rahner exploits this experience, of which scripture itself is full (a). Having stated our agreement in difference, the way will be open for some reflections on Rahner's theological methodology, asking ourselves whether his anthropological conversion, as applied consciously in a theological method, is not *au fond* an anthropolgical reduction (b). If, as Rahner purports, there is a legitimate approach and an 'indirect' method in theology which is called pre-scientific on the first level of reflection, then surely a reaction to his thought in a similar vein is admissible. In understanding Rahner our first remarks are on these lines.

a. In an encounter of love, the concrete person of the other cannot be deduced from human possibilities which we can otherwise know. Rahner, like everyone else, is convinced that such love is an 'occurrence' a happy chance to be accepted. Indeed, the other person belongs to those factual events with which the transcendentalism of German Idealism is unable to deal. These are history, the facticity of human life, the nature of dialogue, our language and hermeneutical experience as Rahner himself assures us. The trouble is that after this admission there is always a 'yet', an 'in spite of this' etc. which arouses our supicious questioning.

Let us direct our questions not to the whole complex scheme of Rahner's conversion to man, but this time rather to his example of love. If John meets Mary and they happen to fall in love, one may ask what is important in this event: (i) that the structures of love, preexisting in both, are now actualized and reach their goal, or (ii) that it is precisely John and Mary between whom the happy and inalienable event of 'falling in love' has taken place? Now to characterize roughly Rahner's interpretation of this event we can say that his approach is from question (i), whereas we should prefer to understand the same from the point of view of (ii). The first approach is a quest ruled by the teleology of the individuals involved, the other, as we shall submit, remains rigorously in the order of free historicality.

We should state, however, right at the beginning that in both cases we have to do with a *hermeneutics*, the one we shall name transcendental and the other personalist. Both should be *retrospective* interpretations of the event, first by the ` partners involved and then by neutral onlookers. Now it is possible that John and Mary may in retrospect interpret the event of their meeting once upon a time by saying 'we were always destined for one another' – , or even 'if we had never met, seperated we could never have found happiness, since something in us would have been frustrated'. No matter how correct it is, there is a certain teleology implied in these retrospective views. And it is precisely this teleological aspect which Rahner seems to pick up and generalize. For he seems to interpret man, every man and woman, as having to love or even having to fall in love by general and transcendental necessity. The concrete objectification of this 'falling in love' (: these precise persons) is contingent and free, and one should (though hesitatingly) add accidental. If the necessary and transcendental obligation is fulfilled by the individuals, then 'love is understood as it should be'. Does it mean that this singular event gains its value, as it ought to, by an underlying transcendental prop?

Surely, there is another way of interpreting the same occurrence. What if we regard it as a unique and singular event in its own right for which none of the persons concerned were prepared by a capacity or potentiality to be actuated precisely in this love (: of John and Mary). There is now something new and unexpected between them which may or may not have a further history. They have not fallen in love with love, but John with Mary and *vice versa* in order to live as concrete persons in this concrete love. Thus we cannot speak of any potentiality preexisting in them for this particular event. This event before it occurs is a possibility not, however in the sense of an Aristotelian *potentia* but rather as a chance opportunity offered from the outside, which for everybody concerned is arbitrary. This event is not the actuation of something prossessed before by the subjects. On the contary one could say that it is in the very encounter that they become subjects, they begin to be person by having met one another in love. We can, of course, speak with Rahner of a certain fulfilment, but we cannot attribute it to the *drammatis personae* before the event. It occurs to the 'we' of the fellowship of those whose concrete life advances towards that fulfilment which is just as unforseeable and surprising as their original meeting. We should prefer to call this fulfilment not a goal, a *telos*, but rather an *eschaton* in order to emphasize its event-character.[44] The account given of this meeting and of the hoped for fulfilment is hermeneutics not, however, from the point of view of the persons' subjective expectation, but from the viewpoint of the event itself in which fellowship was born and which enabled the subjects to be for one another. For the parable of love can, in my view, be 'understood as it should be' only then, when the persons involved can honestly say to the other: *je te dois tout puisque je t'aime*.

With this love-lore we have only pointed out two possibilities of interpretation. The difference should now be obvious: the first is ruled by an all-prevading teleology, the other by a retrospective interpretation of a singular event. The question is whether both, or either of these understandings of the parable are adequate to underpin those subjects for the illustration of which Rahner has introduced it.

b. Our understanding of Rahner's *anthropologische Wende* as being the basis of his theological methodology has been sufficiently emphasized on the preceding pages. Unless the contrary is proved, we can take this as the starting point of our reflections. This would, of course be the place to establish the more than superficial similarity between Rahner and Bultman in their approaches to Christianity by adding to the latter's scheme the central insights of e.g. a Schleiermacher and Tillich. Their theologies, including that of Rahner's, are subject-orientated, in short, anthropological. They all choose to consider a certain point in man from which the divine word of self-revelation can be seen to be in accordance with man's philosophical questioning. For all four of them this point in man is somehow beyond his being and is a common characteristic (i.e. transcendental) for all existents. As we shall presently see the only difference between Rahner and his precursors is that he eventually identifies this questioning capacity of man with the unearned gift of God: it is the theological modality of man's transcendental thrust, as he will later put it. This is the background of Rahner's transcendental theology, on which we have laboured enough on the preceding pages.

Now almost everything that Barth has censured in the hermeneutics of Bultman could be applied to Rahner.[45] Barth complains that Bultman's theology is a desperate existential search for human meaning in the light of the gospel, instead of accepting the meaning of the *Christ-event* inherent in it and independent of the meaning *we* want to read into it. This would also be the place for reviewing Gaboriau's rather muddled attempts at debunking *Le tournant théologique* of Rahner[46] followed by an account on the polemics of von Balthasar against Rahner's transcendental method in theology.[47] It is here that we should remind the reader of Fischer's confrontation of Rahner's transcendental subjectivity (on which his method rests) with Kierkegaard's slogan 'subjectivity is the truth' – resulting in a totally opposite approach to theology.[48] The outcome of these criticisms can be summed up by saying that Rahner, in spite of all his caution tries to domesticate the paradox of Christianity for human consumption. His is an anthropological theologoy.

But does Rahner indeed reduce Christian theology to its anthropological bases? In my opinion: he does not. Once the worry about man and the meaning of his life was admitted to the field of theology proper, we should expect a change in its subject matter. It seems to us *pace* Balthasar and co. that Rahner's anthropololgical conversion does not go far enough. He stops in mid-stream: what theology is about is God in so far as he communicates himself to man as well as about man who is raised by this self-communication and is, as Rahner says 'divinized'. We suspect that in his scheme the ultimate subject-matter of theology, is after all, God. Although this God helps us in our self understanding, he is the answer to man who himself is the question. In this way Rahner holds on to the traditional understanding of *theo-logia*.

This is borne out eminently by the ubiquitous use of transcendental theology rooted in the *Gedankengang* of German Idealism. Sure enough, in 'Methodology' Rahner is cautious in describing this *mésalliance*. One even has the impression that in defining transcendental philosophy within theology it dies the death of a thousand qualifications: any philosophical language game will do, provided it puts the appropriate questions.[49] But these questions are so formulated that they bring out the ontological structure of man which must correspond at least structurally, to the content of faith. It is here in this transcendental method of theology that the decisive step is taken: Rahner raises man to the status of mystery in the minor case. And when the other cautious addition in the third aspect of Rahner's explicit methodology, the *reductio ad mysterium*, is introduced, one fails to see clearly to which side of this two-fold mystery our theological statements are to be surrendered – to the one in minor case (man) or to the Mystery which is God. Rahner's transcendental theology, the centre of his theological method, remains in dialectical tension between these two – but one Mystery – even if it is understood by some of his critics as an exclusively anthropological theology.

Yet in the debate between anthropological theology and, so to speak, 'theological' theology (in whatever way it is proposed) we are on Rahner's side. With this shared anthropological leaning, ought we not to have the courage to affirm that the subject-matter of divinities is man and not God? Theology belongs to the humanities *tout simple*. Of course, we should hasten to add a qualification: theology is the self-interpretation of man *from the point of view* of a religious faith in God. It presupposes man's unconditional commitment to an as yet unknown possibility with the objective content of which he will be acquainted by freely letting it work on himself, on his enviroment, on the world which is at his disposal. To put our view another way: man is the sole *object* of theology, whereas whatever in faith comes under the name of God, this God is presupposed to be the *subject* who interprets man. Though nothing is more hackneyed in theology than the subject-object relationship, it can be useful to illustrate its basic attitude. Whereas in philosophical theology proper it is the other way round: man is the 'object' understanding himself *as being known and loved* by someone who for his sake has become a 'subject'. By this mere fact man will be enabled to understand himself from an entirely different point of view. It is in this way that we should speak of an anthropological theology.

Is not this approach, thus roughly outlined, merely a variant of Rahner's threefold methodology? By the exchange of subject and object in philosophical, viz, theological thought, have we indeed offered an alternative to his scheme? And is not the charge of an anthropological reduction even more applicable to this view than it was to Rahner's anthropological theology? Whereas in Rahner's scheme the encounter with God, who interprets man could be, as we shall see, visualized in a linear way: (man in his interpersonal human love eventually discovers God's love for him), our view will, so to speak, disrupt this smooth lineation and risk the irruption of a divine encounter which could be altogether different from an interpersonal human love: this divine ' irruption' may prove to be the judgement and rejection of human endeavour and human love, but it may also turn out to be the acceptance and endorsement of the same in God's ineffable condescension and benevolence. In this sense, our approach to theology cannot simply be taken as a variant of Rahner's. It is proposed as an alternative according to which man takes the risk of being interpreted by the concrete and categorial words of a divine human-encounter. When we commit ourselves to this yet unknown alternative and live with it we could be surprised by its message, which may not coincide with the goal at which we were always aiming. Yet it will fulfil us beyond all expectations. Thus we are convinced that by strictly keeping apart religious man's indefatigable questioning and the surprising, yet concrete and categorial divine answer, our anthropological theology is more likely to eschew the charge of an anthropological reduction than is Rahner's. As we have seen, in the latter's the contours of the mystery of man and of God the Mystery are blurred, whereas our alternative refuses to use the word mystery as regards man, whose life is rather an adventure into a world of indefinite possibilities, one of which might be his encounter with the living God, The God in whom the Christian believes is the self-chosen *Lebensraum* in which this event may occur. And if it does occur, we live with the Mystery, without being a mystery to ourselves.

That Rahner, on the contrary, holds onto an image of man who is a mystery to himself, can be further illustrated and discussed in the way in which he describes the situation of concrete human life. What then is the make-up of this man who is now at the centre of theology? What are his true origins, his history with its ambivalent outcome: perdition or salvation as wrought in the *deeds* of his life? Is it true that in living out the mystery of human life, one will find the way to God?

We shall now turn to these questions.

Chapter II

The Mystery of Human Life

Main Literature
Hominization; 'Christology' (*Investigations* V, 157-92 = *Schriften* V, 183-221; 'Concupiscentia' (*Investigations* I, 347-82 = *Schriften* I 377-414; *Death*; 'Guilt' (*Investigations* II, 265-81 = *Schriften* II Z79-98); 'Sin' (*Investigations* XI, 247-62 = *Schriften* IX, 259-75); *Foundations*

If man is the methodical centre of theological activity, it is inevitable that this 'mysterious' creature will find his own image in the mirror of Rahner's theology. This section is the place for presenting Rahner's, this time theological, anthropology. The task, in itself, is enormous, since from the beginning he was not doing anything else but reflecting upon man. Fortunately, in additon to Fischer's frequent allusions to Rahner's theological anthropology,[1] we have a fairly reliable collection of texts from Speck[2] and a somewhat oversize article by Andrew Tallon[3] to help us along. Though with some caution, we can refer the reader interested in matters anthropological to this latter article. It is yet another attempt to find a single conducting line pervading the whole Rahnerian corpus, this time in a painstaking genetic and chronological study of his writings about man whose task is to become a person in facing the personally other fellowman. Tallon attempts to show an unbroken line of development in this personalistic view from the hints of *Spirit*s and *Hearers* to Rahner's position on the unity of love for neighbour and for God or on the unity of experiencing self and experiencing God. Were we to follow Tallon in presenting Rahner's full treatment of anthropology, it would necessitate our repeating the whole of his philosophical work and anticipating most of his ensuing theology

of specific topics. Nonetheless, by restricting ourselves to four
major anthropological themes, the becoming and the make-up of
man (1), the becoming of the person in view of the possibility of
sinfulness (2), the finalization of the human person in death and
guilt (3) and the existential situation of mankind in the mirror of
original sin (4), we shall be able to present the absolute minimum
presupposed for the anthropological basis of Rahner's
fundamental theology and, indeed of his treatment of Christian
doctrines.

2.1 On Becoming Man: *Hominization*
Unlike Tallon, we shall not follow a strict chronological order in
the presentation of Rahner's anthropology. It is true that Rahner
never basically moves away from the framework of his
philosophical foundations in *Spirit* and *Hearers*. Yet one could
speak of a kind of development in his thought. His first period can
be characterized as dominated by theology akin to the great
visionary of our days, Teilhard de Chardin. Just as man's
knowing *Spirit* and willing (mainly *Hearers*) are directed to a goal
as disclosed y transcendental deduction, so is the whole universe
in movement towards the emergence of man, and man towards
that of the God-man, Jesus the Christ. It is only in the second
period that a more concrete approach to man in his historical,
social and personal matrix can assert itself. The borderlines,
however, of these two periods cannot be clearly drawn.

When Rahner first turns to the origins of man, he does so as a
theologian whose basic insights, not only in philosophy but also
in theology, are, already formed. The controversies on nature
versus grace, to which we shall come presently, the growing
prevalence of the idea of God's self communication, his attempts
to come to terms with the christological dogma (as we shall see),
leave their mark on his approach to man. So man is no longer
considered in his essential constitution (as in the gnoseology of
Spirit) as someone facing the possibility of God's revelation in
history (as in the philosophy of religion in *Hearers*), but rather as
being immersed in the concrete material and developing world.
Rahner, now dealing with man as spirit incarnate asks not about
his spirit's relationship to matter, but about his origin *from*
matter. *Materia* is no longer the metaphysical principle which he
has tackled in his philosophical works, but that many-faced

reality with the manifoldness of which man must live and with which he must find his world's unity. Thus the matter of this world is the *materia* out of which man was born and as regards which he has a task to fulfil. The first implication, man's material origins, is worked out in the double volume (12/13) of *Quaestiones Disputatae* with the collaboration of P. Overhage,[4] and the second, man's task in this universe, steers Rahner's efforts towards an important recast of christology, now within an evolutionary view of the world.[5] For man's task can only be adequately envisaged in the light of the Incarnation: the presence of the God-man amongst us means God's *becoming* material along with this world,

> precisely *in that one point in which matter becomes present to itself* and the spirit has its own being in the objectifications of the material, in short in the unity of *human nature*.[6]

Human spirit incarnate is the unifying factor of the universe just as the Logos incarnate is the unity of mankind. The origin and the end of man are set, and man's image is shaped, within this teleological framework.

In view of his *Spirit* the above quoted text may be surprising. It says that, in man, the material of the world becomes spirit whereas, as we might recall, in his treatment of sense knowledge Rahner explained how matter 'emanated' from spirit.[7] Does it mean that Rahner the philosopher lets matter be grounded in spirit, and the theologian now contradicts himself by deriving spirit from matter? On closer inspection of *Hominization* we cannot accuse Rahner of self-contradiction. As a philosopher he starts from mind (spirit), which is immediately given to self-reflection in order to explain its reciprocal relation to matter (spirit *in the* world) which is as yet nothing but an unqualified possibility: the *materia prima* in which the spirit will objectify itself. As a theologian he starts from concrete, existing and historical human nature as it is realized in its material circumstances – in the otherness of worldly reality. The same reciprocity is now affirmed on another level, that of existence and history, proper to the theologian. On this level the word 'realized' means a true historical *becoming* of spirit *from* matter.

This latter statement may sound offensive to Roman Catholics

who, under the direction of the teaching authority of the Church,
would suspect any statement suggesting the descent of man from
non-human sources, not to mention from matter: an all
embracing evolution which comprises man's spiritual side
(transformism) is forbidden territory for Catholic orthodoxy.
Man's soul in each and every individual is created directly by
God.[8] In order to forestall the strictures of the Church's
Magisterium Rahner tries, in *Hominization*, to invent a kind of
causality which explains precisely matter's becoming man.
Relying on his analysis of knowing which, as we remember,
disclosed the structure of *all* being, he affirms an inherent
capacity in everything (including inanimate matter) to
transcend and surpass or (if we may coin the word) to 'overbid'
itself and become more (*mehr werden*) than that which it is
(*Selbsttranszendenz* or *Selbstüberbietung*). In the texture of the *whole*
creation which stands under the influence of God's all-
embracing transcendental causality the principle *nemo dat quod
non habet* is not altogether valid.

The philosophical presuppositions of this theory should now
be obvious: we are back to Rahner's *Beisichsein* and to his
transcendental disclosure of the 'whither' in or beyond the
infinite horizon of being. The only difference is that this view is
now extended to the relationship of spirit and matter. It is also
presupposed that being, as *Beisichsein*, is realized in a hierarchical
order wherein a merely physical being is a *deficient mode* of spirit.[9]
There is, and there remains an essential distinction between these
two, yet they are correlated in their dynamic tendency to being
as such. This latter is not only the goal of their movement, but
also their condition of possibility: *Ur-sache* which not only from
the outside gives purpose and meaning to all that is, but somehow
becomes an inner constituent of their movement.[10] From this
follows that matter, due to the creative dynamism of the Absolute
Being, can develop to spirit: a new form of being essentially more
than matter. Thus matter and spirit, though distinct are not only
not disparate realities (i.e, not *Wesensgegensätzlich*, but
Wesensverschieden),[11] but matter, this so to say, 'frozen spirit', has
meaning only in making the historical becoming of the spirit
possible.[12] In 'Christology' Rahner calls matter the fore-history
of the spirit and attributes to it the capacity of becoming *more*
than itself – a self-transcendence, an overbidding of self in a

higher nature or 'an active filling up of its own emptiness',[13] and not only of receiving the new achievement from God's miraculous intervention. These qualities belong to the intimate essence of all beings, otherwise becoming would not be possible at all. This is the only way of 'thinking out' the concept of becoming.[14]

Whereas *Hominization* gives the bare outlines of a meta-physics of becoming, 'Christology' goes a step further and extends this material to the fore-history of man who is essentially a historical being. In man, to a certain extent, the history of nature has reached its goal, yet it continues as the history of the *cosmos*, now guided by man's free action (*Handlung*) towards his own goal which is his transcendence to the Absolute Being of God, to God's mysterious fullness.[15] The cosmos comes to itself in man's freedom and self-realization. The latter is a process in history with a set goal and fulfilment (which by the way, Christians symbolize with the immortality of man's spiritual soul), and by the self-communication of God this history is carried along towards the vision and experience of the divine Mystery.[16] The self-communication of God is then the ultimate meaning of history, cosmic and human.

Although Rahner repeatedly comes back to the same analysis of the correlation between matter and spirit, his purview remains the same and the essential image of man implied within it can be summarized in a few words. He will retain the basic, but now reconciled, dualism of matter and spirit, of body and soul: these are united in the transcendental preapprehension of God, the ground and the goal of everything that is. But beyond this essential image of man, the question about the existential 'living out' of man's task constantly emerges, namely his historical becoming as a person. It is here that he is threatened by the possibility of sin and guilt.

2.2 On Becoming a Person: Concupiscence

In the philosophical part of our first volume we have dwelt sufficiently upon Rahner's approach to freedom and personhood, both human and divine. From our discussion there[17] we must recall that: (a) for Rahner, the concept of human personhood practically coincides with the self-reflecting human spirit, the subject of knowing and willing; (b) although the relationship of freedom and personhood are described in *Hearers* and *Foundations* in slightly divergent ways (the former seems to presuppose that freedom defines the person, whereas the latter takes human personhood as a primordial *datum* which objectifies itself in free action), both presuppose a developing and dynamic force, a transcendental thrust in man's becoming; and (c) both person and freedom become truly themselves in view of the alternatives of 'yes' or 'no' to God.

It is this latter point which will acquire significance in Rahner's fundamental theology: the concrete possibility of opting for an explicit 'no' in facing God is a permanent threat to human existence; it is called (to use the abstract word) *sinfulness* comprising both sin and guilt. The conditions for the possibility of such a 'no' to God are sought for first in the free personhood and then in the universal situation of mankind. The traditional themes which correspond to these conditions are that of *concupiscence* and *original sin*. Both concepts, as anticipating in fundamental theology what belongs to dogmatic, will move Rahner to elaborate his approach to the becoming of the free human person within history.

Here we shall have to forestall our presentation of Rahner's developing thought and say something about the systematic position of these topics. For the time being without comment, we should register that the free person carries in himself the possibility of sinfulness. What is more, to become free and personal largely depends on facing this possiblity. Hence Rahner's dealing with sinfulness on this level of fundamental theology rebounds on the concepts of freedom and personhood which he has already tackled on the level of philosophical theology. It functions as a catalyst to bring his speculative and transcendentalist anthropology down to brass tacks, to the concrete and historical situation of man. The topic of facing sinfulness has a concretizing, *centrifugal* function as regards the transcendental framework of his anthropology, it leads him away from an all-embracing teleological order of things and allows him to give free rein to the historical, the categorial 'facticity' of man's existence. Yet at the same time, as we shall see, he cannot evade his shadow: a *centripetal* tendency, now on this concrete level, will soon reassert itself in so far as he will try to find for these factual occurences of human existence general structures leading to a goal and to an all-embracing ontological purpose. We shall point out these apparently conflicting tendencies in explaining the possibility of sinfulness that threatens the becoming of the free human person.

In an article from as early as 1941 (the year of publication of *Hearers*) he faces first this possibility of sinfulness. This possibility is not simply a matter of man's natural freedom, but is also a problem of dogmatic theology. In this article, 'The Theological Concept of Concupiscentia',[18] in terms of a certain scholastic tradition, Rahner repeats his philosophical understanding of man, but now extended by a new perspective, which we shall term the 'personal'. As compared with a later interest in explaining how matter can become human nature (compare *Hominization* and 'Christology'), here he is asking how man can become fully personal. Whereas the first leap from matter to spirit constitutes human nature with the duality of body and soul, this 'second becoming' concentrates on the person as distinct from nature. Sinfulness can affect man on this second level of becoming. One of its conditions of possibility is called concupiscence.

Whereas Christian tradition has considered this concept in the context of original sin, Rahner's understanding of concupiscence is only indirectly connected with this. He presupposes with Roman Catholic teaching that original sin, namely the first sin, did not irretrievably corrupt human nature and that the sin which every man inherits at birth is not sin in its full sense because the element of personal guilt is missing. Whereas the first sin of the hypothetically first sinner was due to his guilty action, the participation of subsequent individuals cannot be regarded as an inherited *guilt*. Hence 'our' original sin (*peccatum originale originatum*) is, at the most, guilt in an analogous sense, as Rahner is going to state later.[19] In this regard he agrees with a respectable view within Roman Catholic tradition which regards our share in original sin as *peccatum naturae*, but not, *peccatum personae*. Only this second is sin in the full sense (personal sin and guilt), whereas the former is sin only by way of analogy (general sinfulnes).[20] But this general sinfulness could only come about if, in the natural constitution of each and every man, there was a kind of potentiality, or even a disposition, for sin. In order to pinpoint this potentiality, or disposition for sin the traditional concept of concupiscence was assumed.

However, this concept (dangerously similar on the negative side to potentia oboedientialis), according to Rahner, admits an interpretation in a *most generic sense*; a desire (*Begheren*) which is

> any witting reactive attitude adopted to a value or a good ... as opposed to a receptive act of awareness [which] emb races both the free as well as the involuntary acts of human reaction to value.[21]

Yet the same concupisence can be considered in a *narrower sense* as a power of desire (*Begehrungsvermögen* = appetite)

> with regard to a *determinate* good or value, in so far as this act takes shape spontaneously in the consciousness on the basis of man's *natural dynamism* and, as such forms the necessary *presupposition* of man's personal free decision.[22]

This appetitive power, actualized by any value which man encounters, is the immediate condition of possibility for a free and personal decision, and as such is prior to it. In it the *whole man* is involved as facing the chances of his action: from this kind of concupiscence no one is exempt. Yet there is a third way in which one can speak of concupiscence in the *narrowest* (theological) sense: in this regard concupiscence (now: *Begierlichkeit*) is a spontaneous act resisting man's power of desire facing a definite value, a *Begehrungsvermögen* in a negative sense, before a free decision can take place.

> The essential feature of the free decision is thus what is personal and free as opposed to that spontaneous act ... which, because of its non-free character is essentially pre-moral.[23]

But the question is, how can this *Begierlichkeit* oppose free decision, how can it resist that which is personal in man? Rahner's answer is twofold: apart from his spontaneous act man in his free decision 'is explicit or implicity set before God, the absolute Good and comes to a decision in this regard,'[24] and in the second place man's free decision is an act by means of which he disposes of himself as a whole ... not so much with regard to his attitude to the finite good presented to his mind as to his relationship to God's absolute reality as a value.[25]

Briefly the personal in man is (a) free decision, (b) disposing of the whole of what man is, and (c) this in face of God, the infinite good:

> Thus the free decision is essentially a disposal of himself made by man, and one which proceeds from the inmost centre of his being. Now if man's free decision is shaping (in the terms of modern existentialist philosophy) his own being proceeding precisely from his *inmost core* ... from which man's whole metaphysical essence arises ... then the free decision tends essentially to shape and modify the *whole essence* arising from the centre of the person. *The free decision tends to dispose of the operative subject as a whole before God.*[26]

Now concupiscence in the narrowest, theological sense of opposing man's free decision, can arise only from the fact that the person can never absorb his whole nature:

> "And here we lay down *a posteriori* that this tendency of man's average free decision never suceeds in making its way. There always remains in the nature of things a tension between what man is ... (as 'nature') and what he wants to make of himself by his free decision (as 'person'): a tension between what he is simply passively and what he actively posits himself as and wishes to understand himself to be.[27]

It is here that Rahner introduces a duality between person and nature and regards concupiscence as being the tension between these two. Yet this nature is no longer regarded as the abstract and finite essence of man. It almost means in the sense of existentialist philosophy, objective presence, *Vorhandenheit*, whilst person the whole man insofar as he freely disposes of himself by his decision, possesses his own definitive reality in the act of making a free decision about himself. By nature, on the other hand, is meant 'all that in man must be given prior to his disposal of himself, as its object and condition of possibility'.[28] The spontaneous dynamism of man is the material which should be comprehended and transfigured by personal decision in order that man'should no longer be purely natural but personal'.[29]

Nevertheless, in Rahner's mind this nature, like man's essence, is only a potential as regards the person. Thus with the latter, a new, as he says vertical dimension is introduced: his task now is to personalize and thus to realize his own nature. We are in the ethical realm where this 'personal penetration of nature' occurs. This, however, inevitably means a *struggle* in man's ethical becoming where the borderlines of nature and person cannot be concretely drawn,[30] where in the concrete order of things

> free personal decision and self-determination [*Selbstverfügung*] are not capable of perfectly and exhaustively determining the operative subject throughout the whole extent of his real being,... [where] the person undergoes the resistance of the nature given prior to freedom and never fully succeeds. [Consequently], there is much in man which always remains somehow impersonal, impenetrable and unilluminated ... merely endured and not freely acted out. [31]

And this is exactly concupiscence; an experience, not so much due to man's ontological creatureliness but rather manifested in the tension between nature and person, parallel to the duality of the spirit and the senses, of form and matter.[32]

There is a handicap that checks all our personal decisions should these be for good or evil, and this is why man never becomes wholly absorbed either in good or in evil.[33] In this context alone sinfulness is made possible.[34]

The introduction of the duality of nature and person undoubtedly represents an advance on Rahner's merely philosophical anthropology. Yet, unlike Tallon who wants to interpret Rahner as a personalist even in this early essay, we are not sure exactly what Rahner means either by the 'personal' or by its threat, sinfulness. [35] Man's transcendence to God seems there to be attributed to the person, whereas the three layers explaining concupiscence function merely as a pre-moral dynamism. The personal is now the core and centre of man's being: a capacity directing man towards God in spite of the recalcitrance of man's unreflexive nature. This latter, incidentally, is taken on one occasion as a mere passivity and on another as a dynamism apparently aiming at a goal. Therefore both nature and person share a transcendental dynamism: they are tending towards a goal which is ultimately God.

If this is so, we shall have to ask Rahner what is the use of introducing his distinction between nature and person. From his 'Concupiscentia' it appears that, whereas one can attribute sin in its strictest sense as guilt to the person, of nature one could only affirm sinfulness in a vague analogical sense. The possibility of guilt, accordingly, is the only distinguishing mark of the personal: it is its sorry privilege as against nature. These two concepts as well as the notion of guilt are still in the balance. We have not yet reached the full view on the coming-to-be of the human person.

2.3 The Finalization of the Person: Death and Guilt

Now there are several attempts in Rahner's writings which seem to steer his thought in this direction. I am going to take first his most significant, *On the Theology of Death*.

It is difficult to classify this celebrated essay as regards the whole of his theological writing. In my view, however, the first part belongs to his anthropology, the second to hamartology and the third should be treated under the doctrine of the atonement. In presenting Rahner's theory of death, we are, therefore, still moving in his anthropology. As we shall see, the distinction between the personal and the natural of his article on concupiscence is still very much in evidence. Nonetheless, this distinction is now employed in the existential field of man's possible ultimate sinfulness or salvation. It is in this field that he tries to endow the *act of dying* with a significance for irreversible guilt or final salvation. In other words, in dying man does not endure an inevitable fate, he does not passively undergo God's judgement: he 'acts'. On this score, the act of dying is ambivalent. It can be interpreted, it can have its own hermeneutics which, for Rahner, is equivalent to what he calls the *ontology of death*.

Thus death in the first place can be regarded as a merely natural phenomenon, symbolized by the popular belief of the separation of body and soul. Yet at the same time it can be taken for something more 'personal', as symbolized by the end of man's earthly pilgrimage. On this personal level, life ends in such a way that a further development of man's spirit after death is not altogether excluded.[36] At the point of death the immortal yet finite spirit may begin its infinite journey in God's life. Death is, however, an end of moral decisions concerning earthly life and these are now summed up in the very act of dying.[37] We might say: it is the last chance for the person to define himself (his nature) definitively (*endgültige Verfassung*) before he enters his fulfilled state in God's eternity. If this theory is tenable, then within death also there is a choice, and by this choosing the dying can find an ultimate meaning in what was previously perceived as merely 'natural' in the phenomenon of death.

As we saw, the very first step of his argument applies the nature/person distinction to the phenomenon of dying. Rahner also assumes a second distinction between the natural and supernatural in the act of dying, a dogmatic fact borrowed from Catholic tradition. It is the hypothetical state of original justice, containing over and above the gift of integrity (control over concupiscence), that of immortality. Both gifts were believed to have been lost by the guilt of the fall. Death for Adam's posterity is not merely a natural fact,[38] but also a loss inflicted on human existence. In view of a supernatural vocation, death is an absence of immortality, which still causes bitter resentment in facing the necessity of dying. This is why Roman Catholic theology regarded immortality as a 'preternatural' gift. But, as Rahner further speculates, what would this gift have meant for the first man? Surely, it cannot have meant the indefinite extension of earthly life, since death is also a *natural* fact. It would have meant that for men, raised by God to a supernatural destiny, death was to be a *fulfilment*, a 'death without death' as he paradoxically states.[39] Men by freely opting for God would have entered eternity as fulfilled persons. Therefore the absence of death (immortality) presupposes three factors: man's natural mortality (the natural); God's gracious gift of immortality (the preternatural), and man's free option for God's offer (the 'personal').

We now have these three factors of Rahner's theory in a systematic interplay. But quite understandably, he dwells on the third, the 'personal' constituent of the phenomenon of human death. In it death is an act of choice, a fundamental option in which final salvation or guilt can be contracted. If therefore man is NOT to die with what he called a 'death without death' then it is due to a guilty option of the person. This guilt can be radically realized in death. In this case death is the symbolic sign-material of personal sin.[40] This is why death according to Church doctrine is, and has to be, connected with an original guilt, either as its punishment or as its natural manifestation. It can be a symbol of a sinful life now summed up in the act of dying, and an anticipatory sign of what may follow in an after-life. This is why in this actual state the necessity of dying is experienced as an absurd contradiction of existence.[41] Why it evokes fear and trembling, although, in itself, it should be quite natural. It is shrouded in mystery (*die Verhülltheit des Todes*). Yet, owing to his permanent vocation to the vision of God, man can experience the act of dying as a possible beginning. It is not only an 'empty ending', but also a choice for or against God. This second alternative can mean, in biblical terms, that the just man can die in such a way that he contributes by choice to his own final destiny – he can die with Christ (*ein Mitsterben*) whose personally accomplished ending of life is the resurrection. Thus the dying of the just is ontologically different from the death of the sinner: he dies not the shrouded (*verhüllte*) death of sinfulness, but the uncovered (*enthullte*) death of final fulfilment. For this is the ultimate in man's self-personalization.[42]

It seems that Rahner's book on death clarifies at least one aspect of the 'personal': the self-determination at the point of death means not so much man's reaching a goal but being fulfilled by an event of encounter with the hoped for personal God.[43] Though for Rahner goal and fulfilment seem most of the time to be identical, we shall question this identity. However, on the question of guilt only one slight advance was made: guilt in its radicality is now regarded as something expressed in the symbolic material of man's natural actions – in the case of death in man's merely natural dying, without its personal dimension. It is this aspect which is emphasized in a later essay from 1953: 'Guilt and its Remission the Borderland between Theology and Psychotherapy'.

The real emergence or occurrence of human guilt can be due only to a personal deed enacted by a personal decision. An existential situation can never impose guilt. It is always related to an event, a conscious decision and never to blind fate.[44] Yet, it is also true that a person's self-decision before God is always *mediated* through the given materials of his existentially situated nature. This material can be a constitutive sign indicating guilt.[45] In other words, the outward action of an individual may or may not become the symbol of his personal guilt. This is why Rahner insists that no outside judge (he means also the confessor), not even the person himself, can state with certainty that in and through a certain action or in a persistent and visible form of behaviour, guilt can be recognized.[46]

The guilt of a person can only be due to a fundamental option, to personal responsibility before God, however much the material of the action seems to be linked with a presupposed guilt. Thus, to say, 'I did it just because I am like that' is not necessarily the admission of personal guilt. It may be a statement about man's natural inclinations, about his psychological heredity, about the history which every one of us carries within himself. But it may also mean that the person's decision is precisely expressed in this specific act or behaviour. Then it has become a constitutive symbol of personal guilt, which we call actual sin, actual guilt.[47]

Therefore, from a pastoral point of view, it will never be clear whether a man is taken to be guilty because the sign-material of his sinfulness was irrevocably rejectable according to objective moral standards, or whether he is indeed guilty because he willingly expressed his personal aversion from God in *this sign-material*. And this is why 'only through God can man be delivered from guilt,' even if this deliverance 'demands at least a free personal act of conversion',[48] a fundamental option in a reversed sense. But just as real guilt is undefinable on account of its sign-material, so is this conversion: as a

> transformation alone does not yet wipe out guilt. For the wiping out of guilt is essentially a kind of *dialogue*, the adoption of a position concerning God and in the sight of God.[49]

This means that just as guilt, so its wiping out are events of an encounter, this time not with the God of man's self-transcendence (this 'unattainable vanishing point,' as he says), but with the living God in person.

This is the framework of Rahner's 1953 article on guilt: guilt as well as its forgiveness are dialogal events of encounter. It is, however, more important from our point of view to see the anthropological reflections underlying Rahner's position. It is here that the above mentioned centrifugal tendency in dealing with guilt and sin comes to the fore. It is centrifugal, since it does not abide with man's transcendentality, with the core of man's person where man in all his acts of freedom 'is ultimately concerned with himself and his relationship to God' (the two being basically the same).[50] Apart from this transcendental anchorage, man needs an Archimedian point in the world in order to become personal. 'He must diffuse himself,' as Rahner says, 'in order to concentrate himself on himself; he must 'go out' ... in order to be able to enter into himself and into the very core of his person.[51] And in going out of himself he has to go to the 'other' in the world: into the sign-material of his surroundings, into his own bodily constitution, 'in a relationship to something which is neither himself nor the transcendent counter-pole to his spiritual openness for the whole as such. In short, he must constantly achieve himself as a person in an intermediary reality (*in einem Mittleren*) i.e., in things and persons like himself.[52] Since the reality of the 'other' is in the objective order, it can be expressed by means of law.

Rahner attributes this becoming to, what he calls, the seminal (*ursprüngliche*) person in contrast to the achieved (*endgültige*) person, presumably, at the point of death. For the becoming of the seminal person the 'other' is an a priori necessity for the exercise of freedom. Yet in entering into a concrete relationship with others an encounter with God also is hoped for. In this encounter the fully-fledged person can become guilty. In the first case, the necessary relationship to a sinful self-expression of the seminal person is called 'suffering' (*Leid*) which, owing to its own objective structure, can become the sign-material whereby a subsequent sinful state can be expressed.[53]

Guilt, this basically dialogal event of *tibi soli peccavi* is mediated by the 'other', by things and persons and their objective order. Yet the undefinable kernel of sin is always the possible 'no' to God, the transcendent reality, which can become the self-chosen fate of the achieved person in damning himself for all eternity in

In this rather complex description at least two approaches are
involved. We have called these centrifugal and centripetal as
regards Rahner's transcendental anthropology. The first
tendency manifests itself in his inclination to understand
sinfulness (sin and guilt) as intramundane and interpersonal
possibilities, something that happens between you and me,
between concrete human persons. Yet at the same time the
centripetal tendency reasserts itself in his overall approach. It
seems that in dealing with human intersubjectivity as an
ingridient of man's constitution and in making this latter merely
the sign-material of the transcendental 'encounter' with God, he
builds the former into an all-pervading teleological scheme. It is
not the *inter*personal that allows the person to become guilty or its
contrary, but rather an *intra*personal 'encounter'with God to
which the former is subservient.[54] Calling the interpersonal
encounter amongst human persons not strictly guilt but suffering
(Leid) betrays that for Rahner sinfulness, in its strictest sense of
guilt, can only occur in the vertical (i.e. transcendental)
dimension: *tibi soli peccavi*. So the contrary, the becoming of the
person, can be envisaged only on the level on which man faces his
God. Human personhood is not, unless *coram Deo*.

That Rahner, in accordance with this second tendency,
attempts to integrate the contingent and historical occurrence of
sin and guilt into his own system of thought is, of course, not new.
Christian theology right from the early patristics has tried to do
the same, namely, to form, an adequate concept of human
sinfulness which is universally spread and calls for a God who is
the unique source of man's being freed from the bondage of sin.
The paradoxical task of Christian theology is that, in order to
give witness to a saving God, one first has to show the contrary:
man's sinfulness. The topic of *original sin* is the counterpole to the
eu-angelion in the same way as in Rahner's approach the
possibility and reality of sin and guilt are to the coming-to-be of
the human person. But was Rahner's motivation in
universalizing sinfulness the same as that of traditional theology?

2.4 The Existential Situation of Mankind: Original Sin
We need not go in detail into Rahner's view on the complex
theme of original sin. Much can be gathered concerning sin from
his earlier essays on concupisence, on guilt, as well as from his

labours on the history of penance, not to mention his 1954 article on Monogenism.[55] Whilst this latter does not explicitly deal with the concept of original sin, it points to one facet of universal sinfulness, namely to the transmission of sin in the history of mankind. Sin cannot be inborn to man, as if it came from his limited and contingent nature. Nor can sin be identified with the theological notion of concupiscence, the Rahnerian analysis of which we have already seen. Not even the fact that concupiscence is due to the tension between man's nature and the 'personal' corresponds to this doctrine. Yet sinfulness is regarded by Christianity as a *concrete* universal on the shadowy side of the human condition. Now, if we had only the early essay on concupiscence from which to work out his view on original sin, we would conclude that Rahner's position was akin either to the concepts of German Idealism or to those of Luther rejected by the Council of Trent. The former tried to show a priori from man's composition that sin and evil are inevitable, hence universally spread, whilst the latter argued for the concretely experienced fact of concupiscence in which sin consists.[56] If the frustrated desire (which is basically concupiscence on the first two levels of Rahner's presentation) is endemic to man, and if this latter is the source of nature's resistance to the person (concupiscence in the narrowest sense of Rahner) then the sheer experience of it can argue the universality of sinfulness. Yet these are, for a Roman Catholic theologian forbidden avenues. Hence it is no wonder that Rahner' earliest approaches to original sin will be a staunch defence of the historicity of the first sin and also of the first sinners.

It was maintained by Pope Pius XII in the *Humani Generis* that the descent of the human race from a single historical forefather was a tenet necessary to explain the universal spread of sinfulness.[57] The Pope's pronouncement in 1950 was, incidentally, a reaction to modern theories of evolution, and his caution about the one and single forefather excluded polygenism purely on dogmatic grounds: because of the dogma of original sin mankind could only have had one origin. Rahner's apparent defence of the Pope's ruling proposed instead of polygenism a *monogenism*. There is no need to present his arguments, because later he seems to have modified his own views,[58] and in an article published in 1968 he already takes it for granted that the insistence on Adam as the *only* source of the whole human evolution is no longer obligatory for Roman Catholic theologians.[59] What however remains obligatory in the explanation of original sin is to go back to a historical starting point, to an *aitia*, which can be disclosed from man's reflection on history.

Rahner is, therefore, after a cerain historical causality which has resulted in the present sorry state of sinful mankind. It belongs to the generic field of *protology*.[60] But this human inquiry into man and his world's nebulous origins within history would not be enough to explain something which, although not due to God's good creation, is yet universally present. Thus protological reasoning is entitled to assume a certain power in the past which has its effect on everyone in the present and in the future. Rahner calls this research concerned with these powers in the past *etiology*.[61]

Thus proto-history of mankind, as told by the Bible, represents a historical etiology. This literary genus comes about by man's reasoning on his own historical situation. He tries to find a historical *aitia* (beginning, cause, ground) for what he experiences here and now. A historical etiology therefore both maintains this *aitia* as a singular and unrepeatable event of the past, and asserts its universal influence on the present. It has nothing to do with logically conclusive deductions, neither is it a metahistorical speculation, as a merely mythological etiology would be. It is subject to the imagination and its evolving guesswork concerning the unknown event. This explains why the actual story of the fall, as it is told in the Bible, wears the garb of its author(s) and their contemporary experience. This is also why complete certainty is never achieved before the end of history, or before its anticipated end. This power in the past can only be adequately seen in the light of a fulfilled history, in the eschatological event of Jesus the Christ. In other words, the nearer mankind approaches to its fulfilment (which is still partially hidden) the more its origins, its causally determining factors are uncovered to it. This is why the theological awareness of the first sin and of universal sinfulness appear relatively late in the Bible in spite of the story of the fall in Genesis 3. It was probably in the Pauline metaphor (Rom 5) of the first and the second Adam, that is Christ, that the awareness of man's sinful state could appear, since it is there that 'the divinization of man by the pneuma is introduced into the Bible'.[62] Yet the Adam-story is an historical event of the past in a nutshell. Thus the first sinner, his grace and his sin, are to be maintained within history. Adam's sin was an event, an unrepeatable origin still influencing our present. We cannot do without Adam or at least without the historical kernel of Genesis 3 in order to explain mankind's paradoxical involvement in the sin and the guilt that occurred at the beginning. Thus, Rahner reaffirms a point which seems to have been essential in Catholic tradition.

It is this latter conviction which is going to be modified in 'Sin of Adam'. The name 'Adam' is now duly put in quotation marks. It may have been referring to a group of people in the far-away past: the first sinner is now the *humanitas originans* whose free self-decision, in one way or another, can function as mediating power on the *humanitas originata*, if, and only if (as Rahner says) the following conditions are fulfilled: (a) that 'man is inevitably personal *and* communicative at the same time, and both aspects mutually condition one another'; (b) that subsequent mankind constitutes a unity as distinct from original mankind; and (c) that original mankind or any member of it by its free personal decision can specify the existential situation of subsequent mankind.[63] Now the difference between *humanitas originans* and *originata* is the fact that original mankind's freedom was unbiased, i.e.,

> one such that the situation in which it existed was still unspecified by any decision of human freedom (whether that of the individual himself or that of the others).[64]

In other words, the assumption of original mankind with its unbiased possibility of free self-decision is substituted for the history of Adam and Eve. The historicity of original sin is now reduced to

> the existence of a real sin at the beginning. [This is no myth, since] if it were a myth, then ultimately and logically speaking, the same would absolutely have to be asserted of the history of human freedom. For this is the reality which we experience.[65]

But what was this self-decision of the first sinners, of the *humanitas originans* about? How did this self-decision, which in its own setting constituted for the persons involved a real guilt (referred to as the sin of Adam), universally induce an analogous sinfulness for subsequent mankind?

To appreciate Rahner's answers to these questions, either in this comparatively late essay ('Sin of Adam') or in his later reflections from *Foundations*, would presuppose an acquaintance with the notion of 'existential' and its gradual development in his thought. Since it would be premature to introduce this, subsidiary principle, we shall only anticipate it here as applied to the problem of original sin. The next section will explain the meaning of this important principle, the supernatural existential.

The self-decision of the first sinners, according to Rahner's answer, was not strictly int*er*personal – on the human level – but rather int*ra*personal, i.e., in facing God's self-communication and offer of salvation. Traditional theology called this original justice, the supernatural call of God which, though not implied in man's created nature raised to the state of holiness required for the choice and decision of human freedom. Rahner will describe it as an existential *situation* which enters the inner constitution of *historical* human nature. The self-decision of the *humanitas originans* was presumably about this divine call and offer of salvation and their factual option was a (transcendental) 'no' to it. It was their free act and consequently their guilt. What however Rahner, along with Christian tradition, has to maintain is that the original call of God remains unchanged in the form of a permanent *existential* for each and every human being, whereas the original situation of holiness has changed into a sinful *situation* from which there is no escape. What we call original sin is this historical beginning on which our whole concrete history rests: man's decision against God's offer. The original state is withdrawn from us and never recurs. Yet the tragic result, universal sinfulness, is gradually revealed in the light of our future.[66] After the fall the call of God remains a permanent existential, whereas the original situation has turned into that of sinfulness. This sinful situation also is an existential, dependent however, on another: the permanent and 'elevating' call to holiness.

Rahner's answer to our second question is more important for the concept of human personhood. As we explained in our first

volume, freedom and personhood are correlative notions: no one
is a person without being free and, *vice versa*, no one without being
a person can come to any sort of free self-decision. What is not
clear in Rahner's various approaches to these two notions is the
question of priority, at least in its logical sense: if freedom is the
primordial quality of man, it would follow that he in a true sense
becomes a person by freely defining himself; if however, by his very
birth he is a person, then one cannot speak of the becoming of his
freedom, but rather of his acquiring and increasing enslaving or
losing the free quality of his action. In volume I we understood
the early Rahner as proposing the priority of freedom over and
above the person, whereas the Rahner of the *Foundations* seems to
put this correlation the other way round.

Now 'Sin of Adam' and *Foundations*, in trying to explain the
universal spread of sinfulness, follow this latter scheme. The new,
and after the fall permanent, situation is explained by the
influence of one freedom on the other, which then rebounds on
the sinfulness of the person. All are born with sin, since
'invariably we encounter ourselves as those who have already
come to decision....'[67]

But 'having-come-to-decision' means the giveness of the
person: we are born personal and do not have to become persons,
unless in a secondary sense. Similarly, he applies the influence of
one freedom on the other beyond the individual to social units
('since every community has come about through the exercise of
freedom') where everyone is shaped in his free action by the self-
decision of his fellows, since man can only exist in a state of coexistence (*in der Mitmenschlichkeit!*) with others: at the moment of
birth our personality is already shaped and, in fact, wronged, by
a sinful situation. It is, rather, the freedom of the person which
undergoes a development, the personal kernel of man remaining
the same, subject to the history of freedom. Only in this way can
we speak of the history of human personhood, of its becoming,
but the genesis, the coming-to-be, of the person is a given fact at
the moment of birth.

This trend of thought whereby the sinful situation of mankind
is decided by co-determination of alien 'freedoms' in our history,
will be the definitive solution of Rahner's *Foundations*. It is there
that he synthetizes his approach to sin and guilt. Freedom is the
capacity of definitive and eternal self-determination of an

already given person. Its act is an opaque synthesis of what is necessarily imposed and of what is genuinely free: hence it can never be known with certainty whether it involves man in irreparable guilt or not.[68] This guilt, as we saw, is on the one hand of a transcendental nature, deciding against God 'who offers himself to us as the source of transcendence',[69] but on the other hand, it is exercised through the mediation of 'the categorial reality within the horizon of transcendence'.[70] Yet, since its absolute definitiveness can never be known while man is alive, it only appears when man

> has actively passed through the deed of his life and [entered] into the absolute powerlessness of death. [Until then] sin is an existential which belongs to the whole of a person's earthly life and cannot be eradicated.[71]

With this we are back at the themes of death and guilt. Death, though it means absolute powerlessness is, all the same, a total self-decision ('establishing one's final and definitive self'),[72] however it may happen. It is only at this point that the person becomes fully personal: what was there at the beginning becomes definitive at the moment of death's self-decision.

It seems, however, that in this context Rahner uses the concepts self (subject) – person – freedom as equivalents, since he adds that only this last human self-decision can fully underline the difference between God and man ('others being only deficient modes of this real difference').[73] This real difference is now not between the Infinite and the finite, between divine and human nature, but between man as free personal self and God as freely personal. It also means an encounter of two freedoms to which Rahner hastens to add that it is God who establishes human freedom, and with it man's self-actualization and differentiation from the sovereign God who can 'establish freedom as good or as evil freedom without destroying this very freedom'.[74] Freedom is willed and established by God, and its essence and characteristic is that it can say no to God, and thus become *guilty*. The last sentence, apart from being questionable on several counts convinces this interpreter that (a) the givenness of human personhood at the beginning and at the end is due to a developing divine-human encounter on, if we may so put it, the vertical level (intrapersonal), not on the horizontal human interpersonal; and (b) the same view witnesses to the prevalence of the centripetal tendency of Rahner's dealing with the person who faces the possibility of sinfulness and guilt: it reassumes these factual elements (interpersonal encounter, sin and guilt, etc.) into an all-embracing teleology of man's transcendental nature. With it has the central method of transcendental theology triumphed over the third method of *reductio* ad *mysterium*? Or, indeed, does this reduction always mean the surrendering of our thought to the mystery which *au fond* man is?

The Rahner of *Foundations*, in fact, indicates this opinion, which we have put in question form. Still dealing with sin and with the possibility of definitive guilt, he compares these with their opposite: salvation. Already in the very first chapter of *Foundations* he has identified the exercise of human freedom with an implicit question about *salavation*. In accordance with his fundamental theology, he had to do this for methodological reasons: salvation and its attainment are anthropological facts which cannot come from the outside, as if imposed by a divine judgement.

> It means rather the final and definitive validity of a person's
> ... true self-realization in freedom before God by the fact that
> he accepts his own self as it is disclosed and offered to him in
> the choice of transcendence, as interpreted in freedom.'[75]

This last tag, however, 'as interpreted in freedom' means that man accepts his own fulfilled self-salvation as a fact of history. By this Rahner understands the free subject in time, in a world at his disposal, that is, man as he is in a world of things and persons and his relationships to these as an intrinsic element for the exercise and enactment of his own freedom. His salvation and the question thereof is bound to history consisting 'of the *intercommunication* of spiritual subjects in truth and love and in society' – without which no quest for self-actualization can be possible. These belong to the structure of man's personal becoming, they are 'transcendental characteristics of the personal history of every individual'.[76]

From this follows that man in realizing himself in history is 'co-determined by the free history of all the others who constitute his own unique *world of persons*.[77] Man living in this 'personal' world inevitably bears the 'stamp of the history of the freedom of all other men' in his own free and personal subjectivity; on this ground alone the guilt of others is a permanent factor in the situation and realm of the individual's freedom, for the latter are determined by his personal world'.[78] With this, in principle, the access to the idea of original sin is established, as it were, from below: from the experience of man who in perceiving the objectifications of alien guilt feels himself threatened, attracted and seduced by them, even in his apparently good acts.[79]

Yet are these hints enough for explaining the message of Christianity, according to which this co-determination of man by alien guilt 'is something universal, permanent, and therefore also original'?[80] The Rahner of *Foundations* understandably, gives a cautious answer. He would be prepared to drop the word 'sin' from the traditional expression,[81] provided we understand by this co-determination of individual freedom a guilt 'embedded (*eingestiftet*) in the origin of history itself' as an inevitable predicament of man and provided that we assume at the same time the divine self-communication 'as a quality sanctifying man prior to his free and good decisions'.[82] For only then can 'the *loss* of such sanctifying self-communication assume the character of something which *should not be*'.[83] The cause of this sinful state, therefore is the original character of guilt in history; the universal loss, however, which the individual experiences is due to the prior and universal offer of salvation. From the interplay of these two *existentials*, salvation offered to all mankind as a whole and the historical co-determination of an original guilty deed, the Church's doctrine of original sin is understandable. The first (offer of salvation), however, 'comes to man not from "Adam", not from the beginning of the human race, but from the goal of history, from the God-man, Jesus Christ'.[84]

In this last, and I presume, definitive definition of original sin, the centripetal tendency towards an all-embracing teleology has conclusively triumphed over and above that fulfilment in the integration of the person which could have been reached even outside God and his self-communication in Jesus the Christ. For he is the end and goal of *salvation history*. Rahner's anthropological conversion, as a strategy and a persistently carried out methodology, far from *reducing* the Christian message to a humanism in its atheistic sense, seems to *adduce* humanity to its transcendent Source, God. Man's history, whether individual or collective is a dealing with God. He is the beginning, the middle and the end, the alpha and the omega, as revealed in the mysterious transcendentality of human existence.

How this insight concretely and in technical terms is worked out will be the topic of our next section. However, before we discuss the theme of the supernatural existential, some comments and questions are in place.

2.5 *Comments and Questions*

In these four aspects of man's coming-to-be, we have tried to unpack that mysterious character which Rahner attributes to human life. Beginning with man's genesis (hominization), we perceive an all-pervading teleology which he reads into the structure of the world (a); in discussing human life facing the possibility of sinfulness he shows up the mysterious becoming of the person (b); which is then finalized in the act of dying (c). In what follows, we shall try, in a somewhat disordered way to sum up our own reactions, in the hope that from our understanding of Rahner's anthropology the outlines of an alternative position may arise.

a. It is not our task laboriously to go through the *theological image of man* as cast by Rahner within this framework in order to pick holes in his argument. We appreciate his all-embracing Teilhardian *order of teleology*, where everything is ruled by God's transcendental causality. However, we cannot escape the feeling that the whole purposeful scheme of matter developing into man, and man into the God-man, is read into this universe by a kind of *eisegesis* from the point of view of man who already believes. In this case the image of man is a theological construct. Or both Teilhard's and Rahner's understanding of an evolutionary world is a view transferred retrospectively from man to inanimate matter in which man as a spiritual being can find his home, his isomorphic *Doppelgänger*. In this case the image of the world is an anthropomorphic construct. It seems that only from this perspective can matter be endowed with hidden potentialities of surpassing and 'overbidding' its own given nature. One might ask under what conditions the respective exegisis of these views, disguising themselves as scientific (Teilhard) or ontological

(Rahner) theories, can indeed be valid. As hypotheses they seem to be empty theoretical constructs, no more valid then Jacques Monod's on the becoming of man and his universe by sheer chance.[85] Against this, an all-pervading purposefulness of the whole world-process from humble matter to the coming of the God-man, Jesus the Christ, is assumed as a dogmatic fact. Let us call it the dogma of *teleology*.

It seems, however, that there is another important point shared between Teilhard and Rahner. It is the dogmatic fact of man's being essentially different from his worldly environment: he is a conscious and free *spirit*. However, to escape, a spiritualizing Platonism or a dualistic Cartesianism still lurking at the back of the Christian mind, they need to show the coherence between matter and spirit. The result is that they still assume, if not an anthropological dualism, a basic *duality* within man. This means (if we may apply Nietzsche's scathing criticism to a similar trend in western philosophy[86]) that both Teilhard and Rahner unwittingly endow spirit, or mind and soul, with substance as distinct from the substance of matter. Spirit and matter have their own causality and purposefulness even if they are synthesized by the all-pervading teleological order imposed upon them by God, the Creator. Thus beyond the dogma of teleology there is another: the dogma of man's *duality*.

If this is so, Rahner's hominization is a theory arrived at by interpreting the world's and man's origins from the point of view of these two as one dogmatic persupposition. It is a *theological* hermeneutics, and *eisegesis* from the point of view of faith. For indeed faith, on its own level, can and must understand the world in a teleological order and man in the duality of body and soul. These are not only part and parcel of Christian tradition, but also its defined dogmas. The question is, however, are these dogmas also meant to be statements on the scientific and/or philosophical level of cosmology viz. anthropology? Would faith be able to deal with another kind of scientific hypothesis or philosophical concept which contradicted the dogmatic facts of teleology and man's duality? Can we envisage an interpretation of faith which, in spite of an a-teleological understanding of the world, in spite of a monistic (even materialistic) hypothesis of man's origins, could believe in a world directed according to God's purposes and in an image of man only one aspect of whom is meant for a higher destiny? If this kind of interpretation is viable, we should avoid stating with Rahner that man is a mystery to himself. For him it was an apt statement on which to found a theological system, *because* it was also philosophically (if not scientifically) viable.

Precisely at this point we venture to oppose Rahner's position, basic and central as it is for his ensuing theology. Man on the level of his self-experience is not a mystery to himself, neither is the world into which he happens to be thrown, Yet he undoubtedly does have an experience which is primordial: he acts *freely* by choosing from his worldly possibilities, by engaging himself freely in the alternatives of his action and thereby *becoming* what he was not before. It is this basic experience of acting and being free which underlies the concept of becoming observed and seen in the phenomena of a changing world. This fact, however, does not of itself suggest that there is a *substratum* or *substance* which freely acts, engages itself and becomes another, essentially different from its possibilities on account of which it acts. We must not speak, at this stage, of matter springing out of spirit (as Rahner *en philosophe* did), or *vice versa* about matter's hidden potentialities to become spirit (as did Rahner as a fundamental *theologian*). Neither can we speak of an all-embracing teleology which qualifies becoming as evolution, as a development to something better. To do this we would have to presuppose the dogma of man's duality along with that of teleology. Becoming is a neutral fact, the *Unschuld des Werdens*, as Nietzsche would put it. It is experienced without the qualification of progress or decline. There are, as yet no a priori criteria for these qualifications.

Having said this, by starting from these neutral premises we could set up an alternative hypothesis about the origins of the human race *and* of the individual.[87] This origin is due to a favourable constellation of possibilities in which a living organism finds itself. Even traditionally such an organism is said to excel itself by 'immanent activity', i.e., by a kind of action that moves itself without being in need of an exterior mover, other than the outside possibilities offered to it. Since this action can more or less deal with its environment to its own benefit, we can attribute to it a certain degree of freedom. It could be that at the dawn of mankind's history the environment provided that primitive 'free' action with opportunities the use of which enables the organism to come to consciousness, to become aware both of itself and of the alternatives offered for further action. The vistas of mankind's development were opened up and history took its origin.

In the case of subsequent individual hominization the circumstances of becoming are basically similar, of course with the great difference that the human embryo comes to an environment largely patterned by a set of alternatives: its chances and alternatives are more or less stabilized. Its life is, as it were, 'interpreted' and regarded by others in advance as human. At the delivery of an embryo it is no longer the free-for-all chance that initiates new human life, but an already set pattern of human living. Once born, the living organism is challenged freely to enter into relationship with its possibilities, to engage itself in free choice of its alternatives, actively to interpret itself and its given environmnent for its own benefit and thus to become fully human – and not only to be regarded and interpreted as such by others.

However materialistic this counterposition appears to be, like Rahner's hominization, it is arguable on the scientific and philosophical level. In fact, on this *level*, the theologian would be ill-advised to opt for a scientific hypothesis explaining the world by means of an all-embracing teleology (e.g., Teilhard) as against one in which the coming-to-be of the world and of man is ascribed to chance (e.g., Monod). It is not his job. Much less it is advisable for the theologian to take either of these scientific theories into the foundations of a theological system. The dubious merit of Rahner's fundamental theology is exactly the option for the Teilhardean view. Such a world view, if argued from faith, would be acceptable, but only on the *theological level*. Any scientific or philosophical pretentions would expose it to drastic revisions. This applies, above all, to Rahner's main conclusions resulting from this world view: man in his Universe is teleologically directed to a transcendental goal which is a Mystery, therefore man himself must be a mystery to himself. Is this a statement of faith seeking understanding, or is it an anthropological preconception that imposes itself on faith? As Jüngel aptly remarks, the *Aufklärung* eliminated the Mystery of God ('Deus definiri non potest') and gradually transferred God's mystery-character to man ('homo definiri non potest').[88] Does today's theologian have to follow suit and build his theological system on the assumption that man is a mystery to himself?

In order to challenge Rahner's procedure, which in this matter seems to be from a merely scientific hypothesis (that of Teilhard and others) to a theological construct, we shall argue that whilst man may become a myth to himself, he is hardly a mysterious being on which the foundations of theology can be built. In our counterposition about the world's and man's origin we seem to have adopted Jaques Monod's world view as against a Teilhardean teleology. Though we cannot convincingly argue its scientific or philosophical merits, we can safely state that as theologians we can live with it without detriment to faith. This does not mean an immediate appeal to man's inborn destiny towards a divinely set purpose valid for all and sundry. Yet the chances are that man in his free and creative action can impose a purpose on his universe. Religious man did that in the past by *mythifying* the origin and end of his own and of the world's life. This is at the basis of all religious interpretations and, indeed, of all primitive world views. For concepts pertaining to an unknowable origin and end are basically mythical projections to enable one to find one's worldly possibilities and to enter into a kind of dialogue with them. Thus a religious conception of the world is never independent of man's, so to speak, mythical imagery; the word of faith about man and his universe must wear the garb of mythologies, past and present.

Yet the criterion for finding one's true choice from among these manifold 'mythical' possibilities is not an *a priori* possession of man. There is no 'transcendental' hot line between God and man only the commitment of faith to a God who is believed to be able to give sense and meaning to it all. But our commerce with this God in faith is no longer within the competence of a fundamental theology, precariously straddling a semi-scientific or philosophical and a properly theological reasoning. Without this faith man is no more than a researcher whose project is – himself. His myths, his theories, scientific and otherwise, his various attempts at a *Weltanschauung* are but means of finding his way among the manifold possibilities and alternatives offered to him in this world. Perhaps one of these will prove to be the God of providence and the mysterious source of grace.

b. This approach to man, divergent from Rahner's scheme, also rules our reflections concerning the *coming-to-be of the person*. Whereas Rahner in his writings assumes personhood on account of man the mystery in facing (transcendentally of course) the personal God to whom he can say yes or no, it is enough for us to state that man becomes a person *in* facing the personal other and *through* the event of his fellowship with him. Rahner had to labour in his early essay 'Concupiscentia' to extract person out of nature and endow personhood with the capacity for self-transcendence in spite of a recalcitrant nature (concupiscence). But would it not have been easier to tie down the becoming of person to a successful int*er*personal relationship in which as yet there is no need to speak about God? It is difficult for anyone reading 'Concupiscentia' to decide whether nature by its supposedly transcendental dynamism towards God should dominate the person or, as Rahner suggests at the end of the day, the person should absorb nature, the dynamism of which is now conveniently forgotten.[89] Would it not have been better to say at once that what constitutes nature are the possibilities in which free action is thrown with the task of shaping and developing them? In this sense, human nature will not be regarded as a definite and stable construct unalterable by free action. Though nature has its own dynamism its own laws and rules, when we enter into dialogue with its forces it is freedom's privilege to choose its own way. Thus man, being radically free, might expose himself to alternatives which a posteriori prove to be mistaken and wrong, and in the process of his own personalization he might find himself facing what was traditionally regarded as sin and guilt. But failure and its criterion consists neither in nature's nor freedom's own inborn dynamism. It is wrong because of the mistaken relationship to these alternatives. There is nothing wrong in man's dealings with inanimate or animate nature, in his attempts to harness and dominate it; the so-called 'ecological sin' is measured by the result of mankind's mistaken interference with the natural world. If we have understood Rahner's view, the possibility of sinfulness as against the above view, should be judged either by nature's or by the free subject's (for Rahner the person in its primordial sense) inherent dynamism striving with an inbuilt teleology to a set goal. No, the criteria are to be found in between these two factors, man's free engagement and his possibilities out of which he becomes a person.

This is why we must ask him more pointedly about sinfulness and guilt, the possibility of which has played such an important part in man's personalization. In 'Concupiscentia' was it not hard work attributing to recalcitrant concupiscence (in the narrowest theological sense) a tiny bit of sinfulness to be interpreted as the result of 'original sin'?[90] This Rahner did outside interpersonality by (I believe in anticipation at this stage) assuming at the origin of the individual an a priori 'encounter' with a personal God. Would it not have been easier to place the possibility and the emergence of sin and guilt exclusively in the relationship between man and man? Instead, Rahner's 'Guilt' is obsessed (in advance of *Foundations*) with the ultimate choice between yes or no to God under the aegis of *tibi soli peccavi*.[91]

It is our view that the phenomen of guilt is of interpersonal origin: there alone is where man feels himself to be responsible in the fullest sense. Beyond this realm, the feeling of guilt before the world, before society and even before God originates from a justifiable projection of responsibility to these fields in the light of which man now interprets himself as guilty. The legitimization of this hermeneutics of guilt-complex (not necessarily in a pejorative sense) comes from man's awareness of having frustrated the free possibilities of free persons, including himself and perhaps God. This consciousness arises precisely from man's mythifying capacity: he reads into the world, into the structures of his society, into his own self, a partner in dialogue before whom he is responsible. God is projected as such a mythical partner in dialogue. This mythical projection ceases to be such as soon as God is believed to be incarnate in his Word and manifested as a living person, with his own human destiny, ending on the cross. The sin of the whole of mankind in its true Christian sense is man's being interpreted from the point of view of the cross. One *believes* in the *universality* of human sinfulness, one neither knows nor experiences it.

c. Yet, before pursuing our own thoughts, we ought to turn for a moment to the ultimate trump card concerning sin and guilt in the process of personalization. It is adequately expressed in Rahner's *On the Theology of Death*. Since we have to discuss this essay in the context of his soteriology, we will here concentrate on its anthropological and hamartological content. For if we were to try to sum up all the difficulties which have been, and still can be, raised against Rahner's theory of death we would never reach the end of our comments.[92] In any case, it would be a mistake to regard his view on death as a viable philosophical position. Although he insists that his theory provides us with an 'ontology of death', the phenomenon of death is interpreted from the total experience of man in which theological elements borrowed from Christian faith predominate. Whether such a hermeneutics can at the same time be an ontology is open to question in a number of ways.

Nevertheless there is an essential question which can immediately be raised concerning a theory of death which endeavours to incorporate this phenomenon within life itself and so to domesticate it. For this is at the bottom of Rahner's view: death can be 'defined' by means of philosophy and/or theology. In whatever way Rahner's theory is later proposed, for him death is a human *act*, an act to boot which achieves the highest synthesis of man's total passivity and activity. The question is, what sort of act is death? We could say with Gaboriau that we have no experience of death or whatever happens at that 'moment of truth', since no one has come back to tell the tale: our only experience is of observing others die and of our own *moribund* life.[93] Or, on the other hand, we could say with Boros, death is a last, definitive and irrevocable act of decision taken by man, almost irrespective of the *démarche* of his preceding life.[94] Indeed, Rahner's theory was first understood in connection with this latter view. Although in his later writings he explicitly denies this connection,[95] the recasts of his theory still hold that death is somehow an act of man, even if it comes from the deed of his whole life, even if his whole life interprets his death, etc.[96] But as an act, death does remain the end, the goal of life (*das Ende*), which end, being the act of the totality of man, is a fulfilment (*Vollendung*) resulting in the final definition (*Endgültigkeit*) of the person. I cannot help feeling that the pliability of German language leads here to an easy synthesis: all three words are derivatives of *das Ende*. If life's (natural) end is death, then life can be related to death as a potency to its final actuation or as an act to its proper goal (Ende!). If life (as personal) ends in death, then life can be related to death as a person to his fulfilment through decision – this time, however, to a decision not to be followed by others. Hence he can state the definitive irrevocability of death as the result of a final self-definition. Unless we have totally misrepresented Rahner's theology of death, this is the point at which we can hardly go along with him.

For according to our emerging alternative view, the coming-to-be of the person is neither the self-definition of the individual before God (i.e. not an intrapersonal occurrence), nor his fulfilment wherein the further avenues of choosing are definitively cut off. To become a person is due to an encounter with the other person, where fellowship may occur as a hoped for but unexpected event. That this event, arbitrary as it appears to be, can be retrospectively interpreted as a gift without which the persons involved could no longer be themselves and would have remained frustrated – is obvious. Death is certainly not such an event. It can be regarded neither as a fulfilment of the individual, nor as a definitive coming-to-be of the person. On the contrary, it seems to be a definitive depersonalization, an absurd fact in which man's primordial experience, freedom, is radically withdrawn. Death would seem to mean no longer having any possibilities for free action or for becoming, *en rapport* with other persons, with oneself. Is death, then, the total destruction of man, since freedom is no longer possible?

Yet death, *as observed in the dying of others*, is an occurrence in history and as such open to our interpretation. Even in a secular context the phenomenon of death is still interpreted. For what else is the attitude of modern society when the dying are tidily removed from their fellows and restricted to the clinical purity of an emergency ward? This desire to escape the reminders of our own ending is one interpretation of death. On the contrary, others interpret their own future departure as something natural and insist on their right to euthanasia. Of death itself none of us has any experience, only of the circumstances associated with dying, particularly the pain which is feared and the unknown which in anguish may surprise us. Perhaps death is interpreted more explicitly on the philosophical level, where its axiological presence is preconized as a permanent existential of life, as we saw in Rahner, or on the contrary, it is insisted that it simply means *non-being*. Incidentally, this latter was Gaboriau's reply to Rahner's theory of death.[97] On a more theological level we become acquainted with attempts to interpret death as a human act. This seems to be contradicted by Jüngel, who conceives of death as a move contrary to creation, from *esse* to *nihil*, the reversal of 'becoming'. Hence, according to him, death is the point of man's total passivity which excludes any kind of interference as illegitimate (*illegitimer Vorgriff*). This total inactivity is essential: that we are born, that we die are facts to be endured, without which we would not be human. For at both these moments the Creator is highly active.[98]

Thus, in one way or another, death is constantly interpreted. It concerns us; but can it be said that this is an existential concern? The *certa moriendi conditio* cannot be deduced from our natural make-up. To argue that composites of body and soul necessarily decompose, would be a primitive kind of reasoning. Nor can this deduction be performed on the existential level of being: if death (as Gaboriau says) can only be defined as the opposite of existence, as the non-being, NIHIL, we can have no existential experience of it. Our concern about death is, rather, occasioned by other people's dying – it is of social and communitarian origin. The deaths we have seen of relatives, friends and acquaintances will rebound when we face up to our own extinction. Now, if we keep this fact as the basis of our thoughts on death, we shall find that some important traits of an alternative theory will emerge.

First, we maintain, it is most incongruous to speak about the act of death or dying. In this, as against Rahner, Jüngel is correct. Secondly, however, Jüngel cannot be right in postulating an utter inactivity concerning our own dying. For him death cannot but be the reversal of creation (supposing we have correctly understood his view); that they are no longer, leaves the dead as those who 'have once lived', 'once existed'. They left their mark at least on those who witnessed or even regretted their departure. Thus, thirdly, the occurrence of an alien death proves in a certain sense to be a possibility to be reckoned with: we inevitably take up an attitude towards death, including our own dying. Although this possibility to which we actively relate ourselves is no 'interference in advance' with our own concrete death (as Jüngel would have had it), we can, with our mythifying phantasy, transform the idea of death into an alternative opportunity for free action. Death can be made a challenge to life, a spur to the freedom, even as regards death. Fourthly, freedom in our opinion, is no freedom at all if it does not, in one way or another, keep its alternatives open. Man is free in facing even his own self-destruction not by lamely acquiescing in it (which would be fatalism), but by trying to persuade himself that not only the death of others, but also his own dying may reveal yet another possibility.

This last characteristic of death, of course, makes it the most ambiguous of all phenomena in our human experience. And precisely this radical ambiguity *can* open for us avenues for most dedicated action towards others whose death we may witness any time;[99] it can persuade us to interpret life along with death in a religious sense. In that death means the withdrawal of all tangible possibilities, it is experienced as evil. In that it can, nevertheless, be regarded as a further possibility, it fascinates us. Since it is interpreted as evil, man, thinking within his historico-social correlations, will regard it as inherent in the texture of human life and will ask about its origin, which he will blame on fate, on society, on war and violence, on misuse of power – or on someone who may have been its cause. Death, along with evil, will be ascribed to the guilt of a free human self. The problematic of original sin is concomitant with all religious interpretations of death.

Yet, since death also has this element of fascination, it can be endowed with ideas such as that of entering into a new world, into a new kingdom of peace. It can be conceived of as a home-coming to the lost, as the entry of a personal God into one's personal life, as an encounter with an Unknown who judges, as a point at which the already formed person, out of his own human fellowship, enters into communion with his God – or is rejected by him. Briefly, in this human interpretation, death as an alternative possibility can, but not necessarily, become the *point d'attach* from which a religious understanding of history can emerge.

Rahner's theology of death, in my opinion, can only be accepted in this (apparently) reduced sense. Unless, of course, we take his 'ontology' of death, as he wants, as a hermeneutics in awareness of the word of God as received by explicit Christian faith. It is this faith which allows us to speak of 'an act of dying' (meaning man's free action occasioned by the experience of alien death), of an 'existential choice' implied in death (meaning religious phantasies, varying interpretations of one's own dying), of death's connection with evil (meaning the religious search for their origins), of death's becoming the definite 'sign-material' of *a* sin, of its becoming a symbol introduced by a guilty person (meaning the co-responsibility of the whole of mankind, including that of the first sinner, sold to the bondage of sin and death) etc. In the mirror of Christian religiosity we can speak of the origin of death as arising from the sin and guilt of a (hypothetical) human person.

But even in this (seemingly reduced) understanding of death and sin, we are not allowed to conclude to the universal spread of *original sinfulness*. For there is only one convincing way of speaking of original sin, which way Rahner at the end of the day tacitly acknowledges. It is man interpreting himself and the totality of his own socio-historical situation with regard to the death of one particular other: to the cross of Christ through which salvation was and is being offered for all mankind. The doctrine of original sin was introduced into Christian tradition in view of this salvation *valid for all*. Its function has always been to emphasize the one central message of Christianity. But this central message, *the fides quae par excellence*, is just as absurd a fact on the positive side, as sinfulness and death are on the negative. It means, as we shall later discuss, the death of God, the 'becoming' contingent of the Absolute, and the 'becoming' abandoned and forlorn of the Immortal.

That men and women were and are able to believe this paradox of *that* certain death argues that our death can be interpreted in its light. It means that in considering the historical circumstances of *that* particular dying, we can recognize sin in the atrocity of power not only limiting but destroying freedom's *Lebensraum*. That man is able to regard the death of Christ as the most important event in the whole of history, can convince some that violence goes deeper than atrocity and power; that we are able to be sensitive in discovering it in ourselves just as in everybody else: that we can universalize the fact of human sinfulness, because we have seen and accepted its contrary, *salvation* as offered to everyone in Jesus the Christ.

But is this salvation already present and at work in each and every one? In Rahner's opinion, as we shall see, it certainly is. As for its expression, he finds a category, a new principle for interpreting man already in mysterious commerce with the God of salvation. It is called the supernatural existential.

Chapter III

The Mystery of the Supernatural

Main Literature
'Relationship' (*Investigations* I, 296-317 = *Schriften* I, 322-46);
'Nature' (*Investigations* IV, 165-88 = *Schriften* IV, 209-36);
'Potentia', *SM* V, 65f; 'Existential', *SM* II, 304-06

The central doctrine as the focus of a theological system, already implies a choice by the theologian. It is a choice from among many possibilities of presenting Christianity. In it not only personal faith, but also a certain strategy of a theological activity is entailed. Yet both these are only *implicit*: in themselves they remain vague and unmanageable, unless a *subsidiary principle* is assumed in order to express theological topics in technical language. By subsidiary principle we mean a theory which is applicable to various problems in order to show up the recurring basic patterns and/or conflicts to be resolved. How and in what order these are to be pointed out, how and in what order the theologian proceeds in his discussion characterizes his strategy. The articulation of this strategy will as we have already seen result in a (more or less) constant *method* in *theology*.

Now if the basic doctrine in Rahner's theology is God the Mystery and the correlated mystery of man, the first question of a more technical theology will be: what is the basic pattern of this relationship? It is here that Rahner has to develop a subsidiary principle. Its origin was occasioned by a perennial problem in theology which had become acute at the beginning of his career as a theologian, namely the relationship of creation and salvation, human freedom and God's mercy, briefly, of nature and grace. In medieval theology this general relationship and the problems implied in it were tackled with a subsidiary principle,

59

called the *supernatural*. The essential point of this principle was a clear-cut distinction within man's being between what belonged to his created nature and what was an unowed additional gift of God qualifying his life. This quality was regarded as something exceding human nature, to which no one could lay any claim, hence as gratuitous. There is no need to sum up here the origin and development of this, basically, anthropological view [1] which in the last centuries underwent a strange transformation in Roman Catholic thought: it ceased to be a theoretical principle[2] explaining a relationship and became a reality in its own right, sandwiched between nature and grace. In another context J.A.T. Robinson characterized the supernatural as the introduction of a double, or triple-decker universe.[3] Man inhabits its first étage, but its second, and perhaps third, are alien, *extrinsic* to him. The attempt to overcome this view by a Roman Catholic School of thought paved the way for Rahner's entry into theology proper.

3.1 Extrinsicism: the Decline of a Traditional System

Wanting to abolish the so-called 'extrinsicism' inherent in the tradtional view the school referred to as *Nouvelle Théologie* held that God's grace when it affects man comes to its own. It answers man who in his heart expects it. In 'extrinsicism', as Rahner writes,

> grace appears ... as a mere superstructure ... which is imposed upon nature by God's free decree and in such a way that the relationship between the two is no more intense than that of freedom from contradiction ... nature does indeed acknowledge the end and means of the supernatural order (glory and grace) as in themselves the highest goods, but it is not clear why it 'should have much time for' these highest goods.[4]

The roots of this, so called, extrinsicism are already apparent in the medieval synthesis of Thomas Aquinas, who wanted to weld the Aristotelian concept of nature with the platonic-Augustinian world-view of his contemporary Christianity. For, in the view of Aristotle, the nature of all beings is their very essence *in so far as* they are in a process of becoming and of self-unfolding in accordance with their intrinsic potentialities.[5] Thomas, despite his great respect for his philosophical Authority, was non-plussed by this concept. He knew, as a Christian, that the 'unfolding nature' of man *de facto* aims at the God-given (hence gratuitous and grace-like) destiny of the beatific vision. He asked himself, what kind of intrinsic potentialities enable man to reach *this* goal? Aware of the conflict of the Aristotelian and Augustinian views of man, Thomas developed two not entirely harmonious lines of argument. The first, which is an advance on Aristotle, will be the battle-cry of *nouvelle théologie*, and the second the nagging source of objections against it.

According to the first line of argument Thomas admits that, although the absolutely gratuitous vision of God is beyond man's natural reach, yet it is something which is in accordance with nature, since man is somehow capable of receiving it: he was made in the image of God.[6] This capacity of man for grace and glory is explained in the *Summa contra Gentes* as an inborn desire of man, a *desiderium naturale* which cannot be abortive.[7] Though the object of this desire is beyond the reach of man, the capacity for receiving the vision of God's gracious gift impinges on man's inner being: man cannot be thought without his final union with God. The question is, however, how this desire mediates between man's stable nature (in the Aristotelian sense) and God's grace. Here the dilemma begins: if this desire is not to be in vain, God would be bound to give man the free gift of grace for the vision and man could lay claim to it. To be able to live with this dilemma, Thomas will maintain the possibility of a double fulfilment for man, in this life and the next,[8] *and* interpret the desire for the vision as an *obediential potency*. With this latter he enters a second line of understanding the relationship between nature and grace. Though, in his eyes, the double fulfilment of man's life remains correlated, one being perfect the other imperfect, for the former there is only a *passive* receptivity.[9] But what is this passive receptivity in the light of man's otherwise active potentialities? Its clarification gave rise to various interpretations of Thomas' thought in subsequent thomism. Most of these interpretations ended in the, so called, extrinsicism of neo-scholastic theology.

To simplify the line of this development up to the present debate: it consists in the preference of a post-thomistic tradition to figure out the relationship between nature and grace according to *obediential potency*, whilst forgetting Aquinas' theory of the *desiderium naturale* for the vision. Now obediential potency, unlike natural desire, cannot be a mediation between nature and grace. It is not like man's other potentialities.[10] Hence obediential potency will soon be interpreted as a non-resistence of nature in receiving grace and glory — a potency only in an analagous sense. In itself it is not a capacity for man's 'engracement'. From the thirteenth to sixteenth centuries the interpretation of the Thomistic doctrine seems to stiffen in its static Aristotelian sense and produces the concept of *natura pura*.[11] The theory of pure nature entails a certain autonomy of man with his own *natural* goal, and this natural goal is related only by God's positive will (hence extrinsically) to his 'other' destiny in grace and glory. In the post-tridentine debates about efficacious grace and about Michael de Bay's understanding of sin, it became an implicit view of the official Church that human nature, even without God's grace, is capable of a truly human life. This meant that speculative theology had inevitably to assert the goodness of primitive man (Adam) *before* he fell into sin: pure nature was now imagined as a real historical state of mankind to which was added the call of God to a higher destiny – to the supernatural.[12] Human nature was then regarded as an 'elevated' nature. This view, which Mühlen,[13] echoing J.A.T. Robinson, labels a *Stockwerk-Theologie*, was reinforced at the first Vatican Council in the context of a natural *and* supernatural way of knowing God.[14] It seems that the double-decker universe was made the official view of the Roman Catholic church.

By that time a kind of dualism had established itself not only in the theology of that church but also in the mentality of her members. This dualism separated grace from nature by assuming two ontological orders: the natural and supernatural. This theoretical distinction was, correctly, meant to safeguard the absolutely gratuitous character of grace. Yet from the same position it also followed that grace, being entirely beyond human nature, is extrinsic to man. With this we have reached a position which is going to be the whipping-boy of both *nouvelle théologie* and Karl Rahner.

3.2. Intrinsicism: the Challenge of a New Approach

The movement known as *nouvelle théologie* originated with the publication of de Lubac's *Surnaturel* in 1946. It was a challenge not only for traditional dogmatic theology, but also for Rahner to make his entry into theology proper by applying and extending his philosophy of religion to questions concerning the relationship of nature and grace.

Enough has been written about de Lubac's *Surnaturel* and about the raging debate that followed it in Roman Catholic circles during the fifties. His intention, to put it simply, was to remind Roman Catholic theologians of Thomas' *desiderium naturale* which can, unlike the *potentia oboedientialis*, mediate between nature and grace, without detriment to the absolutely gratuitous character of the latter. Strictly speaking, however, his was not yet another interpretation within the thomistic school. It revived a patristic tradition and connected Thomas' *desiderium naturale* with Augustine's *inquietum cor hominis*: man's desire is only fulfilled by God and his vision.[15] At the same time de Lubac's theological approach was implicitly inspired by the mentality of modern philosophy which tends to substitute for the human nature of scholasticism a dynamic human subjectivity. In this de Lubac is a kindred spirit to Rahner. Nonetheless he arrived at statements which were at loggerheads with Rahner. Rahner would agree with de Lubac's motto: 'L'esprit est ... désir de Dieu' ... the desire for God is a constitutive element of the human subject. But when he adds that this desire is absolute ('le plus absolut de tous désirs')[16], Rahner will be suspicious. When de Lubac refuses to think of human nature in a merely static sense and regards created nature, the essence of man, as historical and not as something abstract, he will appeal to Rahner. But when he definitively takes leave of the post-thomistic hypothesis of *natura pura* and regards speculation about *potentia oboedientialis* as insufficient for affirming the one and only goal of human life (i.e., the vision, which is 'le désir de notre nature'),[17] he will evoke a Rahnerian correction.

This correction, however, came first from a more official source in the form of Pope Pius XII's *Humani Generis*,[18] then from de Lubac's otherwise sympathetic theological colleagues.[19] In the first case it was the Roman Catholic orthodoxy of de Lubac's view that was put to the test. Could he safeguard the absolutely gratuitous character of grace? De Lubac was sure he could. He argued, as it were 'from above': if there is a desire in man for the vision, then it is already the gift of God. But this does not mean that because he possesses the desire man can lay claim to its fulfilment; God is not obliged to grant it. It is the other way round: because God wants to give himself to man, man is obliged to try to arrive at the possession of God in the vision.[20] This desire of man for God interiorizes grace and makes the 'supernatural' of traditional theology man's own. Grace remains a free gift: this is de Lubac's explicit conviction. Yet his tendency could lead in an opposite direction from the tradition which it tried to correct; it would be called in lieu of extrinsicism – intrinsicism of grace.

De Lubac's view, summed up briefly by Delahaye in the periodical *Orientierung*, will launch as a reaction yet another theory of the *supernatural existential*.[21]

3.3 Supernatural Existential: the Emergence of an Intermediary Theory

Rahner, in *Hearers*, had already expressed some scepticism regarding the thomistic principle of *desiderium naturale* ... the main support for de Lubac's position.[22] It was from the point of view of his philosophical theology that he then intervened in the controversy about the supernatural. On the whole, he agreed with de Lubac that man's desire for a saving God (beatific vision) is a fact of existential experience. Yet he was not satisfied by a simple appeal to this experience. He wanted to push the question deeper, beyond his French confrère by asking for the *a priori* conditions of possibility that lie behind such desire. The openness of man's being advocated in *Hearers* could be the means of finding a satisfactory answer to de Lubac's problem. Contrary to de Lubac, Rahner appealed to Thomas' *obediential potency*. Yet in *Hearers* this thomistic principle was explained as an *a priori* and self-trancendent dynamism of man towards the whole width of a horizon, towards the totality of being which also includes God's being.[23] In fact, this obediential potency will be the ultimate condition of possibility for grounding the relationship between nature, grace and glory.[24]

Nonetheless the obediential potency of the *Hearers* does not explain this relationship.[25] Granted, this potency – man's openness to the word of God and to his grace – cannot be understood merely as a passive receptivity. Nor is it a mere dogmatic postulate in order to assert man's non-repugnance to receive God's grace. According to Rahner, obediential potency is a dynamism, in itself not absolute, but conditioned, a dynamism now enhanced by the capacity to strive towards a strictly supernatural goal: the vision of God. For this enhancement he introduced in 1950 the term *supernatural existential*. In general, it is a transcendental condition (*Befindlichkeit*) for man's actual 'engracement' not merely his essential openness to God. Hence the supernatural existential is assumed by Rahner strictly speaking to explain the fact of man's desire *trancendentally*, not to identify it with that desire. It is a condition by means of which God concretely 'finalizes' man for the vision and disposes, or let us say 'attunes', him to the concrete encounter in grace. The supernatural existential is already a gift to static nature and not simply its further accomplishment. It shares that gratuitousness which was postulated for grace itself.[26]

The background of this notion in *Hearers* can account for Rahner's choice of the word 'existential'. Now in *Hearers*, as already noted, Heidegger's thought and terminology play a considerable role.[27] Without entering the discussion of philosophical problems implied in Rahner's choice of this term, we should note in advance the intermediary character of the notion 'existential'. It is a permanent determination not however, denoting a 'thing' without any reference to actual existing (these latter determinations should be called logical *categories*, e.g., the location, the disposition of parts, etc). Nor is the existential a quality which accrues to a personal existent on account of his free action. This quality would be existent*iell*, and not existent*ial*.[28] According to Heidegger, an existential characterizes man *before* his free action takes place. It reveals the meaning and structure of human existence (e.g., 'being doomed to death': a determination which penetrates all elements of human existence whether it is consciously reflected upon or not). To ask about the structures, their interconnection and context results in the quest for 'existentiality' – to which the detailed answer is given in the 'existent*ials*'.[29] Therefore, these existentials of the human subject are neither deducible from the abstract concept of a thing (from its 'essence') nor are they contingent facts which may or may not characterize concrete existence. They are permanent, and in the above sense, intermediary determinations.

It is in this sense that Rahner borrows the concept 'existential' from Heidegger. He also names many existentials in man's life,[30] but the existential qualified with the adjective 'supernatural' has something to do with that transcendental horizon of being to which man, in and through his history, directs himself and is directed. Thus from the backgroune *Hearers* it is also apparent that the supernatural existential should be an *a priori* i.e., transcendental notion. But this a priori affects man *not* in his essential being (in which case it would define man's nature as a spirit and would be due to him as such), but rather as a being immersed in a concrete historical situation. The supernatural existential is the pre-condition of man's historicality and not of his essence as a spirit.

If this is so, Rahner is in a better position than de Lubac was. He has found an intermediary principle for interpreting man's supernatural destination which is beyond pure nature yet beneath the full and conscious 'engracement' of the Christian. The existential is sandwiched between these two determinations of man. It presupposes, on the one hand, *obediential potency* (now understood as man's inalienable and transcendental dynamism) and is attributed, on the other hand, to *natura pura* of man. Both concepts were rejected by de Lubac. Now they are reinstated by Rahner on a theoretical level where they neither correspond to their original meaning or connotation, nor are simply equal to the experience of *desiderium naturale* of Thomas as interpreted by *nouvelle théologie*. The *obediential potency* is no longer a non-resistance of nature to grace, but a positive preapprehension of the God of grace; *pure nature* is no longer an Aristotelian constant of human essence which was once realized in history, but a postulate to affirm the gratuitous unexactedness of God's grace. It is rather a theoretical assumption about nature as yet unaffected by the operation of grace, even if we have no experience of this nature. Conceptually 'nature', in this theological sense, is a 'remainder notion' (a *Restbegriff*) from which grace has been abstracted. For in our actual experience we never know what comes from nature alone, and what happens through the influence of God's mysterious presence to us. And this mysterious presence of God is what Rahner terms supernatural existential.[31]

This was Rahner's view at the time of the debate: he developed an intermediary position by introducing the theory of the supernatural existential, apparently apt to overcome the oddity of traditional extrinsicism and at the same time to preclude the dangerous tendency of *nouvelle théologie* towards an intrinsicism of grace with the loss of the unexacted gratuitousness of God's gift to man. As Weger puts it:

> His anthropological approach to theology, which he follows with the help of the transcendental method, reaches an indisputable climax in his concept of the 'supernatural existential', a factor, which, taking the breadth and multiplicity of his theological ideas into account, is the central concept in his theology. It is hardly possible to understand his theology if this central concept is not grasped.[32]

This may all be correct. But whether or not we shall be able to subscribe to Weger's rather sanguine judgement about the solution which the supernatural existential can provide is another question. He writes: 'Rahner knows the problem very well and has found a solution so simple and penetrating that it is hardly disputed today.[33]

This is precisely what we will see in our comments and questions.

3.4 *Comments and Questions*

At this stage we are going to leave for a moment the further presentation of this 'ingenious' concept of Rahner's theology: the theory of the supernatural existential. In our further sections we shall see its usefulness for his theological system. The possibilites which it offers are manifold and, indeed, most of his positions can hardly be understood without it.

We shall, however, see that in the process of applying this principle to the various fields of traditional theology the supernatural existential will be filled with material content beyond the formal and *theoretical function* it was meant to fulfil when it was invented in the debate about the relationship of nature and grace. For just like the medieval assumption of supernatural order, so Rahner's supernatural existential is intended as a mediation between man and God, between what

was due to man on account of his creation and what was God's
unexacted gift, between our present experience and our future
fulfilment in God's plan. Such a mediation is always a theoretical
task, a *Denkaufgabe*, and not the matter of experience. To analyse
matter scientifically in its constituent atoms and molecules is not
to decide by experience whether or not such particles really exist.
Thus the theologian when he tries to harmonize his self-
knowledge with what he believes is bound to produce theories to
explain this state of affairs. He is seeking understanding: *fides
quarens intellectum*. Yet the theory by means of which this attempt
is expressed is always tied to words and concepts borrowed from
the traditional and cultural background from which it emerges.
His question may be correct, whereas his concrete answer could
be ambiguous right from the beginning.

Our question at this present point is whether or not such an
ambiguity prejudices in advance Rahner's assuming and
introducing the theory of supernatural existential. To put it more
concretely: although the assumption of a supernatural order by
the medievals may be *justifiable* as a theory for understanding
man's endowment with god's gratuitous grace (a), can its
Rahnerian version, the supernatural existential solve, the
theological conflicts in which the further application of the
'supernatural' resulted? (b). If the examination of this latter
question does not eliminate the ambiguity of the theory, we shall
have to ask further about its philosophical connotations (c) in
order to arrive at an approach, slightly divergent from Rahner's
original and, according to Weger, most ingenious insight (d).

(a) From the point of view of a theological system the
assumption of an *order intermediate* between nature and grace is
basically sound. Any systematic thought must speak about God's
truth which is at the same time man's salvation. According to
Christian belief, it is for *our* sake that God has condescended to
man. In the same belief this very condescension of God to man
and to his world must have some effect, no matter how this latter
is expressed. On one side of the scale Schleiermacher can
repeatedly speak of the supernatural which is to become
natural,[34] and, on the other, Barth can conclude to man's
'objective redemption' in Jesus Christ. In Barth's theology God
encounters man in a new covenant that presupposes the
covenant of creation as its extrinsic precondition.[35] Man lives in a

universe wherein God's will is the rule.[36] Once this order of God, independent of or even in spite of man's order, is assumed, we cannot avoid speaking of man in terms of human nature within, what could be termed, the 'supernatural'. Such talk about an intermediary order is *justifiable*. The problem is how and with what terminology we explain this intermediary order. Is the term super-natural felicitous?

For most people today, unaware of its medieval setting, the term supernatural is associated with, for instance, parapsychological phenomena, extraordinary and miraculous happenings in the world of our senses. The term can only be used if we introduce our contemporaries to the problem which caused its assumption: how God's action on man can be so characterised that it is in no way the achievement of man, that it is unexacted and yet is the completion of man. Now, as we saw, the further question arising from this was (at least for the medievals in the wake of Augustine's theology), how the good creation of God, man, can be completed and fulfilled by a divine intervention, called grace. The medieval choice of terminology was inevitably Aristotelain: human *nature* in itself was good, but in order to arrive at a higher destiny beyond the scope of its natural potentialities, it had to be re-created or elevated by God himself. Just as nature was God's good creation, so was elevated nature even better; just as nature was a definite ontological state, so was elevated nature a state in which man was capable of perceiving God as he is, of obeying his commands, capable of acting meritoriously. The supernatural was then regarded as an ontological component of man: something granted by God over and above nature's accomplishments. The subsequent conflict arose from this choice of terminology which ontologized the original problem. It was the conflict between extrinsicism and intrinsicism as regards the relationship of these orders.

The Protestant reaction to the same original problem was, unlike the Roman Catholic tradition, precisely the refusal to answer it in ontological terms. We do not know human nature unless in its sinful and fallen state. It is opposed to God. Hence any gracious action of God towards man cannot but be a gratuitous mercy. Thus we must *not* assume a created and stable nature of man, not even in the form of a theoretical *natura pura*. Neither can we assume Thomas' natural desire as something built into man's existence. The obediential potency for grace is inadmissible. On the contrary, when man encounters God's message, the kernel of which is the cross, it will appear to him as a scandal. When we encounter God's mercy we shall have no disposition (either natural or miraculously superadded) for making God's grace our own. The gratuitousness of God's grace, in other words, can only be explained by the existential fact that it suprizes man who is a sinner. This was the foreseeable Protestant reaction to the Catholic debate on nature and grace, including Rahner's intervention.

The ultimate motive of this opposition is easily understood by the basic intentionality of the two traditions. Roman Catholics were out to maintain the freedom of the human subject, and Protestants to defend the absolute sovereignty of God's saving action. In other words the ontologizing habit of the first was looking for an innate *potentiality* of man for grace, whilst the second insisted on the almost arbitrary and *contingent* character of the occurrence of divine mercy. Yet both traditions, in one way or another, implicitly assumed the need for a mediation between God and man. The first, as it were, from below, the second from above, postulated an 'order' without which man in encounter with God would not be understandable.

In this sense the *question* about an intermediary 'order' for characterising the relationship between God and man is entirely justifiable. It is the explicit 'how' of this mediation which divides the two traditions. Whereas Roman Catholics see the need of such mediation already at man's creation, Protestants require such a mediation only for sinful and fallen mankind. Consequently the choice of terminology is already divisive in their approach, and this same approach will influence their different modes of thinking. Thus, for example, the terminology chosen by Barth is that of the 'covenant' between the erring servant and the Lord, whereas the term preferred by the medievals was the God-given destiny of human nature, irrespective of sin. From this originates their theory of the supernatural.

Rahner's intervention in this debate was apparently within the mode of thinking of his own Roman Catholic tradition. This is why he maintains as the first half of his own theory the term 'supernatural'. It was precisely on this point of terminology that his view was proved to be ambiguous by his Roman Catholic fellow theologians and criticised by others of the Protestant tradition.[37]

(b) The objections to Rahner's theory, the supernatural existential, have come from different quarters and the ensuing polemics have questioned its validity precisely for solving the conflict of extrinsicism versus intrinsicism. We cannot follow these polemics here in all their detail. It will be enough just to sample the reaction of those who, like Rahner, intended to overcome that same extrinsicism which has caused the uneasiness in Roman Catholic thinking about the engracement of man. By these objectors I mean the school associated with *nouvelle théologie*.

Von Balthasar, in his penetrating study of Karl Barth, singles out Rahner's postulate for assuming an otherwise unknowable and never realised state of pure human nature as the necessary presupposition of the *supernatural* existential. As we saw, the function of this remainder-concept was to stand for the autonomy of man on the one hand, and the sovereignty of God's grace on the other. 'Is it possible', Balthasar asks Rahner,

to state on the one hand that the meaning of the whole creation is God's willingness to endow it with grace ... that this grace is the most intimate element of human existence, and, on the other hand to try to abstract from this last and ultimate meaning of man [in order to save *natura pura*]?[38]

For if the latter is maintained in any sense, man's endowment with grace remains an extrinsic embellishment. Is Rahner's procedure, asks Von Balthasar, coherent when, on the one hand he sticks to the Maréchalian dynamism in the openness of man's spirit yet, on the other, is not willing to go all the way with de Lubac in identifying this transcendence with man's absolute desire for seeing God? In other words, Rahner accepts pure human nature, endows it with a transcendental dynamism, identifies it with Thomas' obediential potency (and Maréchal's desire for God),[39] and then postulates a certain actuation of this potentiality in the theory of supernatural existential. Does not this procedure lead to a vain speculation about possible worlds in which pure human nature might have been meaningful? In our concrete world it is *not*, since God has from all eternity foreordained man for this and this one purpose alone: to offer his love and grace to him.[40] The theologian has to approach the problem from this concrete *theological* nature of the human creation, man. By maintaining the obediential potency as attributed to an otherwise unknown pure nature, Rahner has arrived at a theologically ambiguous position.

This ambiguity was pointed out, strangely enough, by a polemical reaction not to Rahner, but to von Balthasar's theological conception of human nature. But Gutwenger's argument is equally valid against Rahner's supernatural existential.[41] To put it simply, Rahner wants to have his cake and eat it: he maintains both an extrinsicist and intrinsicist interpretation of the relationship between God and man. The supernatural existential, in plain English, is a nonsense, an *Unbegriff*.[42]

Here, I think, some words in defence of Rahner's theory are in place; not a defence that absolves the theologian of the supernatural existential, but that clarifies his intention as regards the problem in hand. It has already been pointed out that Rahner's intervention in the debate concerning the position of *nouvelle théologie* was not hostile. He had the same conviction as his French confrères: man's endowment with grace affects his intimate being and is not an adventitious quality. Yet he intended to tackle the question on a higher theoretical level according to its transcendental conditions of possibility. Here, however, he is not satisfied with an appeal to the example of human love: true human love, when it occurs, fulfils and gives meaning to the whole person and at the same time it is known to be an entirely gratuitous gift of the other. It is a good paradigm which, as we have seen, Rahner uses repeatedly. But for objective theological writing, to avoid misunderstanding, we have to use categories of theological scholarship and not such analogies. This, I believe, suggests to him a tactical move leading to a highly dialectical position: he will affirm regarding man two universally valid principles which, however, are not opposed on the same level. Pure nature with its obediential potency is a requisite for understanding man on the essential level, its actuation in the supernatural existential is the principle for understanding him on the level of existence. Roughly speaking the first is the result of an *ontic*, the other of an *ontological* way of thinking. Both ways are unavoidable and interrelated. Being in this respect a faithful disciple of Heidegger, Rahner intends to convey in the supernatural existential an ontological principle in which not only the given and definable nature of man, but also his freedom and dynamic intentionality are implied. The first (given nature) is ontic and the second (with freedom etc.) is ontological. When, therefore, Balthasar charges him with vain speculation about possible worlds, Rahner can simply parry the objection: in the *natura pura* he envisages only an abstract, but valid, presupposition for man, not however a world in which it could be realised. Pure nature is not an ontological but merely an ontic principle. On the other hand, when Gutwenger (and others) accuse him of introducing yet another order between nature and grace and endowing man with yet another potentiality over and above his nature, Rahner can say that he is speaking of the concrete essence of man who, owing to God's gift, is in process towards grace and glory. From another point of view, when he is reproached for allowing grace to be adventitious, extrinsic to man, Rahner can distinguish: extrinsic to man's ontic but intrinsic to man's ontological make-up. And when the accusation is made that at the end of the day he joins hands with de Lubac's tendency to intrinsicism, Rahner can point to the sustained principle of pure human nature.

When all is said and done, however, the last traces of ambiguity cannot be altogether eliminated from his theory of the supernatural existential. Weger, in trying to explain his master's thought concerning the distinction between ontic and ontological, writes:

'Ontic' means 'in accordance with being' [*seinsmäßig*], in other words, what is; 'ontological' in the sense in which Rahner uses the term, means becoming conscious of what is 'ontic'.[43]

The question is whether this 'becoming conscious' is a mere reflection of what is, or a human act, free and autonomous, already transforming that of which it has become aware, i.e., the givenness of being. The supernatural existential in the first case, would mean an ontic (*seinsmäßige*) quality as mirrored in consciousness; it would be given to us on account of being created, hence would be intrinsic to our being or nature. If that were so, then the supernatural existential would not be an ontological, but an ontic quality of man, and we are back at square one. In the second case, the supernatural existential would mean a continuous pressure on God's part on man which determines him to such an extent in his knowledge and freedom that it even continues to mould his existence when he refuses it.[44] No doubt Rahner means his supernatural existential in this second sense. As Weger states, he speaks of grace as God himself dwelling at the centre of human existence; it is given in the mode of an offer (*Gnadenangebot*) as a concrete but *a priori* determination (*Bestimmung* or *Befindlichkeit*) of man's coming-to-consciousness. It is universal, since no one is outside a supernatural situation. As Weger concludes: 'The supernatural existential determines man's being ontically and ontologically preceding all his decisions.'[45] This prompts one to ask what possible use this distinction can serve? Or are we forced with Rahner to assume an a priori, hence transcendental act (namely: coming to consciousness) which is both free and determined? Is not Rahner speaking of a choice before free action could take place? It would be an existential beyond our everyday experience.

This is the nagging question which Rahner and his disciples must answer if the ambiguity is to be avoided. As it is, it is carried through into Rahner's further writings on the same subject.

In an article some ten years after the publication of 'Relationship', the supernatural existential reappears on the scene as something that underpins an *experience*, or itself is an experience, namely that of man's orientation towards God which no one can suppress without guilt.[46] This orientation enhances (later 'radicalizes') man's tendency towards the supreme being; God is, somehow given in creation itself which is already geared to the incarnation.[47] The objective of this enhanced orientation is the *formal object* of man's active existence, and by formal object Rahner understands the horizon of man's actions of which he is aware (*bewußt*) even if he does not reflectively know it (not *gewußt*).[48] That is, man in his activity is aware of God's offer of grace as a possibility present everywhere and to everyone. [49]

It is a tacit motive force, indeed an *entelechy* of man's active self-realization,

even when he does not 'know' it and does not believe it, that is, even when he cannot make it an individual object of knowledge by merely inward reflection, man always lives consciously in the presence of the triune God of eternal life. God is the unexpressed but real 'Whither' of the dynamism of all spiritual and moral life in the realm of spiritual existence which is in fact founded, that is supernaturally elevated by God. It is 'purely *a priori*'; Whither, but always there, present to consciousness without being in the nature of an object, but nonetheless there.[50]

All this means, of course, that, first, the supernatural existential is now understood *not* as a theoretical postulate in defence of gratuitous grace, but as a mode of human transcendentality; and that, secondly it is now regarded as a conscious (yet not *gewußt!*), that is, a somehow experienced, orientation of man towards grace and glory. It has left its merely theoretical status in order to become an experience, if not of grace in its full sense, then at least of a felt correspondence between man's a priori tendency and God's gracious action. The grace of a justified man is but the fulfilment of this transcendentality, a felt and experienced desire to see God. With this statement are we not back at de Lubac's position, even if the theory of pure nature is maintained as meaningful and useful? Was not Rahner's correction of *nouvelle théologie* much ado about nothing? For all practical purposes he is of the same view.

This is the ambiguity which, in reading and re-reading Rahner's position concerning nature and grace, we could never avoid feeling. And this ambiguity will call for a radical rethinking of the premises which led Rahner to his conclusions. However, to rethink his premises we shall have first to consider his theory of the supernatural existential, examining its philosophical connotations more closely.

(c). Whilst the use of the term supernatural was borrowed from the Roman Catholic tradition originating in the Middle Ages, its qualifying tag, the *existential*, was a word taken from the kind of existentialism proposed by Heidegger. Now already the coupling of these two trends of thought could impair Rahner's theory and in advance render it ambiguous. But, as we have just seen, the supernatural half of the theory in the 'Nature' of 1960, as compared with the 'Relationship' of 1950, seems to have undergone a transformation according to the principles of transcendental philosophy: to the obediential potency of man (first ascribed to pure human nature) a two-dimensional horizon is attributed – that of being in general and that of the gratuitous endowment of man through grace. The transcendental subject of *Hearers* is now in possession of a higher, elevated, tendency to grace and glory. In order to point out this *a priori* endowment, the supernatural existential too, will be transcendentalized. In this sense Rahner will be able to speak of grace as a 'transcendental existential' – corresponding to the transcendental determination of man's subjectivity through the supernatural existential.[51]

It is obvious that Rahner, in the choice of his terminology, is attempting to weld two basically divergent modes of philosophical reflection. In this process the transcendental gains the upper hand, yet the existential is retained as a useful trump to parry possible objections. When Rahner affirms that the existential presence of grace and glory never fails man (*das nie Fehlende*) yet it 'supervenes', as a consequence of God's universal salvific will, upon man's essence as 'nature',[52] in the first half of his statement he follows the transcendentalist, in the second, the existentialist trend of Heidegger. When he says that 'all men permanently stand under the offer of grace really operative in them', then he speaks of the supernatural existential in a transcendental sense – and when, on the other hand, he asserts that man 'as he really exists is always more than mere nature,'[53] since this 'more' is God's unexacted gift to concrete man – then he voices something more congruous with existentialist thought. Briefly, in explaining his supernatural existential Rahner speaks *qua* transcendentalist and *qua* existentialist: the supernatural existential is conceived as transcendentality as well as existentiality.

Greiner, in his book on Rahner, questions the compatibility of these two trends of thought underlying Rahner's position on the supernatural existential,[54] and concludes, I believe convincingly: first, the transcendentalist and existentialist trends of thinking are basically irreconcilable: secondly, the only possibility for Rahner to be able nevertheless to weld these two in his theory of the Supernatural Existential would be a selective reduction of the two trends in order to suit his purpose.

The objection that the transcendentalist and existentialist traditions in philosophy are incompatible, is adequately argued by Theunissen.[55] The analysis of transcendental subjectivity, as used by Kant and Husserl (and not as transformed by Rahner!) is intended to describe the *subjective* constitution and delimitation (*Setzung*) of the whole of reality,whilst Heidegger's intention in introducing his *existentialia* is precisely to point out its opposite: it is an analysis of those human states in which man experiences himself as *being constituted* by (objective) reality. Whereas Kant's argument in the *Critique of Pure Reason* prepares the way for the assertion of man's moral *autonomy* in the *Critique of Practical Reason*, Heidegger in analysing phenomena like 'being-in-the-world', 'care', 'anxiety', 'thrownness' etc. wants to establish more or less permanent structures in the human existent. These structures are, on the one hand, regarded as possibilities (*Möglichkeiten*) for *Dasein's* (man's) authentic existence, coming to his way, as it were *ab extra*, and on the other do not become constituent elements of his make-up, as they would in Kantian sense. Whereas the intention in the search for transcendentality is to work out the absolute autonomy of the knowing subject, 'existentiality' makes man in search of his *authenticity* to some extent dependent on the world into which he is 'thrown', on the 'other' that he encounters (*Das Mit-Dasein – Der Andere*). However in neither of these analyses of human knowing (Kant) and human existence (Heidegger) is any reference made to God: in the make-up of man and God has no part to play.

And this is exactly the way Rahner attempts to weld these apparently incompatible traditions of philosophical thought. He is inspired by both and as soon as he assumes God as the ultimate point of reference, he feels free to use both Kant's and Heidegger's language-games. With Kant he wants universal and transcendental qualities orientating man a priori to God. At the same time he introduces (this time with Heidegger) permanent structures into man's existence as resulting from his worldly situation (e.g. the all-pervading sinfulness of the last chapter as well as his supernatural existential as resulting from God's condescension in grace and promise of glory). Although these latter are not constituent parts of man's essential nature (Heidegger), they connect smoothly with the former: they extend and fulfil man's transcendental subjectivity which already possesses everything (anima est quodammodo amnia, including God). Man has, in principle, his autonomy (Kant), but only as far as it is due to the theoretical remainder-notion (*Resbegriff*) of *natura pura*. But, *de facto*, this autonomous nature of man can be existentially impaired by sinfulness or enchanced by God's grace in order to be authentic (Heidegger). Briefly: because Rahner *en philosophe* assumes God, Heidegger's existentiality can be regarded as the radicalisation of Kant's transcendentality. And this 'can' of our last sentence becomes a definite 'is' by means of the assumption of the supernatural existential:

That man is really affected by the permanent offer of grace . . . is a permanent and inescapable human situation. This state of affairs can, in short be labelled supernatural existential.[56]

The philosophica¹ combination of these trends of thought, labelled by Greiner as 'selective reduction' is in fact the transformation of both philosophical reflections. Kant's epistemological a prioris are wedded to Heidegger's existential structures so that the latter becomes transcendentally present qualities a priori embracing man to whom God communicates himself.

Granted, the theologian has the right to be selective in his choice of terminology. It may even show up the ingenuity of his thinking. But when this very choice involves him in two apparently conflicting trends of philosophical thought, he cannot escape the charge of ambiguity. This ambiguity on the one hand calls for caution in considering the application of this theory as a subsidiary principle and, on the other, challenges us to find an alternative solution by radically rethinking the premises on which Rahner's was built.

(d). In introducing and defending his theory of the supernatural existential Rahner mobilizes the whole complexity of his underlying philosophical thought. The two preceding sections were meant to illustrate this fact. We shall, however, leave this philosophical sub-soil and return once more to the theological problem for which Rahner's philosophical electicism produced a terminology, since domesticated, as it were, in newer Roman Catholic theology. What we have not emphasised so far is that with his solution Rahner also intended to arrive at a common ground between Roman Catholic and Protestant traditions.[57] The mediation will again be the supernatural existential.

This mediation is, however, neither a linear continuation of the above mentioned ontologizing habit of the first nor a concession to the second, the Protestant tradition in which grace as the gratuitous mercy of God is meant for the sinner. The supernatural existential is not a linear continuation of Roman Catholic thought, because for Rahner it is not an ontic quality, but an ontological (yet *a priori*) determination of man coming to consciousness in knowing and acting freely. Although when cornered by his opponents he tends to fall back from the ontological to the ontic purview (or *vice versa*), his is a definite advance on the medieval theory of the supernatural. Nevertheless, the supernatural existential does not mean a capitulation to the Protestant tradition: at its introduction he insists, with the Roman Catholic one, on the fact that our vocation to a supernatural goal is in itself irrespective of the fall, it is somehow related to creation rather than redemption. True enough, under the weight of objections he will soon concede that the presence of the supernatural existential is *de facto* due to the 'infralapsarian' (i.e., after the fall) salvific will of God,[58] that it is granted in view of Christ's redemption, since creation is basically connected with redemption.[59] In *Foundations*, as we shall see, he is quite positive in his terminology: the divine call means not only a raising of human nature to a higher destiny but also a forgiving presence to man.[60] Nonetheless just as the theory of the supernatural in Roman Catholic tradition, so is his supernatural existential safely lodged in man's creation.

Thus with oscillating emphases, the two trends of thought are meant to be synthesised in this theory. Rahner attempts to harness both horses which, though running in opposite directions (roughly, the Roman Catholic from creation to redemption, the Protestant the other way round), are driven by the same coachman. Their common motive, their tacit presupposition (inherited also by Rahner) is that man would not be man without an essential reference to God.

It is this common premise which we are about to put to the test.

By this, however, we do not mean that there *is* no relationship between God and man in what we might call grace. Neither do we want to deny that this grace is on the one hand a gratuitous, unexacted endowment and that on the other it fulfils, that is, it gives ultimate and irrevocable meaning to human existence. With this we do not want to quarrel. Yet we are entitled to question the premise on which both traditions (including Rahner) build: what does it mean that man cannot be thought without an essential reference to God? We have indicated how differently this 'essential reference' was verbalized, and how sometimes opposing views instead of solving, underlined the dilemma. We are entitled to search for an alternative approach.

The dilemma is to describe satisfactorily the relationship between God's sovereign freedom and man's freedom in the whole of his commerce with God. Whilst the first was sufficiently reflected and, though in diverging ways, correctly upheld, the second – in my opinion – was not. Although in the history of Roman Catholic tradition much more effort was taken to maintain the human side of this relationship, the freedom of man, than in the Protestant, neither of them, it seems to me, had the courage to affirm the *full autonomy* of man's freedom in facing God's freedom. It is this autonomy of man which is at stake.

By this autonomy of man I mean nothing else than that he (at least on a certain level of his being) is entirely undetermined as far as his possibilities for self-realization go; that he is entirely free in settling for one or for a certain combination of these possibilities and lastly that as a result of his option he can freely define himself, without the menacing *or else* of divine censure. I cannot seriously affirm my freedom and autonomy if, at the same time, I know that without conforming myself to a divine plan and destiny I have failed the purpose of my life. Yet both traditions (including Rahner) assume this divine *or else* and all their attempts to save human freedom seem to be merely lip service to the idea of autonomy.

Thus with all modesty and caution I shall submit (irrespective of possible philosophical influences on my thought) that there is something neutral in man's being in the world, as far as God is concerned. By this I mean the primordial fact of human freedom, namely that man is meant to be fully autonomous in finding *and* founding his own self even without any reference to his creator

God. He has been 'thrown' into this world. He has neither the inner potentialities of his 'established' nature for a definite goal nor does he need the contingent occurrence of forgiving divine mercy to determine his destiny. On this initial level, man is his own destiny. It is the task of his freedom. If we do not reject outright this to many Christians blasphemous and secularistic sounding starting point, we could set this neutral element in man in parallelism with what human nature, or even *natura pura* has meant in the past. However, by this parallelism no identity is meant: the 'neutral' in man has no positive determinations in advance. It is not one of the *possibilia* or even *futuribilia* in a scholastic sense[61] that might have been the order of the world, but – owing to God's positive will to the contrary – never was. It is the basic presupposition of man's existence: null-point in starting to achieve his destiny.

Yet, in the supposition of a full human autonomy, in order to achieve his destiny man is still in need of possibilities offered by the world in which he lives. These are extrinsic to human action, wheteher man becomes aware of them in the givenness of his own heredity, or in his worldly predicament. Such an extrinsic possibility for man's self-realization, *among many others* is his encounter with what he is going to acknowledge as God. Man is not a religious being, as it were, *von Haus aus*. He becomes one, if he chooses to define himself with regard to this possibility, called God. I mean here, first of all, a fully conscious choice which, however, may have been influenced, directed, orientated. At this stage I do not see any reason to assume that the source of this apparently antecedent determination of human freedom is God. It is much more man's attitude to nature (not in an Aristotelian sense!) to society and to other persons.What Rahner calls the supernatural existential as an *a priori* determination of man's freedom is only correct in so far as it points out the various possibilities for human self-realisation in advance of a fully conscious choice. That this mediation is not, as yet, God-given but is situationally bound to this world, that it is, as yet, not universal but contingent – is obvious. Nevertheless when this, as it were horizontal, influence on man's freedom becomes an alternative for a fully conscious option, its result is entirely interior to man. In engaging himself, his (extrinsic) possibilities become his own. It is also in this choice or option for his worldly possibilities that he becomes himself. If God now appears to him as one of these possibilities and man refers himself to it, this relationship – in whatever way it is verbalized – will be an interiorized element of his existence. Man, as yet, is not unless he becomes himself by embracing that which was exterior to him. Hence the apparently insoluble dilemma of extrinsicism versus intrinsicism is a false question, and any attempt to provide an answer discloses its meaninglessness in practice.

From this it follows that we have in advance no inkling in what way God may become man's possibility: it has nothing to do with man's subjectivity. It cannot be deduced from his alleged transcendental preapprehension. It is rather the other way round: if God deigns to condescend and become man's possibility – this very fact *could* constitute religious subjectivity, *if* man freely opted for it. In the Judeo-Christian tradition this possibility is offered to man as an object of faith in creation and redemption and is by no means implied in man's (if I may again use the Heideggerian term) 'thrownness' into this world. It is on account of this 'thrownness' that I assert the neutral starting point in man's existential self-realisation; an assertion which I think does not fall far short of Gutwenger's plaidoyer against von Balthasar for the theological significance of pure human nature. Though I do not believe that he would work with the same hypothesis nor would draw the same conclusions, his appeal to O'Connell's analysis of St Jerome's eschatology may illustrate this point. For Jerome, apparently, man's final beatitude consisted in irrevocable peace and quiet, in freedom from worldly anxiety, and he assigned a secondary place to the vision of God, which was the unquestioned and primary *telos* of the debate about the supernatural. This state of final peace and quiet can be regarded as the inamissible ending, therefore the happiness of one's life.[62] One wonders if Gutwenger, also, would draw the conclusion that this ending can be had without reference to God?

For this is the question that my initial counterposition inevitably implies: can man achieve his final happiness without realising himself as regards the possibility of God's gracious condescension to him? In the case of an, apparently impious yet affirmative answer to this *point de départ*, we shall have to rethink our whole approach to man's, relationship with God in grace, in revelation in Jesus Christ and his redemption, because our sole premise so far is the autonomous freedom of man.

That in this rethinking of a theological system we take Rahner's further explicitation of his basic doctrine (The mystery of God and man) as well as his application of his subsidiary principle (the supernatural existential) as a guideline, will not impair our purpose. For Rahner himself is going to explain God's mystery as well as man's, according to him inevitable ordination to the vision, in categories which in themselves more favour our hypothesis than further his own premises. For him the impringement of grace on man is (or I would rather say occurs) in God's uncreated presence to his creation. The 'how' of this *presence* can give us a clue as regards our own question about God's becoming man's possibility. Grace, according to Rahner, is God himself, and not an effect of his gracious activity on man.

To this aspect of Rahner's theological system we shall now turn.

Chapter IV

The Mystery of Grace

Main literature
'Uncreated' (*Investigations* I, 315-46 = *Schriften* I, 347-75); 'Grace',
SM II, 415-24; 'Freedom', *SM* II, 424-7; 'Order', *SM* IV, 297-
300; 'Gratia'; 'Justification' (*Investigations* IV, 189-225 = *Schriften*
IV, 237-71); *Foundations*, 116-37 (=*Grundkurs*, 122-42)

There is a remarkable feature in Rahner's thought: divine grace
is a topic of fundamental theology, a presupposition that
introduces all the tenets of explicit Christian faith.

In *Foundations*, after acquainting his readers with the absolute
Mystery of God on account of which man becomes a mystery to
himself (Chapter 1), Rahner turns to the problem of evil, of sin
and guilt and ends with some desolutory remarks about original
sin (Chapter 2). As man's overall situation in facing the God of
history this will be interpreted by means of a subsidiary principle,
that of the supernatural existential (Chapter 3). But the
Supernatural Existential though introduced as a theoretical
principle, cannot be left without any content. It was conceived in
view of a basic Christian tenet, that of *divine grace*, and anticipates
that which we, for want of a better word, will call man's
engracement. The term which Rahner is going to use for this
anticipated engracement is God's self-communication —
something which man is not only capable of, but has already
received. According to Rahner, man is the event of God's
forgiving self-communication. From this it would seem to follow
that the topic of divine grace (i.e, God's self-communication) is
not a specific field of Christian doctrine: it pervades the whole
message. It is presupposed as man's existential qualification.
Hence to talk about God's grace and engracement does not

necessitate an act of faith in the content of Christian revelation. It is enough to refer to man in his concrete situation in which grace is, in a way, given, and is, therefore, accessible for historical self-reflection. Grace is a topic of fundamental theology.

Of course the miniature treatise on grace in *Foundations* (as quoted above) is the result of the dogmatic theologian's life-long reflection on the reality of divine grace. Presupposing his acquaintance with the intricacies of this field of theology, it demonstrates his decision for a unified concept of the reality of grace; his skill in presenting its manifold aspects from a systematic source; his understanding of grace and engracement in ecumenical dialogue; and his final summarizing of these under the blanket term of God's self-communication. Once summed up under this term, the reality of grace can help, in the whole presentation of Christianity, students as yet ignorant of its various aspects, stimulating and encouraging them to opt for a more thoroughgoing study of the doctrine of grace . This last way of speaking about grace, as Rahner calls it, is on the first level of theological reflection, as it were at an unscholarly – *vorwissenschaftliches* – stage.[1] Yet it can convey the conviction that divine grace permeates the whole of human existence. It becomes the first and last word on the subject, ready to be disclosed and discussed in more scholarly terms.

In our presentation of the mystery of grace in Rahner's thought, we shall not limit ourselves to the last facet but shall try to explain what doctrinal insights inspired him to universalize the presence of divine grace in human existence as God's forgiving self-communication to all and sundry. These insights are taken strictly speaking from articles of a scholarly type on the 'second level' of theological reflection, yet made fruitful for a fundamental theology: grace as the uncreated presence of God (1); grace as the result of God's universal salvific will (2); grace as objective justification in Christ (3). In our view, all these insights point to the simplified statement of *Foundations*; grace is God's self-communication (4). It is a topic to be anticipated before faith can embrace the subject of Christian revelation and explain the relevant doctrines.

4.1 Grace and the Uncreated Presence of God
A theory which is meant to integrate various topics into a

theological system is bound to lose its formal and theoretical status and will gradually be filled with material content. Such is the case with Rahner's supernatural existential. Whereas in our previous section we were mainly interested in the terminological connotations of this theory, we should now ask ourselves how it is to be understood in itself. Is it a kind of potentiality? Does it contain more than what we used to associate with Aquinas's and the Thomists' obediential potency? Can we say, as many of Rahner's Roman Catholic critics took him to mean, that the supernatural existential is simply God's created grace in the soul?

Well before his intervention in the debate on the supernatural in 1939, Rahner had turned the tables on his future opponents. His position on the relationship between uncreated grace and the scholastic concept of created grace will influence the introduction and material understanding of the supernatural existential.[2] We are here not interested in the technicalities of this problem. It is enough to say: Rahner tries to simplify the process of man's actual engracement. Whereas the older Roman Catholic tradition taught that the indwelling of God is the climax of a long process that begins with man's conversion and at the end is crowned by God's presence in the soul, Rahner believes the contrary. Grace is nothing else than God's presence to man gradually actuating his potentialities and uniting him with his divine source.[3]

Although with this, man's progress to God is radically simplified, he has to find a more or less traditional term to express the part God's action takes. In contrast to his scholastic colleagues, he affirms that God is present to man by way of a 'quasi-formal' causality.[4] He wanted to avoid having to say that grace is due to God's efficient causality, because this would result in a created grace regarded as the accidental yet supernatural quality of engraced man. On the other hand, having more or less adopted the Aristotelian scheme of causality, he could not say that in the process of engracement God becomes man's formal cause. This would strictly identify God with man in grace. Yet by using the category of formal causality (qualified with a rather ambiguous 'quasi') in a highly analogical way, he has arrived at what he wanted to say: the process of man's engracement takes place through God's presence to the soul in such a way that it makes man an apt partner. God 'disposes' man for the reception of his own divine self. The introduction of quasi-formal causality allows us to understand the supernatural existential in scholastic terms as a disposition for union with God.

Thus the first and immediate launching pad towards the material content of his future theory, the supernatural existential, is here expressed by the term *disposition*:[5] the supernatural in man lies somehow on the lines of a disposition with regard to God's uncreated presence. Regarding the term disposition, we should note that it is in no way an inborn potentiality of man's created nature in the Aristotelian sense. It should be taken as an ontological and not as an ontic term: it affects man in his free actions on account of his conscious commerce with whatever he deals. From this it would follow that the presence of such a disposition in man should be explained by other categories than efficient cause and its effect. It is poised between man's acting and being acted upon by the objective he wants to achieve. Consequently, on the one hand the disposition precedes the performed act, yet on the other it depends upon the act it is about to perform. In a sense, it is cause *and* effect. Thus Thomas can speak of a *dispositio ultima*:[6] here the act to be 'performed' is the *forma*, i.e. the thing itself, and the disposition which precedes it depends on its 'effect'. It is the modification of the *material* element in the corresponding *agens*.[7]

In his attempt to apply this thought pattern of *dispositio ultima* (inspired by Aquinas) to man's engracement by God, Rahner has hit, as it were in anticipation, upon the material content of his future theory, the supernatural existential. Contrary to the view that the ground and the beginning of man's salvation is God's created gift, he requires rather a disposition for man's engracement. This disposition cannot be an ontic reality brought about by an efficient causality.[8] It is a disposition which is in one way *prior* to grace formally received yet, from another aspect, it could not be present in man without grace being active *before* human action. This grace being active before man's action (prevenient grace in the terminology of the schoolmen) cannot be conceived, according to Rahner, without as it were transposing the usual key of the whole theology of grace. The engracement of man should be thought out not from the single act of man under the influence of God's helping grace (gratia actualis or adjutorium of the schoolmen), but from its very end: the *beatific vision*. Accordingly, the beginning of this process is homogenous with its ending. It consists in the *self-communication* of God as he is in himself along the lines of the above explained quasi-formal causality.[9] Right from the beginning of this process this self-communicating presence of God does not result in an additional potentiality, in an accidental modification of a human act (one might say, as it were a mysterious but God-given 'muscle' of the human soul), but a disposition of the *whole man*, the whole person for encounter with the God of grace. It is as it were a prevenient union of the created spirit with God; a union which is presupposed ontologically both for the actual engracement (*justification* according to the schoolmen) and for its unfolding (*sanctification* of the traditional treatises) in the direction of man's eschatological fulfilment in the vision of God. This self-communication, this presence of God in a prevenient union with man, this disposition for engracement due to a quasi-formal causality is to become the material content of his future theory, the supernatural existential.

Once this latter is formally established, Rahner will be able to conclude: 'Supernatural reality and reality brought about by a divine self-communication of a quasi-formal, not efficient type, are identical concepts'. Furthermore: in the

> self-communication of God ... which must take place by means of quasi-formal causality, we find ourselves faced with the absolute mystery, since God as his own very self must penetrate into the non-divine region of the finite. Here God communicates himself in his own person to the creature, as absolute proximity and as absolute holy mystery; [the actual engracement of man is the] 'mysteriously radical form (or rather the radicalised form) of the Mystery'.[10]

In the first part of our quotes the systematic connection is made between Rahner's early approach to the problem of created v. uncreated grace and his concept of the relationship between nature and grace, whereas the second integrates his position on these two with the central doctrine: the Mystery. For this integration Rahner had to apply his theory, the upernatural existential, summed up under the blanket term, God's self-communication To this man's disposition corresponds.

We shall see presently that this material content of the theory will gain further qualifications as Rahner goes on. At this stage, it is more important to recall briefly the ultimate purpose which Rahner presents as a consequence of his theory about created versus uncreated grace. [11] The concept of quasi-formal causality and its less turgid equivalent, God's self-communication leads Rahner first to the reversal of the schoolmen's view: uncreated grace is ontologically prior to created. This also suggests that the traditional doctrine about the God of grace, the Father the Son and the Holy Spirit, indwelling man's soul can now be understood along the lines of quasi-formal causality and not of an efficient cause. In view of this, God's inhabiting the just is not an action which can be expressed by the category of efficient causation, as in the case of creation. It is an 'action' of God in approaching man in person; it 'happens' within the being of God's trinitarian life, and not merely *ad extra*. That man is indwelt by God, that he 'possesses himself in the Trinity',[12] that he is, at least, disposed to be taken up into God's inner life means radically altered relationship to the God of grace. To use the traditional terminology: man's relationship to the three divine persons is not only by way of *appropriation* (that is, after its 'production' by the divine essence, the created effect of grace is ascribed analogously, according to the various aspects of the created effect, to each Person of the Blessed Trinity), but in a *direct* and *proper* way. Man in grace is, as it were, *personally* related first of all to the Spirit in a particular way, since in his process of engracement the Spirit guides him and dwells in him in a 'mediated' immediacy. And through this indwelling Spirit he gains access to God's own life. He is saved, having reached the homeland of his divine destination.[13]

In this article Rahner proposed a reversal in the relationship between created and uncreated grace by way of a hypothesis. There is no doubt that for him grace will mean God's presence to man in the immediacy of his personal self-communication. At the same time this seems to sum up the material content of the supernatural existential. Whether Rahner remains at this basically personalistic purview or whether he will extend it to the more ontological (or even ontic) manner of speaking about grace, remains to be seen. In any case, 'Uncreated' is basic for Rahner's further view on man's engracement, on man's justification and salvation through God's condescending love.[14] Since these latter aspects also influence his understanding of the supernatural existential, we shall now have to consider their presentation.

4.2. Grace and God's Salvific Will

Among his explicit contributions to the theology of grace, his polycopied treatise 'De gratia Christi' has a special place.[15] We have to be aware, however, that in this treatise Rahner has to conform to a method of teaching which he simultaneously criticises. It is the method of *Schultheologie* that proposes systematically for students of theology the traditional teaching of the Roman Church, as developed ever since the Council of Trent. Now the authors of these traditional treatises on divine grace seem to have been obsessed with a need to find a synthetic solution to the problem of God's sovereign grace and man's freedom in working out his own salvation. Since Rahner's theses were proposed at Innsbruck, a stronghold of Jesuit theology, we should not be surprised that the debates between the two current schools in Roman Catholic theology, Molinism and Banezianism,[16] feature at the centre of his exposition, and Rahner seems first to take up a Molinist stance concerning the possibility of man's free cooperation with God's efficacious grace.[17] The theologian in his own right is hemmed in by the shackles of the traditional thought of his own school.

Nonetheless, in building up his treatise, in smuggling in his own views elaborated elsewhere,[18] and explaining his own position on the supernatural, here in the Latin of the schoolmen, Rahner's independent thought comes clearly to the fore. Indeed, it is in his struggle to reconstruct the traditional treatise on grace that he gradually parts company with the neo-scholasticism of his day and opens up new vistas more accommodating to contemporary thought. This movement away from the (recent) traditions of his own school is inspired by his very *point de départ*. In the systematic build-up of his school-treatise the starting point is already God's universal salvific will which is gradually realised in his helping grace. Grace exists (as he says later: radically realised) as the means of this salvific will. Although it is at this point that there follow the most Molinistic sounding theses about what man can achieve freely without the grace of God,[19] Rahner will soon come to the conviction that the usual 'systems' of grace, as built upon the synthesis of free will and God's help (synergism), are all unsatisfactory.[20] They all tackle a basic mystery (*Urmysterium*) that constantly withdraws itself from any human solution. And this mystery is not so much the coexistence (both in biblical and human experience) of God's effective will and man's freedom, but rather the difference between God's being and the autonomous existence of the creature. [21] In other words, it is philosophically the difference between Being and beings (where being stands for *created* freedom and Being is God, the Mystery), and theologically the all pervading supernatural presence of God's self-communication to sinful man. This difference must always remain unbridgeable. The problem of God's salvific will v. man's freedom is now reduced to and anchored in that same Mystery from which all the particular mysteries are to be approached. Thus 'engracement' is God' self-expression and self-communication in a radical way to the world. To ask what man, relying on his own devices, can conribute to it, is beside the point. For as Rahner later states: 'It is precisely faith, as posited freely by man, which is God's gift and God's deed in him'. The very freedom of man, and its exercise in which man accepts God, is God's endowment.[22]

But let us concentrate for a moment on Rahner's own starting point. That God wills seriously and without reserve the salvation of every man is axiomatic for his doctrine of grace. This also means that belief in God's universal salvific will is not only a true statement along with other doctrines, it is this salvific will which explains mankind's supernatural situation. *Mutatis mutandis*, it is rather the all-embracing ground of the Christian message and its significance is that it universalizes Rahner's conviction about God's self-communication. Briefly, it is the counterpart of the supernatural existential.

Rahner has dealt explicitly with this topic several times and in varying contexts,[23] yet it will be easiest to illustrate the crux of the problem about God's salvific will by his contribution to *Sacramentum Mundi* V.[24] The belief in universal salvific will implies two dialectically opposed statements: on the one hand, we must be convinced that God really wills the salvation of everybody and, on the other, we must know that the *future* salvation of the individual is still in the balance. This is all that we can affirm with certainty in our present situation and all speculation about an antecedent and a consequent will of God, about his conditioned and unconditioned intention to produce the same effect is of little use. Yet the very dialectical tension of our two statements is already relevant, since it can only be maintained if we are convinced that the victory of grace over man's sinfulness and the promise of the availability of grace for the individual is explicitly given. Christ's death and ressurrection (taken as one act) was indeed an eschatological event that changed the whole condition of mankind. *Mankind* in its free history is already accepted by God's love. This means that salvation (as goal of hope and so of God's salvific will)

> is in general, not one of two possibilities, with the other, that of perdition, standing on an equal level with it, so that the free creature autonomously chooses between them. The choice for, or the decision against God, are not on an equal footing, because God] has already decided the totality of the history of freedom . . . in favour of the salvation of the world in Christ.[25]

Man lives in the order of an *objective salvation or redemption*.

With this position it appears that Rahner has not only done his best to overcome his former Molinistic leanings, but has skilfully extended the material content of the theory of the Supernatural Existential. By the belief in salvific will to which corresponds a 'supernatural' order in human existence, God stands in different relationship to *historical* man. 'The whole multifarious reality of the world has the "supernatural" as its inner structural principle': it is a fact of history, yet it is strictly universal or transcendental; it is freely established by God, yet it has the character of a transcendental necessity for man's action within a supernaturally elevated history. There is a radical change in the world, and this change is first and foremost in man's self-conscious but historical subjectivity. It can be called the 'entitative divinization' of man to whom God's grace is offered and is now available.[26]

Though almost imperceptibly, the supernatural existential is opened up to history, the personal presence of God becomes an offer of grace that moves historical man to his *promised* fulfilment. Faith and hope have joined hands, since 'the supernatural order is a personal order, an order of love in faith and hope', where

God's self-communication becomes irreversible and finds it accomplishment in the kingdom of God.[27]

This historical perspective will be the topic of our next chapter. However, before getting down to this theme we must point out the ecumenical significance of this position for the 'objective order of salvation'. Rahner is ready to join hands with Barth in the matter of justification.

4.3 Grace and Justification in Christ

In a long review of Küng's celebrated book on justification, Rahner reinterprets Trent's decree, and in working out his own position on justification comes nearer to the great Protestant theologian Karl Barth.[28]

The object of Küng's book was to revise the Protestant understanding of Trent on Justification. Where Protestant and Tridentine understanding of Justification seem to differ is on the level of *subjective* appropriation of God's justifying grace. That faith alone justifies is the tenet common to both. But how faith justifies the individual is explained differently. The Reformers understood Trent to say that faith *before* justification is an intellectual acceptance of the teachings of a creed and on account of this belief justification is granted to man, his sins are forgiven, and the initial act of faith is now transformed by divine charity (*fides caritate formata*). In this state man can live out his justified life driven by the permanent habit of sanctifying grace. This latter directs man towards meritorious works which eventually constitute his total sanctification. Protestant theologians, on the other hand, in their insistence that justifying faith even in its initial state is a gift of God through Christ, asserted that this grace meets man in his total passivity, as it were, *contre coeur*. By justification man's sin is overlooked and sanctification is not achieved by meritorious works. It is, rather, a process trailed out to an eschatological fulfilment. Briefly, after justification man still remains a justified sinner (*simul justus et peccator*). There seems to be a qualitative difference between justification and total sanctification.

Now Rahner proposes a slightly different understanding of Trent. It is true that Trent held justification and sanctification together. But these two are by no means identical. They are two sides of the same *subjective* process of redemption. Their difference is formal: we can assign acts proper to justification (e.g., faith) and acts proper to sanctification (e.g., love). It would be improper to speak of a 'justifying love' and a 'sanctifying faith'. Yet there is a basic identity between the two. Love is the fulfilment of faith, sanctification is the summit (*die Aufgipfelung*) of justification. The two, mutually conditioning one another along the lines of quasi-formal causality, with acts proper to each, are self-involving realities and their identity in difference is obvious. From this follows that justification is already an anticipated sanctification and that love is already at work in initial faith. Thus if we can speak of faith *before* justification, this faith is not only, as Küng puts it, 'germinally love': it is love's real beginning. In other words, Rahner's refuses to interpret the Tridentine decree with the alleged distinction between *human* faith before and *divine* faith after justification.[29] Both are God's self-communication, for God, in giving himself, to man creates in him the disposition for accepting faith, and by the very same act effects justification as well as sanctification. It is this latter state that man is capable of good works.

To what extent Rahner's interpretation of the Tridentine decree is correct does not concern us here. It is important, however, to note three features of his own view. First, it simplifies the theology of God's grace in the subjective process of man's salvation. Grace, whether it is called prevenient, sufficient or efficacious is the same self-communication of God. Secondly, if this self-same grace is at work in man at the very dawn of faith, before man has done anything towards his subjective redemption, then Rahner must acknowledge with Barth a moment in man's life when he was *objectively* (without any choice of his) under the influence of grace. It is a moment when he is totally passive or receptive as regards God's action (*ein Ansich-Geschehenlassen*).[30] So we can speak, with Barth, of an objective order of justification, of an objective redemption, which consists of the fact that God in Christ has already justified man, the sinner. God has done something to me before I have done anything with my life. As a result, there is a new existential situation where grace is permanently offered to me. I am disposed to, made capable of being redeemed, and this capability is innermost to my whole concrete life. Here Rahner is speaking implicitly of an objective, that is, supernatural order to which there corresponds a subjective disposition in man's existence: no doubt, the supernatural existential. Yet, and this is the last feature of his position, if the same grace is at work in man from the very first moment of his existence and this same grace is the beginning of sanctification in which meritorious works are envisaged, then grace's proper field of operation is man's freedom.

And this is the precise point at which Rahner, on the one hand seems to improve upon Küng's interpretation of Tridentine doctrine and on the other goes beyond Barth's basically Protestant view. As we shall see, both aspects are significant for the further understanding of the 'supernatural' as an objective order and subjective disposition of man.

The problem is how can faith be *free human act* when it is passively accepted as God's gift. It would be incorrect to distinguish, as Küng appears to do, between a kind of faith which man 'makes' as the condition of justification and a faith which God brings about.[31] What is meant by the Tridentine *cooperari* is that

> the very faith which man has as his own free human act is the faith which God gives us in his action upon us, because he can give to the creature not only its passively accepted determinations but the free act of its 'yes' to the grace of God.[32]

This means that not only the possibility of the acceptance but also the free actuation of this possibility by man is the unowed gift of God. Freedom itself *and* its exercise correspond to the call of God's personal self-disclosure or self-communication. By means of this, the very human act as it were enters the supernatural order. From this it follows, as an improvement on Barth, that the triumph of justifying grace is not restricted only to an *objective* order of redemption, but is God's victory also in the *subjective* sphere. For man, as Rahner explains, lives in the 'polarity of two mutually irreducible realities': as a creature he has the possibility of freedom (*Ermöglichung kreatürlicher Freiheit*) *and*, as the one called to God, the possibility of activating his own free action in accepting God. 'But both components are the result of grace, each in its own way; in both grace triumphs.'[33] Rahner speaks of the natural and free man encompassed by a supernatural destiny, and within it endowed by God with the disposition for it, called the supernatural existential.

It is in this article, written in 1958, that Rahner's concept of the supernatural order and the corresponding theory, that of the supernatural existential, gain a certain precision in their material content. He is concerned with Küng's thesis about the basic unity of creation and salvation, and sums up Küng's view:

> The actual order of creation (of man and the world) is founded, even as a natural order, on Christ (the *Verbum incarnandum et incarnatum*) and reposes in him, so that the world, even in its natural state, is in fact everywhere and always a Christian thing, even though it is possible to some extent to 'prescind' from this, and a world without Christ is possible .[34]

Or briefly, Küng's position is that not only the supernatural engracement through Christ, but also the primordial creation is grounded in Christ.[35]

Although Rahner, who will repeatedly insist on the basic unity of these two orders,[36] can accept Küng's view only with qualifications. He shares with Küng the acceptance of the Pauline evidence for this, and appreciates Barth's thesis according to which creation is the condition of the covenant of grace, nevertheless he cannot entirely share the consequences which Küng draws in concession to Barth. One of these conclusions is similar to that of *nouvelle théologie*: the fact that man's created nature, his freedom (which even survives sin) is actually a grace of Christ, and that there could not in any real sense, be another possible world without this christological character endowed by creation itself. Now Rahner, the protagonist of *pure nature* as a remainder concept, holds the contrary view: the world could have been created without the personal self-communication of the triune God. He defends the hypothesis of *natura pura*.

Nonetheless, his own argument develops in the direction of Küng's Christocentric thesis. On the one hand, he insists on the basic difference between a natural and supernatural order, since creation is *experienced* 'as the *one* disposition of the rational action of God', whereas 'the personal self-communication of God ...

must not appear as something inevitably instituted with the creation of man of itself. It must appear as the free gift of God over and above man's being freely created, since

> the mere creation of man is as it were a *transcendent* free act of God, the anonymous miracle which is always man's background. Within his life, however, another miracle is to take place, that of the *historical self-communication* of God which, to *some extent* is a *categorial* miracle.[37]

Note here the distinction between creation and salvation in Christ, that is, between nature and grace, is strictly maintained! On the other hand, and by way of concession to Küng, this same difference does not mean the absolute autonomy of man: it rests rather on the 'graduated' character of God's gratuitous grace, according to which nature is 'always and irrevocably conceived by God as the presupposed condition of possibility of grace, strictly speaking.' Nature remains nature by the grace of creation. And this is the grace of Christ, which is entirely supernatural. It can be said that nature (whilst remaining such) is *modally supernatural* through its supernatural finalization.[38] The reason for this 'supernatural modality' of nature is nothing else but the presence of the supernatural existential which, in its turn, is explained by our *de facto* being created in Jesus Christ, as Küng's thesis tells us.

This delicately poised stance implies a, to me, surprising conclusion: Küng is right in his interpretation of Roman Catholic theology as regards the unity of creation in Christ. However, by maintaining the distinction between nature and strictly supernatural grace, Rahner does not mean to attribute to human nature an autonomy such as would be indifferent or neutral with regard to man's justification in grace. For in the actual order of things nature is already, and in a certain deficient sense, grace: this creation actually exists on the grounds of God's absolute and irrevocable will for his personal self-communication, on his will to impart himself to man in his (revealed) word, and in his (incarnate) Logos.[39] The actual order in which we live is entitatively supernatural, the order of Christ, the order of God's salvific will, the order that endows man's nature with a permanent supernatural modification, briefly, with the supernatural existential. It is the order of grace. The Christological re-shaping of the theory of the supernatural existential, at the point of Rahner's reaction to Küng's book in 1958, may well perplex some of Rahner's readers: man's created nature is not necessarily due to the personal self-communication of God. Even if this nature in the actual order is irrevocably directed to supernatural grace, this directedness, the supernatural existential is, as he surprisingly states, natural rather than supernatural.[40] Nonetheless the same nature along with, or on grounds of its orientation, is or should be called, grace in a deficient mode, since it was *de facto* created in Christ who in God's self-communication in the highest degree.

There is no need to emphasise the unbalance and possible inconsistency in this type of argument – wanting to have one's cake and eat it! It is this apparent inconsistency which Rahner will have to overcome in his *Foundations*. But does he?

4.4 Grace in God's Self-Communication

In his article on justification we saw that Rahner strove to assert the reality of a created human nature which did not necessarily seem to be due to the personal self-communication of God. The thesis of his *Foundations* seems to contradict the way we have understood him in 'Justification': Man is the Event of God's Free (and forgiving) Self-communication. Undoubtedly his language and mode of expression have changed: he does not speak here of created human *nature* and employs the word 'event' (*Ereignis*) instead of 'effect' or 'result'. Does this alteration of terminology also mean a change of his viewpoint on man's engracement as a whole, now due to God's self-communication?

The definition, or rather, the repeated description of this term reveals the eel-like quality of Rahner's thought: you just cannot pin him down. One thing, however, is certain: God's self-communication is the very centre of what Christianity really is;[41] a conviction which is, of course, not new to *Foundations*. An earlier contribution to *LTK* has asserted that this concept comprises a 'good deal' (*ein gutes Stück*) of the Christian message.[42] Its meaning contains a reference to God's *uncreated grace* (and *not* grace created in the soul); it refers to a *direct* (proper) *presence* of the divine Persons to man (and not indirectly ascribed by way of 'appropriation')! Self-communication is a term in which the supernatural order is summed up; in this word the *basic unity* of grace and incarnation (i.e., the hypostatic union), the *unity* of creation and redemption in Christ (*Christozentrik*), the *unity* of God's salvific love and his creation by way of efficient causality (as the condition of the former) are summarised. The word self-communication comprises the unity and difference of God's relation to the world which consists both in a real participation of man in God's own being (that is, communication in an ontological, entitative sense) as well as God's gifts to man in truth, faith and vision (communication in a gnoseological sense).[43]

We already have a mouthful in this description, and there is more to come in *Foundations*. Let us look at some examples. Self-communication means that God 'in his most proper reality makes himself the *innermost constitutive element of man*'[44] It is a communication between God as personal and absolute Mystery and man as a 'being of transcendence'. It means that man himself is an event of this divine self-communication in a strictly ontological sense, that is, as an event that affects (*entspricht*) the very essence of man: his being-present-to-self (*Beisichsein*), his personal responsibility and conscious freedom.[45] Self-communication is an event in which man is in unity with the one who communicates: the giver himself is the gift.[46] Self-communication means that the 'whither' of man's transcendental thrust is allowed to reach its *object in itself*. Self-communication is the word which subsumes both (the 'whither' and its object, i.e., content), however these differ, into a more original and ultimate unity which, Rahner adds, cannot be adequately expressed in our concepts. In it the Mystery communicates itself as an abiding presence.[47] Self-communication means, furthermore, that God can impart his own reality without ceasing to be the absolute Mystery and without man ceasing to be what he is, the finite existent.[48]

Self-communication means the immediacy of God to man, because in it

the original horizon [of man] can become *object*; that the goal which man cannot reach can become the real point of departure for man's *fulfilment* and self-realisation.[49]

This, therefore, is the 'event' meant by Rahner in speaking of

God's self-communication. For the first level of theological reflection, appropriate to *Foundations*, the 'how' of this event seems to be unimportant. As he says, the real thing about God's self-communication is the relationship between God and the finite existent.[50] Although within this framework almost all the elements of Rahner's doctrine of grace are alluded to, what I believe he is after is to point out the event-character of this self-communication. And with this he is going to restate the the theory of the supernatural existential.

Rahner's *démarche* in *Foundations* is to some extent novel. The term supernatural, a generic attribute for grace and glory in traditional theology, is now interpreted entirely from the point of view of this event. He takes it exclusively as an 'act of most free love'.[51] From this follows its gratuitous, unmerited character, even if it is coextensive with creation. Over and above creation, Rahner repeats himself, the supernatural is a further miracle (even prior to sin), and adds here: it 'is most self-evident thing of all, and at the same time it cannot be deduced from anything else.'[52] Yet, and this is the next customary topic of Rahner's view on the supernatural: it is intrinsic to creation, it is intimate to man the creature of God.

There is, however, a slight change in the explanation of this last statement: the purpose of creation is the success of divine self-communication (man 'was created as the possible adressee of divine self-communication')[53] This well known idea of Iraeaneus, however, is explained by an allusion reminiscent of Lalement's spiritual doctrine.[54] God in creating man also creates ("out of his freest possible love"!) an emptiness within him which God alone can fill.[55]

Although in Rahner's procedure this void and emptiness in created man seems to be mentioned as a passing remark, it has, I believe, an important function to fulfil. Nothing in a physical entitative sense (or as Rahner would say, in a categorial way) is superadded to man's created being (no double decker universe!), yet by means of this gap there is a possible correlation between man and the freest love of God. This emptiness (apparently constitutive in man) also makes it understandable that, if it is filled by God, it fulfils man's intimate being, man 'can become himself through what he is not', namely through God's self-communication. To the emptiness in each and every man's heart there corresponds God's love, at least (as Rahner hastens to add) in the mode of an offer. *Enter* the supernatural existential.

Although we do not here find a clear cut definition of his theory, we can attempt to reconstruct Rahner's advance towards its description. Let us concentrate first on that 'emptiness' created in man by God himself, which he has just mentioned. I take it, it stands for what used to be called the 'obediential potency'. True enough, this was characterised as man's unlimited self-transcendence to the far away, transcendent God. Yet from the point of view of man's free act this self-transcendence offered only a vague alternative of a 'yes' or 'no' to God: in itself it was empty and void as far as the object of choice was concerned. Now God's self-communication as a free event on his part alters the situation and the supernatural existential is exactly the modality of the same. Owing to this event an offer or call of God to man's freedom can now be presupposed.[56] Indeed, he now stands under God's efficacious will to save all mankind, and the supernatural existential is the modification of this state of affairs: 'the once again twofold modality of the response to this offer . . . in the modality of an acceptance or . . . in the modality of rejection by man's freedom'.[57]. This situation of choice, of accepting or rejecting God's already present self-communication, is the permanent existential of man.

Let us now try to understand this rather complex position. In Rahner's mind, man in this one and only concrete situation is always challenged *from within* (as we shall presently see) to accept or to reject an offer of divine love. His very freedom, without its being knowingly exercised, is already nudged from two sides to prevent the event of acceptance and surrender to it that might occur in him.[58] In other words, man, and every person to boot, in the situation of the supernatural existential is like someone who is in a way *aware* of being loved, and through this interior awareness he is challenged either to refuse this love happening to him or to surrender to love offered, to fall in love, to let love happen in himself from the first holding of hands to its consummation. This 'being challenged' by divine love, in itself, is the supernatural existential (the twofold modality of man's situation of choice in facing God's self-communication). The resulting state, or rather process, of 'being in love' is what we mean by grace:

God's self-communication in grace [is] a modification of
transcendence in and through which the holy Mystery ... is
present in its own self and in absolute closeness and self-
communication. . . .[59]

If the above is a correct translation of Rahner's definitive view on
grace, of man's engracement and its condition of possibility, of
the supernatural existential, his position in *Foundations* has
clarified at least three points of detail. First, grace is now
considered irrevocably in terms of God's continuous *personal*
approach to man, rather than in the more static categories of
uncreated grace and divine indwelling. It is an all-pervading self-
communication to man as a person, and awareness of this fact
must take into consideration the historical event of God's
revealed Word.[60] Secondly, the process of engracement is now
indeed a surrender of man's free will to a person who loves us
freely, and thereby actively liberates our freedom in his
unbounded freedom: man freely lets God, who communicates
himself, work *through* his human actions. And last but not least,
the supernaturally modified human nature of which Rahner
spoke (rather infelicitously) in his article on justification[61] is now
the twofold modality of man's self-transcendent freedom before a
God who has already encountered man in the proximity of his
loving self-communication: to accept or refuse God's dynamic
presence in man's intimate self. Nature, the debated remainder
notion, which Rahner has constantly upheld, has now shrunk to
that 'created' emptiness (or rather objectlessness) which man's
'original and unthematic subjectivity' would have reached in self
transcendence, had it not, through God's self-communication
been given alternatives for a genuine choice. The supernatural
existential impinges not on man's nature but on his freedom
towards his self-realisation in the God of grace.

To return to the dilemma at the outset of this section. In
'Justification', Rahner deals with the fact and necessity of pure
nature and its obediential potency. Of this he says that it need not
be the effect of God's personal self-communication. *Foundations*,
on the other hand, does not speak of this possible pure nature but
of the whole man, including his personal free action. This he
states to be the event of God's personal self-communication. The
two statements need not be contradictory. For as pointed out,

Foundations seems to substitute man's created emptiness for 'obediential potency'. This void cannot be God's selfcommunication, even if it impinges on personal freedom. The reason for this substitution was probably not only to avoid technical terms (emptiness is vague enough for what he wants to say), but rather to avoid the use of a category – obediential potency – more appropriate for characterising a situation in which verbal communication takes place. It will be the task of our next section to examine what exactly Rahner means by it. It will be his approach to divine revelation.

But before we go on this topic, let us add some comments and formulate our questions on his conception of divine grace as a whole.

4.5 *Comments and Questions*

It was to be expected that our presentation of Rahner's approach to divine grace would confuse the reader. There are two main factors to account for this. First, we have endeavoured to analyse his thought, as it were in a genetic way, i.e., by taking samples from his early writings up to the apparently definitive position on grace which he has – to our mind – proffered in *Foundations*.

In the course of this presentation we had to consider ad hoc essays of various types. We thus found ourselves at one moment dealing with a problem proper to a neo-scholastic theology of grace ('Uncreated'), at another with a scholarly summary of the whole doctrine of grace ('Grace'); and again, we chose to analyse a painstaking review of Küng's book on justification which, at the time of its appearance, aroused great interest ('Justification'); then we were faced with a brief view on grace drafted for students not yet acquainted with the intricacies of doctrinal theology (*Foundations*). Our attempt to pinpoint Rahner's interest at each stage of these writings must have left the reader conscious of the variety of unintegrated aspects of divine grace which converge in his thinking.

Secondly, another factor may have impaired the clarity of our presentation. In introducing this section, it was mentioned that Rahner's thinking on grace, and, what we have termed man's engracement, belong to the forecourt of a dogmatic theology which already presupposes an act of faith in the Christian message as a whole and tries to make its *content* understandable.

The treatment of divine grace by Rahner is a matter of fundamental theology, hence it goes on to dwell on the mystery of man in general, even though it is the work of a theologian whose thought is firmly grounded in explicit faith. Therefore all that is said about divine grace can be taken as an attempt at 'filling with content' that theoretical principle, the supernatural existential, which we have discussed in our previous chapter.

This is why, in analysing these particular essays, we could not avoid pointing out the general trend underlying Rahner's thought, the purpose of which is, by means of the supernatural existential to give an integrated cast to the grace of God in all its various aspects. Thus in our comments and questions we shall first have to sum up what seems to be essential in Rahner's approach (a) before any criticism can be raised (b) as arising from a possible counterposition (c).

(a). It is an undoubted merit of Rahner's early approach to grace that he reverts to the course along which this notion has developed during its history. Up to the Middle Ages grace and 'gracious' were used to characterize God's condescending action, his *hesed* towards man. It was an attribute of God. Yet beginning from Anselm of Canterbury and systematically worked out by high-scholasticism the same attribute was transferred to man. Also in view of God's gracious action they began to speak of man's 'engracement', of the different kinds of grace-like gifts he was going to receive (the charismata) until finally he was transformed by sanctifying grace. The medieval *gratia gratum faciens hominem* was regarded as a supernatural *entelechy*, an Aristotelian *forma* of man's soul. Grace was thus thought of as something possessed by man.

When Rahner, in his article 'Uncreated', considers grace from the point of view of indwelling, of personal presence, the perspective has radically changed. Of course, he was not the first to do so.[62] But he was among the first to make this reversal palatable for Catholic Scholastics by introducing a newly coined terminology in order to satisfy a need of explaining man's engracement in causal terms. He employs the category of *quasi-formal* causality as a means of making the thomistic *dispositio ultima* for the divine-human encounter understandable. This subsequent procedure in handling, by means of quasiformality, his otherwise remarkable insight, viz., grace as personal presence, will have to be questioned.

The next step in Rahner's developing thought was the insight of systematically organizing the whole treatment of grace, in its very diverse aspects, under God's universal salvific will. Discussion of the biblical and theological foundations of this basic belief is reserved for elsewhere,[63] but, as an all-embracing systematic approach to man's engracement, its place is here. For it assumes an efficacious power in this divine will that not only alters mankind's historical situation, but whose result is regarded as in fact already achieved and victorious, as something that becomes an inner structural principle of the whole creation. It is seen as an inescapable order of salvation, indeed, grace for all and sundry. We shall have to ask how and in what way, if there is such a *universal* salvific will, its *universal* effect can be assessed.

This theme is further expanded in Rahner's review of Küng's book on Barth. At this stage we drew attention to a certain vacillation in his thinking on grace. On the one hand, he hesitates wholeheartedly to admit with Küng the organic unity of the two orders of creation and redemption, on the other, he makes Barth's objective redemption his own, explaining it, however, as a triumph of divine grace in the subjective sphere of man's autonomous choice also: not only God's gracious call but also its free acceptance by man is the efficacious work of God through Jesus the Christ. As we shall see this hesitation on Rahner's part is significant.

Whilst at each stage of his developing thought in considering grace and the process of engracement there was a tacit pointer to God's self-communication, in *Foundations* this expression seems to gain a monopoly. The term itself, as we shall show, is ambiguous enough. However, it becomes even more ambiguous when, under the event of self-communication, not only 'the even greater miracle' of man's engracement is summed up,[64] but also the very coming-to-be of man. If the creation of man is already due to God's self-communication, then all the more so is grace. And if creation can be experienced (transcendentally, of course!) in the intimate self of man, grace and the process of engracement, too, as the modality of man's transcendental thrust, are open to human experience. This 'supernatural transcendentality' (as he calls it) is real though not ontic, and within it God's grace can be felt. It is not ontic since 'it can at most, if at all, be made thematic in subsequent reflections and thus objectified in a concept'.[65]

Grace is not like 'some definite thing which exists alongside other things, but rather it gives expression to the nameless God as someone given to us.' It is a matter of 'our transcendental experience which is beyond words'.[66] That is to say, grace is such that 'basically and originally man does not encounter it as an object', yet at the same time 'it is something in which the infinite, transcendental horizon becomes and object'.[67] On the one hand, this experience is 'inconspicuous and cannot by psychological introspection be differentiated' – it 'cannot be made reflexive', since the 'self-communication of God is absolutely beyond the subject and his consciousness'. Yet on the other hand, being real, it can be discovered in a 'transcendental experience which is its own evidence'.[68]

When he speaks about the 'experienced' (?) self-communication of God, Rahner seems to be hunting the shark. Now the shark is real and self-evident, yet a most elusive creature. The reason is that 'everyone really and radically *every* person must be understood as the event of a supernatural self-communication of God'.[69]

The theme of God's self-communication, seminally present in all Rahner's writings, is meant to integrate all the previously discussed elements of supernatural grace. No doubt, as we tried to present this term up to its unfolding in *Foundations*, its ambiguity will have struck the reader, just as it has left the present commentator with an uneasiness about Rahner's approach to God's grace.

(b). But before we try to pinpoint the cause of our uneasiness in detail, a general question should be raised. In these writings is Rahner speaking of God's grace itself or of man's state as resulting from it? In view of our attempt at summing up his thought, such a question is almost rhetorical: his approach to divine grace is from alpha to omega anthropological. It characterizes man in his allegedly supernatural situation which is now filled with content borrowed from a strictly theological consideration of grace. The supernatural existential, not yet grace itself, means the personal presence of God, the result of God's salvific will, objective justification and redemption – since God has communicated himself to man.

In view of what we have said earlier we should have no

objection to this sample of anthropological conversion:[70] theology is about man as he is interpreted by God. Yet we might ask, is this God and the way it interprets man known already at this stage in which there is no explicit faith in and acceptance of the Christian message? Does not Rahner try to proffer statements about man in a vague assumption of a generic idea of God without asking with what kind of God we have to do, with what kind of action this God has undertaken to convey to us his own understanding of man? Unless we first assess this faith in its objective content, our talk of 'grace' and 'engracement' will remain just another theory about man, another anthropological *Weltanschauung*, and at the end of the day the gracious God of Christianity will be put into brackets. About this grace we have as yet said nothing. As for the corresponding state of man who infinitely transcends himself, it can only *per accidens* be called supernatural engracement. To treat grace in such an anthropological way (even within a fundamental theology) evacuates the very notion with which it explains man. This, the source of our most acute uneasiness concerning Rahner's approach to grace, is borne out by the various aspects of his procedure in dealing with it.

First, there is an underlying imagery in the whole of his approach. We shall call it *nautical*. As in his philosophical theology, Rahner characterizes man as moving within a *horizon* which stands for the totality of knowable and real being. Since God is real, too, he belongs to this horizon. But God is real in a superlative sense: hence he is at the margin of this horizon as a goal that 'draws' the navigator. It is this same image which underpins not only our philosophical but also our theological search for God. Yet, in order to distinguish these two, Rahner extends his nautical imagery: the God of our philosophical horizon is the far-away goal and ground of our navigation, whereas for the 'theological navigator' this far-away God suddenly comes close. Somehow the ineffable One, the Mystery at the end of or beyond the horizon has become someone to be seen with a growing immediacy, as in a kind of anticipated home-coming at the completion of the voyage. This modified view in the mind of the navigator is roughly equivalent to the subsidiary principle of the Supernatural Existential. It is introduced by an event and stands at the beginning of a process which we have called engracement. Man, this indefatigable navigator, is now in grace, that is, in the presence of God's all embracing love, under his effective will to save *all* navigators. He is in the order of objective redemption where God's self-communication triumphantly prevails.

We have no quarrel with this imagery, which is as good as any. But we must ask whether, in the way it is applied, it does not contradict Rahner's own transcendentalist principle according to which God cannot be an object alongside others? If he comes near to us must he not become (at least) a quasi-object and a known objective of human action for all and sundry?[71]

Secondly, in order to avoid objectifying the God of grace, Rahner has to revert to the suspect causal scheme. We know the God of grace not as an object of our knowledge but through the effects of his gifts in us. This simple reasoning would, of course, militate against the immediacy he requires for the personal presence of God which is his leading category for grace and engracement: it would again introduce the priority of created grace preconized by his medieval predecessors. Hence he constantly employs (perhaps only for the benefit of his fellow schoolmen) the bastard category of the *quasi-formal* cause. As we saw, one can hardly understand this otherwise than as a cross between formal and efficient causality, combining also the other kinds of Aristotelian causes: what has been made (efficient) by its constant direction (final cause) toward a definitive *dénouement* (exemplary cause of Platonic origin, here identified with the vision) becomes by its interior finalization (formal cause) that which it is meant to be. The quasi-formality of supernatural grace is in this last class. It may be a happy marriage of two or a polygamous union of all these Aristotelian causalities, but can it express that personal encounter between God and man which is presupposed by God's presence as grace? Can it express that love between God and man which is the culmination of engracement?

Thirdly, when Rahner organizes his whole treatise on grace under the axiom of God's universal salvific will, he is inescapably committed to the traditional causal understanding of engracement. In this tradition, even in considering grace, God was the all-powerful being whose will necessarily produces its purpose. In fact this presupposed image of an omnipotent God, the creator *and* the giver of grace, was destined to be the source of all the calamities to befall the thinking about grace in Western theology. Augustine's desperate fight against the Pelagians; the subsequent controversy of his ardent followers with a semi-pelagian piety which maintained man's autonomous freedom at least for the beginnings of faith; the predestinationist quarrels of the Carolingian age; the clash between the Reformers and the Romans, the embittered debates between the (Dominican) Banezianism and the (Jesuit) Molinism, Baius and Jansenius and their opposition to the mentality of the post-Tridentine Catholic Church – were but stages in an attempt to solve the insoluble dilemma of grace and free will: the God of grace being the cause of an effect within the realm of man's will. The strategy chosen by Rahner under the maxim of God's universal salvific will, for a safe passage through the ruins of this often disreputable past is, to say the least, infelicitous. It can be misundertstood either by taking it literally or qualifying it out of recognition. In the first case, the universal will to save must have its universal effect and all men and women will infallibly attain the salvation intended for them by God. In the second case, the divine will is qualified by several conditions (dependent either on its restricted divine meaning or on its free human acceptance) and one is no longer able to speak seriously about a universal will since its effect is particular. The first leads to a salvation optimism (a theory constantly tempting Christian minds from Origen's *apokatastasis* to Karl Barth), the second to an Augustinian predestinationism or a Molinist synergism.

Of course, Rahner is more than aware of these pitfalls and takes refuge in the supernatural existential. What is universally effected by this salvific will is not grace as such, but the concrete offer of grace, an all-embracing situation in which no one can evade an obligatory choice between capitulation before or rejection of the God of grace. The result, however, of this subterfuge is that we are landed with the same dilemmas which burdened traditional theology – now transferred to an entitatively supernatural order. This, being produced by the same absolute divine will, is in itself a grace-like reality. Briefly: to choose the universal divine will to save as the organizing principle of man's engracement encourages a programme which will try to determine a divine causation of grace, of forgiveness and of glory – just as the world was caused to be as it is by its divine Maker. The offer of grace, though declared by Rahner to be an ontological reality, an event of freedom, is nonetheless implied ontically in man's creation. Hence in *Foundations* Rahner will require from the gracious and loving God the 'creation' of a void in man to function as a peg on which to hang grace. This 'emptiness', however, in Rahner's view is never empty: it is immediately filled with the grace-like reality of the supernatural existential coextensive with creation. The ontological offer resulting from God's salvific will unmasks itself as a situation of choice without genuine alternatives: it seems to be basically an ontic reality entailed in man's now 'divinized' historical nature.

In the *fourth place*, from this point Rahner's hesitation is understandable when in 'Justification', as we pointed out, he accepts only with reserve the organic unity of creation and redemption. There he sees clearly that unless a certain autonomy, due to man on account of his created nature (*natura pura*) is maintained the process of engracement will coincide with that of creation. But no sooner is his correction of Küng's view made than it seems to be withdrawn: one can only maintain an autonomous human nature, in so far as it is seen as relativized by the fact that it is created in and by Christ, that it is neither indifferent nor neutral with regard to grace, that it is in itself a grace-like reality. When this nature comes under the (universal) spell of Christ's grace even man's free choice, which s his nature's highest accomplishment, is in its subjective execution effected by God's will to save. Yet the question remains: how can God infallibly effect man's action whilst this remains free and genuinely his own, even when this question is transposed from actual engracement to the transcendental option *before* any categorial and free choice? Is the only valid answer God's self-communication of which we are the beneficiaries in being created and redeemed?

Finally, we doubt that the introduction of this term, self-communication, can overcome the difficulties inherent in Rahner's conception of grace. According to him, the result of this self-communication is the *reality* of the supernatural order, of offered grace – the reality of objective redemption. Owing to the self-communication of God these are real events, they really take place. They are so real that 'freedom as transcendent *is* and remains always confronted really and inescapably' with God's gracious offer.[72]

True enough, since even if we envisage the event of God's self-communication as words having been said and their meaning having been understood, we still have to do with a historical 'reality' which no one can undo as if it had never happened. Factual protocols can only be altered by falsifying history. If we, therefore, understand the word, *Selbstmitteilung* in this communicative (or as Rahner calls it, gnoseological) sense, we can hardly argue the universality of its result: it depends on its being heard *and* understood. No one doubts that the gospel lays bare a (theologically speaking) supernatural offer of grace. But is it by necessity that *everyone* will hear it and will be able to take it for their greatest *opportunity* for salvation?

This is why in speaking about God's self-communication Rahner uses a *subintelligitur*. For, according to him, the other sense of this word is 'ontological' that is, *self-impartation* of God to man. However this sense is explained (e.g., by quasi-formality, by 'divinization' etc.), for Rahner it means a new relationship between God and man, insofar as it is woven into our historical existence as a structural principle of the totality of what is. The question, however, is, what kind of relationship between God and man is brought about by this event? Certainly not the same as in creation. Though, according to biblical imagery, God creates throught his *word* and the world *is*, that the world can hear and understand this creative word is another matter. For this not a subject-object but a subject-subject relationship is required.[73] In such a relationship I can manifest myself, that which I am and want to be; I can give myself away. But does it follow that the other will hear, understand and respond; unless, of course, my words, in communicating myself, also impart a power to make the other responsive. Certainly, as Paul says, the gospel is not only a message, but God's power (Rom 1:16). Yet this power only begins to work in us, when we in faith have understood what its 'offer' means and have found in it God's love that encompasses and supersedes our feeble human attempts at loving. That a gnoseological self-communication, in Rahner's sense, may become 'ontological' faith such that hears and knows in what it believes is required. Only by means of an act of faith on our part can the offer of grace be imparted, and only then are we made new.[74]

Now can Rahner's presuppositions support such an interpretation or shall we have to sketch a possible counterposition to his thinking on the mystery of grace?
(c). If there is need for an alternative hypothesis to counterbalance Rahner's approach to divine grace, its foundations suggest themselves in our previous comments and questions.[75]

Thus I shall start again from the basis already mentioned: the autonomous freedom of man in facing God's freedom. It implies every man and woman's neutrality: we are 'thrown' into this existence and the basic characteristic of our being human is that we are neither determined in advance nor is our freedom nudged by unequal alternatives. If there is such a thing that can be termed 'supernatural call', it certainly cannot be thought of as the effect or result of man's creation. But neither can it be thought of as an event which took place *with, alongside, concomitantly* with creation: it is not coextensive with it. If it really is an event, it can only be figured out in the contingent way in which history can affect man: by way of chance or, if you like, by way of election. If that is so, then the 'supernatural call' etc. can only be a categorial possibility for which human freedom alone is competent. It does not happen to every one of us, free though we try to be. Some are, others are not confronted with it. Some have, as yet, no alternative to choose and others have a genuine choice, a 'yes' or a 'no' to the offer of God's love. And if in their life's journey they are made conscious of this situation of choice, they may indeed surrender to Love offered to them and be freed in the unbounded freedom of God.

Therefore, contrary to Rahner, I shall regard the very presupposition of man's engracement, his 'supernatural existential', as a contingent fact of history. Should I, with him take it as an a priori and universal quality of man's existence, as present to everyone in its immediacy, as a theologian, I could then hardly argue for its genuinely gratuitous character. It would only be unexacted insofar as creation is believed to be a free gift of God's autonomous freedom. Hence, if nonetheless I speak of a supernatural call I mean that it is embedded in history, that it is one among its events which offer themselves as alternatives for man's free action. Thus historicality is the first requirement of the 'supernatural'. It is enough to know that there are categorial clues in certain events of our history, certain words spoken in it which present themselves as *opportunities* for entering by means of them into a different kind of relationship with what we call God

Now to keep our own terminology straight: that there is a God, the ultimate ground of our being is in itself a *neutral* fact. To this corresponds the neutrality of our being here, of our 'human nature'. When, however, God is sighted as a *possibility* of our free action and we begin to act upon it in whatever way is deemed appropriate, we can speak of man as a religious being in commerce with the Ultimate, with the personal Creator. It is this commerce that can become an existential search for God; we are on the 'lookout' for clues of God's presence in our history. In finding these clues, sometimes by way of trial and error, God ceases to be a mere possibility: he can become an *opportunity*, not yet for any kind of religious action or behaviour, but for a relationship in which one is deeply engaged. Man, instead of remaining a searcher and questioner wants to become an 'answerer' who responds to the opportunity which he has perceived. In this engagement God might become the greatest chance, indeed the supreme possibility of his existence.

This is all I can make of that complex reality which Rahner tries to explain by his supernatural existential: a historical opportunity for man's self-realization in an intimate relationship with his God, not a modification of his transcendental being due to an a priori determination. It is not experienced as a universal structure of our existence, of our created nature (as against Rahner: 'The personal history of experience of self is the personal history of the experience of God').[76] Nor is it a foregone choice which in one way or another has taken place in man's mysterious self wherein God's love already dwells (as against Rahner: 'What is given to everybody realizes the real essence of grace in a radical way').[77] It is rather an opportunity to choose oneself as given, understood and willed by another. And this other is God.

Hence this *de facto* desired relationship with the Ultimate, apart from being thoroughly historical, should in one way or another also be *personal*.[78] As we have already stated,[79] by 'personal' we do not mean just the individual self. It is rather that aspect of man's becoming which arises out of his encounter with the other. Only in this relationship does he become a person – as a gift thankfully or grudgingly received from the other. For not only friendship and love, but also fear and hatred can reveal that correlationship in which the person is posited. Now someone becoming aware of and using this opportunity for correlationship with the 'other' who is God somehow encountered, can become a person made *capable* of living out this encounter. If this living can be characterized as love instead of fear and hatred, then we have arrived, by an anthropological path, at that which Christianity is wont to term *grace*. Man is engraced insofar as he is, out of this relationship, made capable of an attitude of love which embraces not only his fellow human persons but also the person of God.

We are strictly speaking not permitted to call this attitude grace and the preceding process 'engracement' *in a Christian sense*. For use of this term depends on a condition, namely, that we have gone through the event of an act of faith in which God is indeed accepted as a Person, not only allowing us to be related to him personally but endowing us with the capacity to act as such. For this act of faith neither a vague assumption of the Ultimate nor the desire to meet God in person is sufficient. A certain knowledge is required in which one becomes aware that the Ultimate is not only a 'He' but a 'Thou' who, as such, is; a certain knowledge of what in our response to him he wants us to be. Once this insight is gained then, and only then, can we speak of his call addressed not only to some, but to all men and women. It is from this faith alone that the Christian can assert Rahner's universality of the supernatural order in which grace is offered to all and sundry.

He, therefore, is right in that we do not 'encounter' grace as an object alongside other objects. It cannot be encountered, since it is a pure relationship between free and autonomous persons which is neither effected by nor of itself effects anything. Even in an Aristotelian sense, *relatio* is a category to which belongs the *minimum*, or even the void of being.[80] Yet it does occur and it challenges those who come to be personally related more than any effect of a causal power. This is why Rahner's essay, in envisaging grace as a personal presence to man, can provide a common ground between his and our position. Where, perhaps, his approach and our briefly drafted counterposition differ is in the process in which grace happens to surprise man. We have refused to speak of man's engracement in terms of any kind of causality (including that of a quasi-formal cause). Nor did we make any attempt to explain this process starting from God's universal salvific will, since the universality of this will to save is not a fact to be experienced in or alongside creation in which the order of objective redemption, God's universal self-communication in its ontological sense, reigns. We know that God is not imparted in our universe. However, he communicates his will to us in his word and in *his* history in our world he gave us sufficient clues to respond to his call. These clues are the possibilities of our worldly action and, when we freely choose them, if we are engaged in pursuing them, they become opportunities for an encounter with God. Whoever in this encounter finds himself capable of responding with love does not abandon his freedom. Rather, in surrendering to the love of God, his freedom will be freed in the freedom of his beloved. This is not so much the mystery but the miracle of grace.

However, to go into this in more detail does not belong to fundamental theology. It is the matter of a dogmatic or doctrinal theology which lies beyond the scope of this volume. What does belong to this volume is a question which still has to be faced in our Rahner-presentation. It concerns the one and only condition of this process that ends in the miracle of grace: man's coming-to-faith. It is man's act, since it is free. It is the beginning of God's grace since in it and through it we are allowed to encounter the God of grace. He communicates himself through his word, but is man able to listen to it and perceive what is says?

We shall now turn to the discussion of this topic.

Chapter V

The Mystery of Human Faith

Main literature
Inspiration; Visions; Revelation; 'History' (*Investigations* V, 97-114 =
Schriften V, 115-36); 'Integration', *SM* V, 348-55 and 358f;
'Faith', *SM*, 310ff; *Foundations*, 131-75 (= *Grundkurs*, 143-79)

The topic to which we are going to address ourselves in this last
section of our present volume may well seem to be a repetition of
our first. It is concerned with man's coming to faith, into which
we had some preliminary insights in dealing with Rahner's
philosophical theology. In fact, our first anticipatory glance at it
was in the introduction to our work,[1] where an attempt was
made to characterize how and what Rahner the theologian
believes. Our purpose, at that early stage, was not to understand
in detail how an act of faith according to the lines of a traditional
analysis fidei can be explained in Rahner's sense, rather was it to
whet the appetite of the reader for those philosophical
praesupposita which will be formative in Rahner's mind when, as a
fundamental theologian, he will *ex professo* deal with that subject.
This latter will be supplied in this volume.

There was, however, a second instance where, though not
directly we came near to presenting his approach to human faith.
This was in our section concerning man's philosophical
approach to God's historical word in revelation.[2] There we
showed how man, this self-transcending being, in his historical
situation is not only able to hear the word of God's self-revelation
but, when it occurs, is obliged to listen. We went on to present
and discuss this view of Rahner's at two stages of his theological
writings, separated by a gap of more than thirty years of
developing thought, from the 1940/41 first edition of *Hearers* to

117

the 1976 *Foundations*. Have his ideas changed, have they been clarified in this period? Or have they become more muddled by being complicated through the integration of those elements which he has worked out *en théologien*?

In this chapter we will work out in more detail those points touched upon in volume I. To start with we shall have to recall certain tenets of his philosophical theology in order to see their development enhanced now with the achievements of his fundamental theology (1). Only then shall we be able to address ourselves to what, for Rahner, seems to be the revealed word of God (2), resulting, as it does, in the synthesis between God's spoken word and man's act of faith (3). These three sub-sections will then inspire our friendly comments and questions put to the one who has since become a kind of universal god-father to contemporary Roman Catholic theology (4).

5.1 From the 'Philosophy' to the Theology of Revelation

In volume one we have already discussed the implications of the concept of revelation in *Hearers*. Sure enough, this early work was not mean to tell us what revelation is. *Hearers* was built up as an 'ontology of *potentia obedientialis* for a possible revelation'. Its task was to show that a

> revelation from God is . . . possible only if the subject to whom it is supposed to be addressed *in himself* presents an *a priori* horizon against which such a possible revelation can begin to present itself.[3]

This presupposed a priori, as we already know, is man's transcendental subjectivity which encompasses all that is: its openness is correlative to being in general. Since, however, being is by its very definition knowable (*ens et verum convertuntur*), or luminous in itself (*Beisichsein*), it can also disclose itself, communicate itself as *logos*, as word to human hearing. And thus man '. . . has an ear that is open to any word whatsoever that may proceed from the mouth of the Eternal'.[4]

This is all that is said, except that, in principle, if it comes, man is able to listen to God's word. At this point, Rahner, very correctly, takes the conditional clause, 'if it comes', seriously. For it means that its coming is due to a free act on the part of the

Revealer, God; it means that its coming is contingent, an event, an occurrence in history; it means that an actual revelation can only be the gratuitous benevolence of God's offering us a chance, an opportunity really to encounter him in his historical word. For the divine word does not lie within man's sphere of power (*Machtbereich*)[5] even if, owing to his self-transcendence, he can embrace everything knowable and act upon it freely.

Now this anticipation of the divine word by means of a philosophical disclosure is not enough for Rahner. He adds two points as a spin-off, both of which were mentioned in volume one. He first assumes that if the word comes, it does so as an event of history and must be of such importance that all men are obliged to listen to it and act upon it, because only such a free obedience makes man able to fulfil himself, attain his goal and, in general, lead a meaningful human life. Secondly, this obligation regarding a possible revelation is such that, even if God's concrete historical word is not offered to man's encounter, he is bound to listen to God's silence (which Rahner strange enough characterizes as *abweisendes* – 'dismissing').[6] For God's silence in history is a kind of answer which challenges the listener for the word to an option in which either of two things can happen:[7] man *can* to a certain extent fulfil himself in 'listening to God's silence', even if in the depths of his heart he remains dissatisfied. Or else, if he refuses to act the part of the characters of '*Waiting for Godot*' to his life's end, he will fade away into the insignificance of mere human existence.

At the time of *Hearers* first publication, Rahner did not yet have at his disposal those insights of his fundamental theology with which we are now acquainted. Man was not yet characterized as the mystery in minor case facing God *the* Mystery. The magic word, supernatural existential, was not as yet operative and the triumphant presence of God's uncreated grace embracing the whole of mankind had not become the centre of his thought. Furthermore, Rahner had not yet come to the insight that man's transcendental thrust, owing to which he is obliged to listen to the word, is itself historical; it occurs in history and has its won history. On account of this insight the *abweisendes* silence of God, the equivalent 'answer' to man's search, has become a negligible alternative. For in any case, God has already spoken and man, at least initially, has consented to the Revealer.

For Rahner these facts of 'God's having spoken' and of man's 'having half-way consented' are events of history. The name given to these elements is *transcendental revelation*.

The second edition of *Hearers*, the text of which has been slightly changed and provided with additional footnotes, was amended under the influence of Rahner's later theological writings. It belongs to the period following the gradual introduction of the supernatural existential. In volume one we also saw that, in Metz's footnotes, with the approval of the author, the term transcendental revelation suddenly appears.[8] Metz was not, therefore, an unwelcome midwife when he extended the first edition with notes reading into Rahner's thought of 1940/41 the insights of the period up to 1969, during which the nature-grace debate raged and his master's thinking developed. Now the reasoning behind the connection of the supernatural existential with transcendental revelation is very simple: just as God's grace presupposes the supernatural elevation of man (supernatural existential), so does the concrete historical word of God presuppose something of revelation itself in the intimate being of man. Therefore Metz can safely state:

> In the light of factual Christian revelation, the concrete ability to hear the divine word of revelation is constituted by two moments: by the spiritual transcendence of man (his 'subjectivity') and by his 'elevation' through grace or, his 'illumination'.[9]

Whereupon he goes on to explain the theory of the supernatural existential. This addition, of course, implies more than our summary reasoning above, namely factual (i.e., categorial) revelation, which we can now assume as given and as such reflect upon. That is to say, confronted with this fact, we can now, *après coup*, see that the ability to hear is safely lodged in man's transcendental thrust. In other words, this latter is, on the one hand, the remote subject of an act of faith; on the other, the Supernatural Existential, can now be taken equivalently for the grace-like illumination of the person.

That the connection, the interdependence and, as we shall argue, the merging of these two (supernatural elevation and transcendental revelation) are not alien to Rahner's initial thought in the 1940/41 edition of *Hearers*, can easily be shown. The problematic out of which they arise, the manner in which transcendental revelation will be described, run parallel to that of the supernatural existential. Their relationship to man's ultimate end, the vision of God, etc. are practically the same. Rahner too, already in a footnote in the first edition connects the 'light of faith' and the 'infused virtue' of faith with man's natural self-transcendence.[10] Already at that stage, he is thinking of faith in revelation as a 'modification' of self-transcendence, just as its radicalisation is the supernatural existential. To say that man is ontologically raised to a supernatural end is, for him, tantamount to saying that man is aware of God's word already spoken. It is *bewusst* in a kind of initial reflection, even if it is not *ge-wusst* in clear and explicit terms, namely, in the concreteness of history. Hence the ontological re-direction of man by the supernatural existential as well as the 'initial reflection on it' (the 'yet another *new* subjective openness, through the interior light of the grace of faith.'[11]) have suddenly become historical and religious *a priori* in contradistinction to an obediential potency transcendentalized by Rahner. Whilst this latter was the a priori of natural man, the other two are to be found in that history which *de facto* contains in itself the story of God with man, *die Heilsgeschichte*.

Thus, beginning from *Hearers*, where a betrothal between the supernatural existential and transcendental revelation took place, the way is now clear for Rahner to procure the happy marriage of these two with a view to consummation in the beatific vision. Both spring from the self-experience of historical man, both build on roughly the same historical a priori. So he will affirm that it is not only the desire for God which can be experienced, but also its cause, namely God's call in the supernatural existential and his transcendental revelation. His insistence at the next juncture on the *experiential* character of these two is, I believe, a turning point in his theology.

For his claim is that we have a certain awareness, if not clear consciousness, of this divine presence (supernatural existential). It engages our historical freedom. That which in his earlier view was an ontological principle, hence non-objectifiable, now, as we have seen, appears as a choice between a 'yes' and a 'no'. It is a challenge demanding a fuandamental option. Yet this option is not, strictly speaking, an existenti*ell* choice (as in the case of

Bultmann) in which the alternatives are given in clear contours. The *Deus absconditus* has not yet become the *Deus revelatus*. This will only happen in man's actual encounter with the gospel.[12] Before this occurs man must somehow have an a priori experience of choice. In fact, this a priori is the condition that constitutes his freedom by making him able to pronounce the yes or the no to revelation. 'We encounter God everywhere radically as an actual question put to our freedom.'[13] Briefly, for Rahner the transcendent God is the only 'other' of man's transcendental freedom in history and, in this sense at least, transcendence also 'has' a history.

It is the historical, yet transcendent, God who also engages man's knowing and awareness. What is offered to his option is the God of grace who cannot be altogether outside his concrete experience (*bewusstseinsjenseitig*). Grace, even when it appears under the veil of faith, always means a change in the structure of man's self-consciousness.[14] On account of this Rahner, unreservedly now, introduces implicit faith into his two a priori but historical principles. This entails that man is always possessed by grace, prior even to his existenti*ell* choice.[15] For just as the supernatural existential is experienced in man's historical life, so is transcendental revelation. Whilst the supernatural existential directs him towards his actual engracement, transcendental revelation leads him to the actual acceptance of Christianity in faith. The supernatural existential is now, as we have already seen, regarded as 'offered grace' (*angebotene Gnade*) as distinct from 'accepted grace' (*angenommene Gnade*).[16] In the same way transcendental revelation can be regarded as 'faith offered' before being 'accepted faith' (*lumen fidei* and *fides infusa*). Furthermore, unless it is to remain extrinsic, this offer must, in both forms impinge on man's natural self-transcendence. Thus we can speak of the basic identity of the supernatural existential and transcendental revelation.[17]

This means that God's call in these two forms 'radicalizes' human self-transcendence. And this radicalization means that our dynamism towards the unknown God is somehow realised and, in a way, fulfilled in our supernatural subjectivity. The individual accepts implicitly that grace which is explicitly accepted by the Church and witnessed to by Jesus the Christ. On account of this, he stands in a new relationship to God. His secular history is subsumed under the history of salvation.

Thus we can witness the gradual concrescence of these two principles, the supernatural existential and transcendental revelation. Their *factual oneness* is then subsumed under God's self-communication. Under this blanket term the supernatural existential fucntions as an ontological communication of God's grace (resulting in supernatural elevation), wheras its other aspect, transcendental revelation, is the gnoseological self-communication of God through his word (resulting in supernatural illumination). They are to all intents and purposes one and the same. From this it would follow that, even prior to the historical revelation of the categorial word, man perceives the word within his own historical being. Hence if we take transcendental revelation as initial knowledge or reflection on the fact that God has already spoken, and the supernatural existential as the presence of God's personal love, initially reciprocated by man, it will be realized that the two principles are self-involving realities. I can know something about God's word because I am initially engracd (that is, I am in a supernaturally raised order). And *vice versa*, I am initially engraced because I am aware of God's call to me. I am *bewusst* of his self-communication in words. And so is the whole of historical mankind.

In following the gradual merging of these two principles we did not only see their step-by-step unification, but also the explanation of the act of faith implicit in Rahner's approach. To be more precise, man's coming-to-faith was foreshadowed on its subjective side. Rahner has shown, what is called the *fides qua* corresponding to the word of God in transcendental revelation. Will he be able to integrate this with the other side of the coin, *fides quae*, as corresponding to God's concrete and categorial word? In this God tells us *what* to believe.

5.2 Groping for the Categorial Word

Any Christian theologian in working out an adequate concept of revelation and faith will inevitably have to chart a course between the rocks of Scylla and Charybdis, between immanentism and dogmatic fundamentalism. In the first case, revelation would not mean more than that which we can experience in our created being, and the corresponding faith

would be entirely subjective, a *fides qua*. In the second, revelation
would be a divine message, made known in its definite contours
('statements dropping out of heaven') and received by the
human obedience of a *fides quae*. Now Rahner has always
emphasized that the word of God was not contained only in
man's supernatural elevation (in the supernatural existential)
nor only in transcendental revelation. The objective and
categorial word adds something to what we experience
existentially. Thus in spite of his laborious analysis of the human
subject in facing God's self-revelation, he was all the time groping
for the categorial word of God in history to which the response is
objective faith. There should be a primacy of the categorial word
over and above the transcendental, of the objective message over
and above its subjective reception. God's word is before man.

Whether or not he was successful in finding this categorial
word in history will be seen from a summary of some of his
contributions to this and related subjects.

5.2.1 Visions, Prophecies and Inspiration

We start with *Visions and Prophecies*, an early essay dating back
before the debates on nature versus grace.[18] It is in this work that
his anti-modernistic leanings are implicitly manifested. The
word of God is not a private interpretation, emerging out of the
individual's religious experience. It is *de facto* 'heard' and
received in history. But what is this 'hearing'? From his analysis it
becomes clear that for Rahner (at least at the time of this
publication) visions and prophecies presupposes an immediate
communication of God and of his message to certain individuals.
In this respect they are similar to, whilst being different from,
revelation. First, they are granted to select people. Hence there is
a need to distinguish between private and general ('public')
revelation. Secondly, the basis of this distinction is the fact that,
whereas in Christ everything needful for man's salvation was
once for all transmitted,[19] individuals in subsequent generations
do not receive a new message. They rather receive imperatives
for their concrete situation: 'Not new assertions, but new
commands'.[20]

What is meant by these imperatives? Visions and prophecies,
while being deep, mystical experiences, are expressed and
objectified in human words and images. Rahner's question is: is

God the immediate cause not only of the inner experience, but also of its objectification? In his answer there appears a distinction, to the best of my knowledge, now applied for the first time to a more theological topic: God is present to the visionary, viz.,the prophet, in a *transcendental way*, not so that the laws of nature are thereby suspended in an 'empirically verifiable sense', but as the transcendental cause of his inner experience. As for the second part of the question, God acts in a *categorial way*, so that by his 'miraculous' intervention he promotes the objectification of an inner experience. Hence, one can speak of a transcendental and categorial action of God within history.[21] And this, incidentally, is why a vision or prophecy can be authenticated by a miracle.[22]

Although this long essay does not deal directly with revelation, it · contains within a related context important hints. First, Rahner's starting point is undoubtedly the historical and categorial. Yet, secondly, all that is of importance in God's word has been summed up in Jesus the Christ: he is the only source and fulfilment of revelation with an objective content. When, however, this is applied to communications, preceding the event of Jesus (prophecies) or subsequent to it (visions), the source of these 'commands and imperatives' is not so much the historical event as the general experience of grace produced by God's transcendental action. To this accrues God's categorial assistance in their objectification. It is he who projects the imperatives the prophets speak and the visions the visionaries see – they are not just *human* words and experiences.

In this essay, however, the exact relationship between the transcendental and categorial action(s) of God in history is not yet clear. Nor is it obvious which of these is regarded as primary. Only a later summary of the same topic in 1963 leads us to surmise Rahner's bias for the transcendental: God's intervention in explicit and categorial words 'is the objectification of divine grace in a transcendental way to the prophet'.[23] Otherwise, the word of God would be subject to a priori states of the human mind. Thus the principle of prophetic speech, although mediated through the experience of grace, is God himself. 'The history of the prophets is the history of the objectifications of God's grace.'[24] With this emphasis, of course, the balance tips over to the transcendental. Yet the latter, despite being an historical action of God, is another kind of a priori, an a priori within history. In it the later principle of transcendental revelation is foreshadowed, whereas the categorial word shifts its weight from the initial event, the prophet's encounter with God, to the result of the whole happening. It is the objectification of grace.

This categorial word of God in history was regarded by a dogmatic fundamentalism as being found in the words of the Bible and (at least in the Roman Catholic Church) in the traditions and teaching of the *Magisterium*. However, Rahner's stance is not as simple as that. In his 1956 essay on inspiration he emphasizes that the theologian has first to explain how the Bible came about and in what sense tradition and Christian teaching are a continuation of God's categorial word.[25] His main question is: in what sense can God be called the literary author of the Bible while not only allowing, but positively promoting the human contribution to its actual writing? It is obviously not enough to say that God, in as much as he gives the grace of faith to the sacred writer, 'inspires' the writing. The Bible is not merely the sacred writer's own expression in human words of his inner experience. In its coming-to-be, besides God's engracing, hence transcendental, activity, we also have to assume his categorial intervention in that dimension in which historical man is at work.[26] Therefore the activity of God who inspires (causes?) the very writing of the biblical words, must also be regarded as God's categorial word.[27]

This answer, however, could still be understood in the sense of a dogmatic fundamentalism. Rahner goes beyond this. It is not necessary to explain in detail his whole theory of inspiration, since an important insight for the understanding of revelation emerges from his premises. Approaching inspiration from the side of God's historical activity (causality?), he asserts that there are two 'moments' in the self-same intervention. God wills absolutely the coming-to-be of the Church in general, and with it, he also wills its main constitutive elements in particular. One of these is the genesis of the inspired Bible. In other words, God's inspiring activity is implied in his intention to found the Church. Thus the Church becomes a mediation not only for subsequent tradition and teaching but also for the Bible, in which we ought to recognize the categorial word of God in history. In this view the Church's mediation, now replacing the prophet's experience of grace and apparently even substituting for Christ, the quintessence of all possible revelation, is something transcendental. And this transcendental willed by God implies the categorial word which we read in the Bible. Categorial revelation (at least from God's point of view) is entailed in his will causing the Church to be. From our point of view, however, it can be seen the other way round: the presence of the same will can be known through the mediation of the categorial word. In this way, the 'action(s)' of God are self-involving realities: the one can be known through the mediation of the other and *vice versa*.

With this, I believe, the basic view of Rahner's concept of revelation is laid bare. Whatever he will write about it later will merely be variations of the same theme. In fact, in his later references to revelation he seems either to forget the tension between the transcendental and categorial word of God or to take their unity in difference for granted. In his contribution to *Sacramentum Mundi* the whole problem boils down to the assertion that revelation is 'the highest and most radical case' of a relationship between the God of grace and supernaturally raised historical man.[28] This relationship, however, only indicates the generic and transcendental term under which all possible 'revelations' can be summed up. It seems that, for the later Rahner, it is enough to speak about this transcendental side of revelation, without exposing his flanks to a modernist type of immanentism. That he is able to do this derives from yet another insight: both the transcendental and the categorial word of God's revelation are historical events: they occur in the contingency of salvation history.

5.2.2 Revelation and *Heilsgeschichte*

The basic relationship between God and man, in which the concept of revelation is summed up, is through and through historical. Hence 'it is granted to every mind by grace but inescapably and always',[29] and within this grace the occurrence of God's word is historically implied:

> Revelation is the historical self-unfolding in categorial terms of the transcendental relation of man and God which is constituted in God's self-communication.[30]

Through insistence on the label 'historical' the dangers of a revelation-immanentism have faded away without falling over on the other side of dogmatic fundamentalism. However, Rahner's use of this adjective is to be understood according to his theory of history, which he tackles in the important article already referred to, 'History of the World and Salvation History'. We are going to present it in so far as it further witnesses to his search for the categorial word of God in its relationship to the already assumed transcendental revelation.

The aim of the article is to sum up what is meant by salvation history and the process within it by which the transcendental and the categorial word of God attain unity. The article presupposes what Rahner has worked out elsewhere: first, revelation is 'divinizing' grace in so far as it must be 'thought of as a change in the structure of human consciousness;'[31] secondly, both grace and revelation are just as widely distributed as God's universal will to save – though historical, both are a priori realities; thirdly, the presence of grace and revelation is felt by man in his basic condition (*Grundbefindlichkeit*) as an initial reflection, viz., choice, as an initial faith granted to everybody.[32] In other words, man's freedom is, however incipiently, engaged a priori.

This last statement serves as an access to what he is going to affirm as the main message of 'History': there is a sacred history within the profane; a history which is coextensive with the events of world history; a history 'hidden' within history, even if it does not appear in the same concrete forms as profane history, even if the term 'historical' can only be attributed to it in a wide and watered-down sense.[33] So on what grounds can we attribute the word 'historical' to the transcendental side of this happening'? Rahner's answer is that both the categorial and transcendental sides are carried by human freedom, both together make up the history of man's freedom. For the same freedom, by its very nature, is exercised in two realms. Through it man encounters *simultaneously* the God of grace *and* the world with its profane history. Freedom combines the transcendental and the categorial:

Hence the freedom of acceptance or refusal of salvation [i.e., transcendental dimension] ... always occurs in an encounter with the world [i.e., categorial dimension] and not merely in the confined sector of the sacred.'[34]

Thus man's freedom as regards both dimensions can be called 'historical', since it is enacted in free action, in encounter, in intercommunication as objectified in various forms.[35] It is a matter of really free acts, decisions and communications which take place in an ongoing history.[36] And the concurrence of this free 'happening' in both dimensions, the interaction of these two 'histories' can be termed *Heilsgeschichte*.

In order to visualize this interaction Rahner says that the 'history' of transcendence strives to realize itself in the history of the world on the one hand, and on the other, certain events of profane history point to the hidden history of man with God. On the one hand, it is expected that sacred history 'will try to objectify itself in explicit expressions of religion, in liturgy, in religious associations, in prophetic protests against misinterpretations of [our] basic experience', etc., that is, in secular events.[37] On the other hand, these events will invite discernment of God's saving acts, perception of God's own words giving them sense and meaning. In this discernment, viz. perception, we can, in a sense, encounter God's *categorial word* of revelation. However, insists Rahner, this categorial word is not simply the divine word expressed in human words. If it were, we could not speak of *salvation* as history. It would only be the history of individual or collective faith recognizing, as it were in a flash, certain events humanly *interpreted* as God's saving acts and words in an otherwise profane history. The history of the world can become sacred history if and when, through its events, 'God as such becomes present ... when the word [i.e, of God] which expresses and interprets them is added'. And this word is *not* added by us from the outside or subsequently, but is their inner constitutive.[38] In other words, Rahner seems at last to have reached, over and above God's transcendental revelation, the categorial word in history. It consists in God's interpreting 'a particular part of this profane and otherwise ambiguous history by his word ... by giving it a saving or damning character.'[39] In this sense the categorial word in history has a restricted field, it is selective regarding the events which it intrinsically constitutes. But in constituting them, it is recognisable as God's categorial word in our own history.

Thus the concept of salvation history, as distinct from yet related to profane history, is the achievement of 'History'. Yet

there is a further precision in this article which will play its part in
the treatment of revelation in *Foundations*. There is a general or
universal as well as an official or particular salvation, viz.,
revelation history. *Foundations* will thus insist on the possibility of
a genuine history of revelation outside the Old and New
Testaments, provided 'that *this* categorial history of revelation is
understood, or can be understood, as a self-interpretation of the
revelatory and transcendental experience of God'; that it is
driven by that 'immanent power of divine self-communication';
that it cannot be deduced by any *human* a priori, but is
'experienced, suffered and accepted in history itself.'[40] With this,
of course, we have conceded the revelatory nature of non-
Christian religions, and there is need for a further distinction.
The general or universal revelation of God which we can see in
other religions comes to its own in the official or particular,
whereas the latter keeps the orientation of the particular towards
universality, 'towards the mediation of an ever more adequate
religious self-understanding for *all men*.'[41] That is to say, non-
christian 'revelations' tend toward the Christian, and the
Christian in a reciprocal way tends to their unification in an
adequate religious self-understanding of all men!

In this, for our topic important excurse on the history of
religions Rahner, of course, takes for granted that Christianity *is*
the particular or official form in which God's word can be heard
and obediently believed. As I see it, the ground for this assertion
seems to be a pragmatic success-principle. He states that all
religions (including Christianity) are historical; they have a
beginning and an ending between these two points there is a
tension like a strung bow. Furthermore he assumes that, in a
sense, in all of them there is an objectification of transcendental
grace in an intimation of God's historical word. Primitive
religions which express themselves in myths, etiological tales etc.,
can be taken as the beginning of revelation history. At the same
time they are incipient histories of human freedom in which man
becomes conscious not only of his transcendental reference, but
also of the inner dynamism of his own religious expressions
towaards a more advanced form. Thus world religions seem not
to be God's revelations as far as their definite *content* goes, but in so
far as they are interpreted by subsequent religious
manifestations. One among these is the revelation contained in

the Old Testament. But even of this one can say that it is not its content that makes it a definitive revelation-history.[42] The Old Testament, too, is in need of a radical reorientation in the event of Jesus the Christ, *the* successful revelation-history. For he alone is the ultimate criterion of all categorial revelation. In the incarnate Word of God

> the God who communicates himself and the man who accepts God's self-communication become irrevocably one and the history ... of [categorial?] revelation reaches its goal.[43]

In the God-man the history of transcendence as well as its counterpart, the categorial history of God's word, reach their concrete unity. Christ is the unique and unsurpassable criterion of all positive revelations of the divine world (transcendental and categorial). In fact, what the event of Jesus Christ contains is the ending of salvation history, the second caesure of all *Heilsgeschichte*. Sure enough, history does not end with this event. But it has achieved its main purpose in view of *the* eschatological ending (the god-manhood of the whole of mankind).[44] In Christ the history of mankind has now reached its goal categorially and within this goal it directs itself towards its *eschaton*.

With these Christological panegyrics Rahner appears to have found the categorial word of God, which sums up all that God ever wanted to reveal. This word is now in the major case: the Word of God.

5.3 The Synthesis of God's Word and Human Faith
The topic of revelation entails that of corresponding human faith. This statement, however needs to be qualified. By *revelation* we usually mean God's explicit word, the categorial message of God's self-disclosure, not just a vague conviction that 'God has spoken'. We mean the *what*, i.e. the objective content of God's revelation.

By *corresponding human faith* one ought to mean a human act or process of acceptance and consent to the revealed word. In technical terms: a *fides quae* is required, a response in explicit human words to the summons of God's explicit word. We mean belief in a truth offered by God.

In saying that the word entails faith (or *vice versa*), we mean a necessary or inevitable link out of which there arises an obligation: man in facing this word 'is made to', must or ought to believe. The description of this obligation, dividing as it does the various approaches to the act of faith, can commonly be summed up as *analysis fidei*: an analysis of what happens when the word is heard and the individual consents by expressing his newly gained conviction in a profession of faith.

It is this analysis of faith which we shall now have to tease out from Rahner's fundamental theology. In doing so, we shall not be covering entirely unknown   ground. As mentioned at the beginning of this section, Rahner's analysis of faith was implicitly dealt with in volume one when we tried to understand his new formulation of 'creeds' in a contemporary setting. There we could see the general trend of his solution, without explicitly facing the question in hand. We shall have to recall it now: man's coming to faith is an *event*, an occurrence in history. Although it is a single event, it has various aspects which need not take place in a temporal sequence, yet constitute the whole.

Faith is, *first*, an event which takes place in an encounter with the word of God's historical self-revelation; faith is, *secondly*, an event which transforms both the preacher (who mediates this divine word) and the human listener; faith is, *thirdly*, of both human and divine origin. This unity and difference is, *fourthly* a matter of transcendental experience which can be objectified in a confession of faith or in 'creeds' in their contemporary setting.

In the above summary an encounter is mentioned in the first aspect alone, where it obviously refers to human interpersonality: a human mediator conveys the message of God's word to the would-be believer in what could be a chance meeting. But this encounter in itself is not enough to explain the other aspects of the event; it might remain an exchange of merely human words; it seems to be only an occasion of coming-to-faith, but not its ground. Furthermore, 'Faith is never awakened', says Rahner, 'by someone having something communicated to him purely from outside, addressed solely to his naked understanding as such'.[45] That is to say, at this level the encounter does not contain the categorial word of God as such.

Thus the encounter needs to go deeper or, rather, as he says, 'to its further explicit stage',[46] i.e., the second and third aspects above. There we have used 'faith' as a substantive: faith transforms, faith is the result of God's and man's action. This indicates that faith which 'transforms' is already thought of as a power equivalent to man's supernatural elevation. Rahner thinks in terms of the Supernatural Existential which is at the same time transcendental revelation, that is, an event which, prior to man's coming-to-faith, has taken place in the would-be believer. 'To lead to faith is always to assist understanding of what has already been experienced in the depth of human reality as grace.'[47] Or to put it another way: it is presupposed that (a) every human being is 'always potentially a believer', and what is more, (b) is already in possession of faith 'prior to his freedom as to what he is to believe' – because (c) 'faith may be assumed to be present'.[48] Therefore the human preacher of the word or, more precisely, his preaching, like the addressee's listening, is being transformed into an apt vehicle for the divine word. In a short sketch of 1970, Rahner expresses the same, as we can now see, central 'happening' in the ineradicable duality between a statement and what is intended by it. Thus, when the preacher's words are heard, it can happen that not 'only what his statements are about will come home to the listeners, but what is stated takes place by the very fact of being stated',[49] meaning, presumably, a skilful preacher does not only inform; he is empowered to convey his own conviction to the hearer. But this conviction in being conveyed is, in Rahner's idiom, God's divinizing presence[50] in the innermost core of man, common to both preacher and hearer. Both the preached word and its obedient hearing here and now are borne by God himself.[51] Thus coming-to-faith as a whole is a *word-event* that encompasses not only the preacher but also the listener: under the influence of the divine presence in both of them, it becomes the constitutive element of their historical dialogue.

Bear in mind, however, that with these two aspects of the fourfold event, we have not yet reached the last stage, namely, that of explicit faith consenting to the categorial word and to *that which* it conveys. In the second and third aspects Rahner still speaks of the transcendental word on the one hand, and of a subjective disposition for faith, of a *fides qua*, on the other. Yet this latter is, for him, already faith[52] which has to 'grow up', to be objectified, just as the categorial word of God is the objectification of the transcendental. Explicit faith, as distinct from implicit, is a kind of objectification of the latter.

How is this to be understood? We have tried to formulate the fourth aspect of man's coming-to-faith as arising from the transcendental experience of the unity between the divine and human origins of implicit faith. This latter projects itself into an objective confession of faith. It is an objectification. Now, if this summary presentation of ours is correct, then Rahner must have assumed two kinds of 'transcendental experience': (a) out of a vague awareness of the disposition for faith (of which everybody is in possession) there arises, (b) an experience which is still a priori and transcendental yet with more definite contours (i.e. of the unity of the divine-human origin of the faith event). This second kind of experience can, under certain circumstances, express itself in definite words and statements.

In 'Integration' Rahner tries to explain this state of affairs with parallels borrowed from sacramental theology, ecclesiology and Christology. For instance: the faith of the would-be believer

> lays hold of a sign, and is, therefore truly faith *only* if it grasps the sign [b] *through being itself held in the grasp* of the unutterable mystery [a] of the presence of God mercifully communicating itself.[53]

This tortuous text is patterned on sacramental theology. In the first sentence it is said that the sign and the signified (i.e., the proposition and its meaning), though different, find their unity in faith (trascendental experience [b]) on account of God's transcendental presence (experience [a]). Faith is the unity and difference of these two experiences. It seems that (a) infallibly grasps that the sign and signified (i.e., the proposition and what it contains), that is, experience (b) is correct. Both (a) and (b) are transcendental experiences as it were rolled into one. Therefore, it is not that the would-be believer brings these elements into oneness, but rather that their unity is warranted by God himself. It is given inseperably and unmixed, as Rahner's Christological allusion would have it. Or, as he later adds, the would-be believer 'implicitly' believes what the community of the faithful professes (experience [a]), hence the words of the creed basically coincide with God's categorial word (experience [b]). Although the Community of the faithful (i.e. the Church) is a finite mediation, yet this 'mediation has its ultimate truth in what is mediated', as Rahner's ecclesiologal reference would have it. The sign and God's transcendental presence are, though unmixed, one and the same complex reality. What the words of a proposition wants to state is ultimately one with the explicit statement. Thus implicit faith in the divine-human origin of Jesus the Christ gradually matures into the dogmas about the Incarnate Son of God. They are, at bottom one and the same. Once this experienced unity is expressed in definite terms, we have reached the stage of explicit faith, the *fides quae*, by means of which man is enabled to respond to God's categorial word.

What we have gathered, mainly from Rahner's incidental writings, will be confirmed in his approach in *Foundations* to man's coming-to faith in accepting God's word of revelation. There is only a slight shift of emphasis in this late work, understandable in view of the nature of a *Grundkurs*. Here the whole process is taken in a dialogal context, not so much between man and man as between man and God. It is, however, a dialogue in which the roles are somewhat inequitably distributed: man is the one who asks the question and his questions are directed to God who, even if he remains silent, is *the* answer. The unfolding of this dialogal event is the coming-to-be of both revelation and of corresponding faith.

Its stages are, roughly, as follows: in becoming aware of being a questioner, man realises that he is 'made' to question by that answer whose existence he transcendentally experiences. In this fact Rahner refers to God's transcendental presence to the questioner. (This is more or less correct, since one does not ask a question without suspecting that there is an answer to it). He is, however, hardly convincing when he goes on to explain that within this experience we do not only ask, but also become aware of being challenged by the answer itself: are we ready to ask the absolute question, or do we refuse to do so? (Remember, *mutatis mutandis*, there was something similar in Rahner's procedure in *Hearers:* does one want to listen to the silence of God when no difinite answer is forthcoming?). In other words, he crams into this initial experience of dialogue, as has so often been pointed out, an obligatory option for man the questioner, before his free action faces its alternatives in their concrete contours. By means of this the supernatural existencial (equivalent to transcendental revelation) is introduced, and on this ground he will affirm that every man is, in a sense, a believer: he is gripped by the transcendental word of God.

God, however, *de facto* wants his categorial word to reach man. He wills the salvation of everybody. In this will our 'absolutely unlimited question is fulfilled and answered by God himself as the absolute answer.'[54] This answer is in categorial words and has some news for man, since 'in it God speaks to man and makes known to him something ... which is still unknown, [namely] his inner reality and his personal free relationship to his spiritual creatures.'[55] If this disclosure is accepted, then the event of encounter blossoms into faith, hope and love. This is the overall setting for the revelation – as well as for the event of man's coming-to-faith. *A word of promise* is given to hope, but love already has its fulfilment in the personal God with whom every spiritual creature enjoys a free relationship. In fact, if the whole history of mankind has been borne by God's self-communication ever since its coming-to-be, then there does not seem to be anything else to be concretely revealed 'except the manifestation of God in the beatific vision'.[56]

Is this what is ultimately meant by the categorial word?

Thus, by the time of *Foundations*, Rahner seems to be speaking the language of dialogal personalism: both revelation and faith happen to occur in a dialogue. Both have a history, for these events 'have to be mediated categorially'. Once, however, we consider more closely this dialogal situation, we shall have to ask him how seriously he takes the language which he adopts in *Foundations* and occasionally elsewhere. Is it not just a disguise, by means of which transcendental revelation in communicating God himself *inevitably*, or even by necessity entails man's coming-to-faith? Is it not just a cover leading to the acceptance of the transcendental in historical circumstances as God's categorial word? Whereas the first is meant for everybody, the second will obtain for some who, indeed, found God's definitive message in Jesus Christ and in the vision at the end. For in Christ Rahner sees God's absolute (categorial) answer, as well as man's absolute acceptance as projected, objectified in our history. Something similar to Christ's coming-to-be happens to us on our way to faith. God's word of transcendental self-revelation is about to incarnate itself in the corresponding answer of human faith, now explicit and articulate. Should not this strategy, by letting revelation-history run parallel with mankind coming-to-faith, advocate a still closer synthesis between these two: God's message comes to its own categorial manifestation in man's explicit faith? From this mutual involvement between revelation and faith would it not follow that God cannot reveal himself successfully, unless there is human faith to accept what is revealed – and that human consent to explicit faith is simply God's revelation?[57]

Instead of a summary of Rahner's view on the mystery of human faith and revelation, we seem to have finished on a critical note. Indeed, we have anticipated our ensuing comments and questions to be addressed to Rahner's whole scheme in fundamental theology.

5.4 *Comments and Questions*

We were only able to present and understand Rahner's view on man's coming-to-faith in its wider context, namely, in his theology of the divine word. These two are inextricably interwoven in the gradual development of his thinking from the philosophical theology of the *Hearers* to his later fundamental theology, the main insights of which are more and more influenced by his own Christology. At the latest stage of this development, especially in the *Foundations*, revelation and faith are not only correlatives, but self-involving realities. This means, in Rahner's idiom, that the transcendental word of God, owing to the supernatural engracement of everybody (supernatural existential), as it were incarnates itself in the community of believers (Church) and becomes the categorial word (kerygma, prophecy and Holy Writ) in order to reach its fullest realisation in the explicit belief of the individual. Man's coming-to-faith is a process of radicalized self-discovery that one already has (and always has had) the faith, or, rather, is possessed by it. What is missing for the would-be believer is to accept himself as he was always meant to be and commit himself to God in and through those historical circumstances in which he has perceived the divine word in its categorial shape. If he is enabled to take this ultimate step, then revelation has come to its own in him, i.e., it has become the realised word of God: Christ lives, dies and is risen in *his* faith.

If this is indeed a correct summary of Rahner's theology of

faith, it inevitably raises several questions, some of which we shall have to formulate. First, his overall strategy which goes under the name of fundamental theology will have to be put to the test (a). Secondly, from the analysis of this method we shall discuss its validity against the background of the *Modernismusstreit* in the aftermath of which our contemporary theology proceeds (b). Thirdly, we shall have to ask whether his fundamental theology is an apt vehicle for the acceptance of explicit Christian doctrines, or whether it is a self-sufficient discipline substituting for doctrinal or dogmatic theology (c). Lastly, depending on our answer to this last question, we shall either have to improve upon Rahner's scheme in approaching faith or offer an alternative as regards the direction in which our further search should go (d).
(a). One cannot help feeling that in the approach to faith the strategy of Rahner's fundamental theology is, on the one hand, an uncomfortable mixture of a philosophy of a *possible* and a theology of a *factual* revelation and, on the other, a combination of two traditions, Roman Catholic apologetics and the propaedeutics of Protestant orthodoxy.[58]

We have already discussed in volume one the possible relationship between a philosophical approach to the obedient listening to the word of God, as exemplified by the early work of *Hearers*, and a more theological concept of what revelation is. Eicher;[59] in his very penetrating study, points out convincingly that whereas the philosophy of religion in the *Hearers* is ruled by a basically theological insight, what rules the later theological concept of revelation is a sustained effort of (transcendental) philosophy. As for the first, the main intention of *Hearers* is still to maintain the absolute transcendence and historicity of the divine word in its most traditional Roman Catholic sense. Its formal definition indicates that revelation is a summary of statements and imperatives guaranteed by supreme divine authority and not accessible to human experience.[60] However, this somewhat dogmatic viewpoint has an anthropological significance which is then expressed, as we have seen, in man's absolute obligation to listen either to God's speaking or to his silence. The said obligation cannot have its ground in a merely philosophical reasoning, unless it is theologically presupposed that man in his essential being is meant to be a listener; if he fails to fulfil this obligation he cannot be human. This, in *summa*, is the anthropological message of *Hearers* which, however, rebounds in Rahner's theological understanding of the divine word: it must be a correlate to man's essential self-questioning; it must be a word in human language, expressed in human concepts; it must be such that we can basically understand its drift; it must be a (sacramental) symbol of what God in his hidden personal being is and what he requires from us etc. The philosophy of revelation is thus mediated through a theological insight.

As for the second, when the later Rahner, after the merger of Supernatural Existential and transcendental revelation, speaks *en théologien* about the word of God, his concept seems to be ruled by his transcendental philosophy. Roughly, as Eicher sums it up: Rahner's main thesis will be that revelation is not an irruption of God's transcendent word into our history by means of an efficient causality (as it was in *Visions*), but rather a supernatural transformation of human existence through the experienced presence of God. Thus revelation becomes an *existential* of human being, given in our ontological constitution as grace and in our actions of knowing and willing as our (transcendentally) experienced (*bewusst*) faith. This is what enables us to confront ourselves with categorial statements to be embraced as objectifications of an already possessed faith.[61]

Such an understanding of the divine word-event cannot be arrived at otherwise than through a massive borrowing from the sub-oil of his philosophy. As a consequence we are still undecided about Rahner's strategy concerning the theology of revelation and faith. It could be a philosophical or theological construct – if not both, without the border lines drawn.

Nevertheless, this uncomfortable mixture of philosophy and theology can throw light on the peculiar nature of his fundamental theology employed as a means to explain man's coming-to-faith. As we have already said, it lies between Catholic apologetics and the hermeneutics of orthodox Protestantism. Catholic apologetics has restricted itself to the preliminaries of faith (*praeambula fidei*) as a rational inducement. Since the sixteenth century Catholic scholars have laboured to draw up the criteria on account of which a statement worthy of belief (*credibilities*) could be formulated and arguments for its obligatory acceptance (*credenditas*) put forward. In fact, in the late nineteenth century this was attempted on grounds of natural reasoning without the aid of grace.[62] Philosophical self-knowledge (especially natural theology or metaphysics) as well as certain events (e.g., miracles), certain words spoken (e.g., prophecies) in history were regarded as sufficient motives for the first move to faith before, on God's ultimate authority, the grace of consenting to revelation was granted. However, such apologetics were regarded as an inducement to faith and certainly not as its foundation.

It was understandable that an othodox Protestant tradition should regard with suspicion the Romans' efforts at apologetics in their fundamental theology. For them, faith and that which it contains were an either-or and and any reasoning towards its acceptance would smell of the rat of semi-pelagianism: no antecedent inducement to faith can substitute for the grace given *initium fidei*. This is why, for instance, Barth's propaedeutics to theology is a *doctrine* of the word of God and contains without any preliminaries a trinitarian affirmation. In *summa*, until recently Protestant orthodoxy renounced any kind of fundamental theology; theirs was a propaedeutics from the centre of Christian faith, from its doctrines.[63]

Now Rahner's initial position in this state of affairs seems to have been in accordance with the Catholic tendency, however, with a certain twist. Although he shared the intention of the old apologetics in arguing on philosophical grounds for the necessity of believing, yet he did not imitate their appeal to exterior and miraculous facts. He looked rather to the inner ontological structure of human being which finds in its self-reflection the grounds for the obligation to the obedience of faith. His *transitus*, however, from the 'is' to the 'ought' or even 'must', as we said, anticipated faith, in so far as already in *Hearers*.[64] His analysis of man led him to the acceptance of a personal and free God who grounds man's freedom: God, out of his *free grace*, discloses himself to the listener as a *free person*. This definite content of faith is anticipated in a philosophical reasoning – a content which the later Rahner will specify as something that categorially extends the transcendental word in us. God is the Absolute Answer, as he will say in *Foundations*, when he 'speaks to man and makes known to him *something* ... which is still unknown (namely) his inner reality and his personal free relationship to his spiritual creatures.'[65]

The obligation to believe, in view of this revelation, is only understandable if grace is already granted as a vehicle for objectively acknowledging God as person; on merely natural reasoning it is unacceptable.[66]

This qualification concerning his initial agreement with Catholic apologetics is one of the reasons which will cause him to move in another direction. In fact, after Vatican II the traditional manner of argumentation of Catholic apologetics came into a certain disrepute, not entirely without Rahner's influence: in *Revelation* and 'Integration' he distances himself from it.[67] By then he had a better device to found not only man's preliminary access to faith, but also faith itself: since faith is already given and available in man's self-reflection, he is in a supernatural situation in which not only grace, but also revelation, although in a transcendental sense, are immanent. With this not only is the objective of Catholic apologetics fulfilled, but also the human foundations are laid for the subsequent life in and with explicit faith. Not only is a rational task performed but, at the same time, the either-or approach of othodox Protestant propaedeutics is, in a certain sense, satisified: his argument is from faith to faith.

Rahner's fundamental theology, with that of many of his contemporaries, now claims to have achieved this synthesis, i.e., first, between a philosophical and theological, and secondly, between a Catholic and Protestant, access to faith. At the same time, this kind of fundamental theology has safely lodged itself not only in the forecourts of belief, but in the very heart of doctrinal and dogmatic theology. To a certain extent it founds not only the access, but also the content of faith. The newly coined English word *foundational* theology, an ill-sounding neologism, nevertheless characterizes its peculiar procedure. It is a discipline relevant for both the would-be and the *de facto* believer.

(b). This analysis of Rahner's strategy poses the question of its validity. But first an apparently grave objection, at least to his later conception of revelation and faith, should be discussed. This is not new as regards his fundamental theology: it can be exposed to the charge of *Modernism*. Now to evaluate it against the background of the *Modernismusstreit*[68] would seem to be preposterous as regards his early writings. In fact, *Hearers* tries to steer its way between the two types of Protestant philosophies of

religion: liberal theology and Barth's orthodoxy. Rahner is
aware that liberal Protestantism from Schleiermacher to Ritschl
has made its way into nineteenth century Catholic modernism.
Both hold that revelation is nothing other than the objectification
of man's subjective religious feelings, the projection to the thin
layer of rationality of the irrational or emotional. Against this
Rahner's whole effort in *Hearers* appears as a serious rational
argumentation leading up to the threshhold of faith. He has no
intention of being counted with the modernists.

In the period beyond the publication of *Hearers* Rahner should
easily be absolved from the charge of straightforward
modernism. In what we have summed up as his struggle for the
categorial word of God, one could be convinced of his persistent
anti-modernist leanings. At first he insists that God is the cause
both of the prophets' and of the hagiographers' inner inspiration,
as well as of its objectified expression.[69] God himself, with his
providence guides the individual and/or the society in
pronouncing the message of Christianity, otherwise the word(s)
of revelation would be due to a prior state of human minds. He
emphasizes that it is not enough to assume interior grace given to
the sacred writers for the objectification of what is going to be the
categorial word of God;[70] they are also under the influence of
God's categorial causality. In his later period, for the very same
reason, Rahner insists on the event-character of transcendental
revelation also; he attributes importance to the concrete
encounter with God's word preached to engender faith; he
appeals to the need for this, as yet subjective, faith to express itself
in definite and objective terms, etc. All these are devices to fend
off the danger of nineteenth century modernism.

Nevertheless, after the merger of man's elevation to a
supernatural order of grace (supernatural existential) and the a
priori status of transcendental revelation, could it not be said that
his theology roughly corresponds to the religious feeling or sense
of the modernists? Has not an attempt been made to regard
historical revelation as a series of worldly events as interpreted by
man through his religious experience? Did not Laberthonière,
for instance, hold that human life was already penetrated by
divine grace which had become the innermost being of man's
natural self;[71] and again, did not Tyrrell think that the
incarnation made visible what was already happening within

man?[72] Compare with these Rahner's statement appealing for transcendental experience:

> This transcendental moment in revelation is a modification of our transcendental consciousness produced permanently by God in grace. But such a modification is really an original and permanent element ... as the basic and original luminosity of our existence ... constituted by God's self-communication ... [it is] already revelation in the proper sense.[73]

Reading this after Tyrrell at least a whiff of suspicion remains.

Thus what used to be the interior sense of religion of the modernists is now the God-given presence of the transcendental word or of implicit faith by means of which secular history can be interpreted. An event in itself is not revelation until, at least, these two a priori facts (transcendental revelation and implicit faith) establish its meaning. Without these two historical a priori owing to God's work in us, there can be neither an objectification of the divine word in history nor objectifications of subjective faith. Both 'objectifications' are historical, if not in the sense of historicity, at least in that of historicality,[74] i.e., they are transmitted through the sieve of human subjectivity[75] which inevitably mediates the categorial word of God. God's word in itself, as an event in history, like any of his 'mighty deeds', has to be mediated not only by the individual hearing and witnessing to it, but also through the various, more or less successful, forms of world-religions, and finally, as preeminently intended by the God of grace, by the Church. In these God's universal, viz., special, salvation history realizes itself. In a sentence: without the humanly experienced transcendental presence of God to the individual and to mankind in general, neither revelation nor faith in their categorial and explicit shape can come about. For Rahner this experience is not only the prelude, but part and parcel of man's coming-to-faith.

A kind of modernistic leaning seems to lurk in Rahner's later concepts of revelation and faith. Nowadays, however, modernism should not be regarded as the arch-enemy of Catholic theology. In fact, this is implied in Brüngel's contribution to the latest *Rahner-Festschrift*.[76] The author does not defend him against the suspicion of modernism, but tries to

demonstrate how skilfully Rahner mediates between the
rationality of old fundamental theology and the emotional
appeal of the modernist movement. Brüngel intends to show how
in Rahner's fundamental theology the kernel of truth in
modernism was dexterously adapted without the danger
inherent in this movement. Thus the Rahnerian mode of
thinking smooths the rough edges (*entschärft*) of modernist
emotionally and softens up the crisis it evoked in the Roman
Church. What enables him to do this is that, on the one hand, he
posits the *experience of the Spirit* at the centre of his theological
thinking (which, in itself, is an emotional or even irrational
factor) and, on the other, maintains that it is to be rationally
reflected upon. For reflection, according to Brüngel, is a kind of
mirroring of this experience, yet in a manner which is beyond its
inherent emotionality and ready to be taken up by a rational
discourse. However, this reflection has always to return to and
exemplify itself in that in which it is rooted, namely, experience.
This is something given, but human freedom in facing it has a
responsibility towards it. Thus Rahner concedes to the modernist
that experience is the alpha and omega of any religious
movement of the self or of society, however with the underlying
duty of bringing this experience through reflection to its rational
and conceptual aspect. With this the dichotomy between an
irrational or emotional sense of religion and the rational and
sober acceptance of faith's explicit tenets should have been
overcome: Rahner, as it were, has brought modernism home into
the bosom of the Church. Or would it not be better to say that his
fundamental theology is of a neo-modernist type?

As for ourselves, however, we are still far from evaluating the
validity of Rahner's strategy with the shibboleths of
(neo)modernism. In spite of all the rancour which the modernist
movement aroused in the police network of the post *rinascimento*
Vatican, it is by no means obvious that it has not done the
Church a service. In subsequent decades, instead of taking refuge
in an irrational and emotional religious sense, as the first
modernists did, the scholars of the Church have correctly fought
for the freedom of research and tried hard to re-establish the
scientific status (*Wissenschaflichkeit*) of theology. We are not called
upon to judge Rahner's method from the point of view of his
concept of and self-estimate in scholarliness. Yet one thing is

certain: owing to the ambivalent status of his fundamental theology, Rahner's advance to a reasoned, but explicitly theological discussion of Christian doctrines could be impaired. When the borderlines between reason and faith, philosophy and theology, apologetics and the positive presentation of the Christian kerygma, are blurred the clear-cut contours of what Christianity is could well fade into nebulous insignificance.

(c). This *in nuce* was Cardinal Ratzinger's suspicion in reviewing Rahner's first level of reflection in that masterpiece of fundamental theology, the *Foundations*. He asked, though in other words, is Rahner's scheme of introducing as well as of founding and organizing Christian doctrines on the first level of reflection apt for working its way to the second, namely to a life inspired by an unconditional dedication to what Christianity stands for and to an earnest scholarly interest in considering the objective content of divine revelation?[77] Certainly no one doubts Rahner's own dedication and no one should detract from his earnest scholarship. His life's work has been aimed at establishing within the realms of the sciences the right of citizenship for a mode of thinking, whether it be called philosophy or theology, speculation or faith, which neither insists on observable phenomena nor tries to impose on these a verifiable super-structure. For him, disciplines which examine these phenomena belong merely to 'regional' sciences (in the German sense of *Natur* vs. *Geisteswissenschaften*). They deal with the mere categoriality of tangible or observable objects, whereas theology does not reflect upon the categorial as such. Its aim is to uncover their foundation in God, or better, in God's mystery, in God's self-communication, thereby making them in their turn mysterious. Theology as a science projects and objectifies this kind of thinking, and its conceptually objectified statements can be discussed on an objective, i.e., categorial level. This discourse, then, is on a higher level of scholarly activity.[78] All this is, of course, under the aegis of fundamental-foundational theology in which the grounds of divine revelation and corresponding faith are at work. This is the basis of theological scholarship.

It would be beyond the scope of this volume to test whether, in dealing with doctrines as the objective content of Christian revelation, Rahner *de facto* reduces them to the scheme of fundamental theology. If he does, then Ratzinger's suspicions are well founded: fundamental theology remains a self-contained discipline substituting for dogmatic or doctrinal theology. Now we cannot decide about this in advance. However, we can indicate under what conditions an otherwise necessary fundamental theology can be reductive as regards the doctrines of faith. For any such enterprise should go beyond itself, while it may be used to organise Christian doctrine systematically.

The main difficulty in Rahner's approach, in our opinion, is his adherence to the question-answer scheme of fundamental theology. In opting for this he enters the circle of those theologians who understand their subject in a similar way,[79] in facing God one asks, and revelation answers. This pattern, however, becomes radicalized in Rahner's rendering – man in his very being *is* a question, in his mysterious self he is questionableness itself, whilst God is the Absolute and radical Answer. In such a suppostion it can hardly be imagined that the questioner, man, does not suspect at least the tenor of the answer, otherwise he would not question at all. Questioning can be determined by the answer to come; worse, it can manipulate the answer, and it is for this that Rahner is reproached.

We are not alone in picking on this line of criticism. For instance, Gaboriau, a rather ill-tempered critic of Rahner's position, can say that in this view the historical word of God does not reveal, but rather reassures man as to what he already is in a hidden and implicit way. Rahner's man, says Gaboriau, moves towards God's word not because he had realized his misery, but because of his nature's spiritual self-transcendence. Thus God's word is not stictly a saving word that succours man's misery; it does not heal man's deformity, but elevates his nature. This is why it should be the other way round: not man who asks while God dutifully answers, but rather God who calls and expects man's answer in obedienct faith.[80]

Gaboriau's harsh understanding of Rahner is repeated, perhaps in less emotional language, by Simon's critique in his *Philosophie der Offenbarung*: if self-transcendence is itself *de facto* disclosure of God, then one would not be able to speak of it as a free event for both man and God.[81]

Pannenberg singles out the same aspect when he says in an essay, possibly more applicable to Tillich than to the later Rahner, an allusion to the correlation between question and answer does not suffice. It leaves as yet in balance how far knowledge of the question inevitably depends on God's answer. On the other side, it is not clear how far the questionableness of human existence has anything to do with revelation in a Christian sense.[82]

The same uneasiness is felt in the already-mentioned work by Eicher: if God's self-revelation is discovered in reflecting upon one's own subjectivity, then 'to what purpose is history, the finite world, the cross and the resurrection?' They already seem to be implied in 'man's directedness to the transcendentally felt presence of God who for ever forgives us.'[83]

We are not however, going to add our own protest against this basic feature of Rahner's fundamental theology because, whilst these criticisms are more or less correct, it is our opinion that they overlook a basic facet. The historical situation in which man could address any question at all is, in view of God's revelation, that of a concrete encounter where an actual dialogue can originate. But this encounter can only take place between autonomous and free persons who in meeting confront one another with questions or complaints, with words springing from common need and shared joy, of thankfulness and praise or of bitter reproach. Such an encounter between God and man could only be envisaged when, and if, communication had already been taking place and exchange of words had been established. Now Rahner is aware of this, but his device of projecting this communication and exchange of words onto the transcendental plain of God's self-communication in everybody's being mystifies the matter. If communication of being means man's participation in God by being so and so, i.e., already constituted by his creative will, then there is either no freedom of dialogue or the words spoken therein are of no significance. One could do without their expression. What is important is the previously established nexus of persons. In this case, it would be better to substitute for the word 'communication' that of 'dependence' in its unconditional absoluteness (cf. Schleiermacher). If, however 'communication' means exchange of words in the freedom of a dialogal encounter, then words have meaning, the counter-arguments and debates have significance for man's final end.

Job, wrestling with his God comes to his conclusion in faith after he has seen not his own miserable self, but God's mighty deeds.

This, however, is only a paradigm, Job being the best allegory for man. In it we could perhaps envisage the revelation and faith event, although in a changed key, as a question and answer affair. But it does not usually happen like this. Hence neither Rahner's nor our alternative scheme are able to make revelation and faith understandable for a concrete fundamental theology. Yet the dialogue which is supposed by both is valid, provided we do not immediately assume it to be between God and man. We do not meet God in person. Yet we are told by our fellows, with whom we are, as a rule, in dialogue, that God is a person who has spoken and told us something; that he has acted and that paradoxical facts arose contrary to our expectations; that he disclosed himself in his teaching and in his imperatives. Those of us who have had the fortune or misfortune of being born and educated in religious faith hear all this in a human interpersonal dialogue. We are all thrown into this world, but some of us are also thrown into the world of religious persons, communciation with whom might or might not fire our imagination and challenge our free decision to try it out. In a sentence: only through the *what* of revelation are we able to wrestle with *the* Person who entices our freedom to a divine-human dialogue. Our creative, or as we said, mythifying phantasy plays a considerable role in this happening, as does our memory in recalling what was narrated to us by our fellows. Yet the *sine qua non* of this imaginative dialogue is the content of the communications which assures us about God's having spoken to the world. The concrete categorial *what* preempts the *how* of that personal relationship between the would-be believer and the God of revelation.

To speak of a strict obligation to listen and to answer within this sort of dialogue seems to be a misnomer. If we are really free, nothing can compel us to this. For there is a much stronger motive than obligation and necessity in man's coming to faith. It is love for the other person, letting oneself be freely held in their spell. Ultimately, the way to faith is by unwarranted love which cannot be buttressed by arguments. This holds true after one has heard, or even in spite of having heard, God's word.

Thus the fundamental theology we envisage in this kind of

dialogue will have to be just as retrospective as is the justification of a love affair. It starts from living with the entirety of Chrisitian doctrines, however paradoxical they might appear. Following the lines of this approach we shall be ready to re-think and re-shape this world of ours according to the light we have and the skill at our disposal. In doing so, we may find that in the praxis of the day some of these doctrines have less significance than others. But this does not mean that they are theoretically reduced or absorbed by the others. They might temporarily stand apart, respected and acknowledged, in the hope of finding their way back into the focus of our mind and into the outcome of our praxis.

To find out whether this emerging scheme of fundamental theology offers a real alternative to Rahner's, or whether it falls prey to an inherent inconsequence, we shall have to take a closer look to see exactly how man's coming to faith can be envisaged. (d). With the preceding points of our *Comments and Questions*, the set-up in which man's coming-to-faith (*pace* Rahner) could be envisaged is adequately prepared. The first impression, no doubt, will be that our view is at loggerheads with his. Our suggested concept of revelation, according to which it is the content, the categorial *what* as offered for our acceptance in a *fides quae* that is primary, seems to contradict him. In 1973 essay he writes:

> Christian faith possesses, then, of its essence no particular categorial content which is exempt from the doubts and threats attached to such facts, nor is it immune to the process and experience of ideological criticism.[84]

In apparent contradiction to this we were not afraid to imply that the divine word is communicated in the first instance in Rahner's gnoseological way and nor in the ontological. It 'informs' man; not, however, in the sense of a scholastic *informatio* or by way of a quasi-formal causality; nor is it a communication of something divine, i.e., God the Mystery himself as a divine force in a supernaturally elevated progress to faith. The word, first and foremost, informs us. And this information can neither be deduced from man's inner make-up (Modernism) nor is it an answer to a transcendental quest (Rahner's well-nigh neo-modernistic view). It is simply a *novum*, unasked for and unexpected as it is, a surprising fact that befalls us.[85] These words of 'information' cannot but be categorial. Hence, again *pace* Rahner,[86] there must be an element of arbitrariness, a chance-like facticity of this word-event as well as a similar contingency in man's coming-to-faith. Both are inexplicable. Briefly, Rahner's conviction that in faith the categorial object is secondary[87] seems to conflict with our insistence on the objective content of faith with which the word of revelation confronts us.

Looking at it from this different point of view might expose us to the danger against which the whole of Rahner's fundamental theology is directed. From the early days of *Hearers*, as we saw, he had to navigate between the Scylla of a liberal-modernistic and the Charybdis of an orthodox-Protestant approach to faith. Whilst the first was banned from his Church, the other was labelled as fideism and revelation-positivism (or, in its Catholic version, even as traditionalism). Now by assuming as primary the *what* of faith offered for acceptance, we shall be forced either to opt for the thought-pattern of dialectical theology (Barth) or to renew the rational argumentation of nineteenth century Catholic apologetics. Whereas the first implies that the divine word itself makes the subjective receptivity in the elect, the second assumes that one can argue on rational grounds for one's obligation to accept the tenets of Christian faith.

Though the direction of our search is similar to both the above, we should not be afraid of the reproach. With Catholic apologetics we do acknowledge that there is a human process before the act of faith (*praeambula fidei*), yet we shall be wary of admitting that the act of faith is the logical result of this process. We shall claim that man's progress to faith is accountable not to syllogistic logic, but to the reasonableness of human *action*. We also acknowledge that the positive contents of the word are mediated by the society in which we live yet, as against Rahner's scheme, this society is neither *the* Church (as it were a 'transcendental mediator' of the written or spoken word) nor is it the dogmatic teaching of its *Magisterium* (as in the case of the Catholic apologists). The mediator is rather the small community of persons which by words and example 'indoctrinates' those who are born and educated within it. Our point is not that this preparatory process, along with its social mediation, can rationally convince the would-be believer that he might come to faith, or that this process is steered by God's transcendental or even categorial action in order that we might believe. It is enough that these words happened to be spoken in our history, they happened to influence and permeate the culture which some of us inherited. They are given, and we have, willy-nilly, to live with them.

This 'living with them' is the next point which we intend to raise, this time as it seems, in contradistinction to Barth's purview. For in facing these words (as when we are about to face our own death) we are not inactive. Although standing before these words we are not yet asked to understand their message; the events reported, the actors and the narration of their story, the imperatives conveyed, speak in such a way that it is not our knowing that is appealed to, but our freedom that is challenged. For not awareness, but courageous action announces the dawn of faith. Challenged by the contents of these words some of us will freely relate to them as possibilities of human action, despite the fact that others would regard them as 'impossible possibilities'. Nonetheless, what the words tell us become alternatives for a new sort of living, opportunities for an as yet unknown fulfilment, in hope of which one begins to reckon with and rely on them. They become a freely chosen and no more *ab extra* imposed objective, a *telos* of one's life from the mirror of which oneself and the whole world can be reinterpreted.

In this brave engagement, however, there remain two completely uncertain facets. The first is the eventual outcome of it all, i.e., not the *telos*, as our freely chosen objective (for which the individual is ultimately responsible no matter how he was 'indoctrinated' by his fellows), but rather what will be achieved thereby, the *eschaton*. By *eschaton*[88] we mean the existential difference which intervenes between a desired end and its concrete realisation. For those who actively commit themselves to and engage themselves with these words do not know what the outcome of their actions will be. The darkness of our way to is not to be ignored; it is of its essence. Any imagined certainty of being in possession can petrify the ongoing process[89] or, when faced with a difficulty, expose the whole edifice to radical doubt. However, this darkness is supported by the dim light lent to us by our fellows, because of whom we have dared this leap into the unknown, and by, what we might call, the word of promise contained within those words which we have heard.

This leads us to the second facet of our uncertainty: the ultimate source of the words challenging our action. Our freely engaged courage is sooner or later confronted with a subject, with a personal centre within this enterprise. In facing this, it is not only our free action which is called forth but also the, yet again, free acceptance of a concrete personal relationship to be lived out. For at this level it is not a free choice but a free decision which is asked from us, a *scio cui credidi*. This refers to a Person and demands a personal relationship: ignoring or even disliking or, on the contrary, loving and trusting this other. In the first case, the result can be a mere going through the motions of faith, frustration and eventually a depotentiation of the word; living according to it was a 'mistake'! In the second case, trust in the outcome of one's own action with all its trials and successes is preserved in the embrace of another. This not only verifies the reasonableness of the process that went before, but also re-evaluates even that which has gone wrong within it. At this point the self is forgotten for the sake of this other, not however, the words according to the possibilities of which one has lived. Just as the witness to others of one's own dying,[90] so a life lived in the hope of a promise will verify both one's life-long commitment and will recognise the source of this hope in the One who initiated it. Likewise the words according to the possibilities of which one lived, will be recognized as His words – no longer in their human tenor (they remain human words!) but in their outcome. Out of life's courageous engagement, if we may so put it, success has dawned. The outcome is faith, and the success achieved by it can be called salvation.

Thus man's coming-to-faith (as we know it in a Christian sense) can be defined as a way of life according to the word, the outcome of which proves to be the person's permanent and active attitude towards himself and the world, which is in accordance with God's active attitude towards the addressees of his self-revelation. The act of faith, the essential event crowning this process, is precisely to see this accord.

In this description and final definition of faith, we have purposely used terms as yet unburdened by the controversial pedantry of customary scholarship. It had to be so, since our aim was not another theory of the way to faith or of the *analysis fidei*, but a hint as to the way in which the main problems of fundamental theology of the Catholic type or Protestant propaedeutics are dealt with. As it stands, it is still exposed to a number of queries from the point of view of both competing views and religious praxis. To formulate these and attempt to answer them would mean entering into an extended scholarly intercommunication, inappropriate at the end of this volume. Here we should, rather, restrict ourselves to the confrontation of our proposal with that of Rahner who inspired the dialogue. Having seen his struggles to describe what revelation and corresponding faith are, one could say that our proposal could be understood in accordance with his. This is – *au fond* – correct. We pointed out an apparent and seeming contradiction and suggested an alternative view which may prove to be basically an improved version of his. Whether this is indeed so, the reader will have to judge.

Nevertheless, if there is no real conflict, there may still be some points of divergence. For our view could give the impression that we have only inverted the terms of Rahner's analysis. What was for him primary, namely the (transcendental) relation, has become for us secondary. We seem to have missed Rahner's point that primary and secondary, transcendental and categorial, are not meant in temporal succession but rather as 'moments' of the same event. However, if Rahner keeps speaking of events, of a history both of their transcendental and categorial aspects, one either has to understand them as in the succession of time or one has to regard his word 'history' as a meta-history hovering above the course of our time, briefly, as a theoretical construct. Though in discussing transcendental revelation Rahner qualifies it as being history in a 'watered-down sense,'[91] this 'watered-down sense' is soon going to be forgotten and history without any such qualification added to the transcendental word and to its corresponding faith.

Now, according to our purview, the irruption of the divine is historical in a real sense, since not only is it tied down to its objectified manifestations, like the spirit to *materia* in Rahner's view, but also to a living and historical society whose antecedent mediation is inevitable. Otherwise the word of God would not at the same time be a human word. Granted, this mediation of the word often reaches us in a distorted form, often being imposed by the misuse of human power. It is freedom which may or may not liberate man to get rid of these and reach out for the kernel of the message. Nonetheless, if the word reaches us in such a way, it is none but a thoroughly historical process.

There is another, connected point where our understanding and Rahner's view can diverge. It will be remembered that he argued for the historicity of revelation and faith from the fact that it was and is borne by freedom, divine as well as human.[92] What, however, this freedom really is for him we can learn again, from his own formulations. In discussing faith between rationality and emotionality, he takes refuge in the act of freedom as something of itself inexplicable, yet which holds both rationality and emotionality in control. Freedom is the synthesis of both. The way he puts it is indeed 'reasonable', but we suspect and oversight. He says:

> I would state as a thesis, without offering any further argument to support it, that the essential nature of freedom is not in itself a neutral possibility whether to act or not to act with regard to this or that particular categorial object of choice experienced in an *a posteriori* manner... It rather consists in the capacity of the spiritual subject to exercise definitive control over himself even if this self-determination occurs in space and time ... The subject and object of freedom is constituted by the whole man acting with ultimate decision.[93]

All this can easily be granted, however with a slight change: freedom itself is *not only* a neutral possibilitiy for the particular. But does not any free act in facing a fundamental option have its alternatives before and *after* the decision has taken place? Cannot an apparently discarded alternative remain, though possibly in another shape, as a possibility of a further action? Life goes on, and so does the history of freedom, steering its way amongst its alternative possibilities without becoming constituted in one way alone. Thus, in a sense, despite the self-determination resulting from it, any free action in its very depths remains neutral and undetermined. This, indeed, is of the essence of freedom.

This is why we cannot go along with Rahner's next thesis.

Taking his concept of freedom for granted, he says:

> According to Christian understanding the realization of
> freedom is identical with faith ... [since] wherever freedom as
> decisive self-determination is positively realized and the object
> of freedom, namely the human person, is unconditionally
> accepted for what he is by the subject of freedom which is that
> very same person, wherever, that is, a person, does not reject
> himself in a final denial and does not utter an ultimate protest
> in total scepticism or despair ... then there is present what
> Christians call 'faith'.[94]

Should this statement be accepted without reserve, then we
could not reckon (with Rahner) with secular history initiated by
unbelievers also, for according to him, they could never realize
the essence of freedom, and we should acknowledge (again with
Rahner) that all history is salvation history, because freedom is
identical with faith. In this case there is no coming to faith and no
falling away from it – for in the first case it is already given and, in
the second, no one can be held responsible for the loss of it: it is
'done in unfreedom'.

Would it not be better to consider faith as a temporal outcome
of a process of human action engaged with the word in history, in
the sense we have just described? The course of life winds through
its unavoidable revisions and wends its way towards ultimate
success. Looking back, life retrospectively interprets its own
history as a history of salvation in opposition to its alternative, the
history of perdition; it will be interpreted as an experience of
grace in those moments where action came to its fulfilment; and
looking forward it hopes for the successful outcome of its labours.
At present, the only criterion of this kind of life is that it works.
That is, we and our world are increasingly felt as enveloped by a
personal presence, and this gives the believing person, though not
a certainty, a sense of being safe and secure. In faith man can
reach a kind of salvation which might be the only one ever meant
by God.

Epilogue: Faith and Salvation

No word is more frequently used in Rahner's writings then *Heil* and its derivatives. His is, or wants to be, a *heilsgeschichtliche Theologie*, which was indeed realized in the seven outsize volumes of *Mysterium Salutis*, composed with teutonic earnestness. Since this word, salvation, is ubiquitous, we shall single out one basic line in Rahner's thought concerning it.

It was almost foreseeable that in *Foundations*, urged by his transcendental method in theology, he would connect the question of salvation with the exercise of personal freedom (or rather with the freedom of the person):

> Salvation is the final and definitive validity of the person's . . . true self realization in freedom before God by the fact that he accepts his own self as it is disclosed and offered to him in the choice of transcendence, as interpreted in freedom.[1]

This definition, which summarizes all the elements of his later thinking, would be accepted by modern man only in its first part. While salvation in its Rahnerian sense is obviously moulded to match man's need for redemption, that is from sin and guilt, our contemporaries seem to separate these two concepts. Salvation, if not *ipsissimis verbis*, can be and is a concept relating to an exclusively secular context: one speaks of happiness, of wholeness, of integration, of sanity, of expanded freedom or even of welfare now and in the future. One speaks of a *heile Welt*. But for Rahner, along with the whole Christian tradition, there is but one way to salvation and this is through faith, the subject and object of which is Jesus the Christ. However, that freedom in its transcendental sense is identified with faith in a Christian sense, the unicity of these two ways to salvation, can now be argued: not only faith is a given fact, but also salvation for all and sundry. This is what is meant by God's universal salvific will that cannot fail.[2]

With our alternative conception of faith we are, I am afraid, not in the same position as Rahner of being able to argue the salvation of all and sundry. It remains to be seen whether man in encountering and living with particular objects, with the categoriality of his faith, can come *ipso facto* to the conclusion summed up in Jesus the Christ. In fact, for us the modern dichotomy concerning the concept of salvation is a theological fact to be seriously considered. Should we not ask whether man can reach salvation in its secular sense if he never encounters, or even never cares to consider accepting Christ and his message? Can he be free, can he ever be fulfilled and safe in what he makes of himself out of this world, without an explicit Christian faith? We are asking about the salvation of the unbeliever and the atheist, yes, about the sinner who does not know God.

This indeed is Rahner's innermost motivation in theology, which we cannot but wholeheartedly share. If our dialogue with him, especially in the *Comments and Questions* of these volumes, was understood by some as a radical departure from his thinking, they were mistaken. Rahner's efforts to explain the mysterious character of human existence, the theoretical constructs by which he tries to bind man into the mystery of grace, are all attempts to witness to the love of God, the origin and end of our life in faith. Nonetheless, no theology can be of permanent value. This is the fate, as well as the fortune of the theologian. For the God of our salvation has many ways of achieving his ends with us, which means that there are bound to be alternative expressions. One such alternative has been gradually emerging while we were trying to read Rahner's mind.

In the last section on faith in the divine word, in pursuing our shared motivation in theology, namely the way of the unbeliever to salvific faith, we were implicitly confronted with the whole of Rahner's strategy. We trust that in our presentation, in spite of any unclear and tortuous passages, which were unavoidable, we have made him understood. From him we have heard how facing the world of unbelief one has to appeal to man's reflective discovery of what he already has – he is a mystery to himself.

Granted, this may be legitimate, it does not exclude other alternatives. One might think, under certain circumstances, of this strategy as a kind of accommodation, of which in my opinion, we had enough in the decades following Vatican II. Although there is nothing wrong with it and a great deal of good has been achieved by it, it might be time to change one's attitude. The answer to the question concerning the faith, which we, by God's mercy, claim as our own, should not be *how* we came to it, but *what* in fact we believe. An alternative position would be to give an account of the content of our faith, to explain to the world the *pattern of doctrines*, according to which the praxis of our life can be made understandable. One does not know whether the strategy achieves the objective of our shared motivation. Yet it should be legitimate in any dialogue first to clarify the positions of those concerned. If this kind of dialogue fails to achieve its desired end, provided it does not condition faith, nothing is lost. For the ways of the God of grace are as variable as their outcome and success. Salvation is offered to everyone, yet the manner in which in each case this salvation is realized is not within our competence to decide. We leave it to the freedom of God, whose word of promise makes us hope in the salvation of everyone.

In pursuing this alternative strategy we intend, *Deo volente*, to continue our attempt to understand Rahner, dealing this time with the tenets of doctrinal and dogmatic theology. It remains to be seen whether his concept of God, of Jesus Christ, of his work in saving mankind in the mystery of the Church now and in the world to come, are a sufficient witness to what we believe. For it is on account of this belief that we Christians hope to be saved.

Notes

Notes

Notes to the Introduction

1. See the somewhat uncritical essay by K. Füssel, 'Die Wahrheitsanspruch dogmatischer Aussagen: Ein Beitrag zur theologischen Wissenschaftstheorie', *'Wagnis' – Theorie: Erfahrungen mit der Theologie von K. Rahner*, ed. H. Vorgrimler, Freiburg-im-Breisgau 1979, 199-212. A much more critical approach is that of E. Rupp, *Zur Kritik der transzendentalen und analytischen Wissenschaftstheorie*, Berlin 1972 (a polycopied dissertation). More accessible is H. Peukert's, *Wissenschaftstheorie und fundamentale Theologie*, Düsseldorf 1976, esp. 43-9.

2. See the early presentations of Rahner's work by D. Gelpi, *Life and Light: A Guide to the Theology of Karl Rahner*, New York 1966, and L. Roberts, *The Achievement of Karl Rahner*, New York 1967. Though the latter attempts to introduce some critical remarks, it remains basically a presentation of Rahner's thought.

3. See our Foreword to vol 1, *A Theologian in Search of a Philosophy*.

4. J.H. Newman, *On the development of Christian Doctrine*, London and New York 1960, 69: 'You must accept the whole or reject the whole.'

5. See R. Niebuhr, *Schleiermacher on Christ and Religion*, London and New York 1964, esp. 238-43: should the sequence be redemption-creation, or vice versa? Compare with Rahner's remark in *Foundations*, 13f (= *Grundkurs*, 24f).

6. See Barth's reflections on his relationship to Schleiermacher in *Schleiermacher Auswahl*, Munich 1968, 290-312; and *Church Dogmatics* I/1 Edinburgh 1960, 39 and 141ff (where an anthropological method is contrasted with Barth's own). See also K. Barth, *Dogmatics in Outline*, London 1966, 9-14.

7. F. Schleiermacher, *The Christian Faith*, trans. H.R.M. Mackintosh and J.S. Stewart, Edinburgh 1968[2], esp. paras. 20-31.

8. E. Brunner, *Die Mystik und das Wort: Der Gegensatz zwischen modernen Religionsauffassung und christlichen Glauben dargestellt an der Theologie von Schleiermacher*, Tübingen 1928.

9. Paul Tillich, *Systematic Theology* (3 vols.), Chicago 1951[1] and London 1960[2]. See especially I, 11-76.

10. See Chapter 7 of our first volume.

Notes to Chapter I

1. P.K. Fischer, *Der Mensch als Geheimnis: Die Anthropologie Karl Rahners,* Freiburg-im-Breisgau 1973.
2. Karl Rahner, *Meditations on Priestly Life,* London and New York 1973, 21f: our italics.
3. 'Anthropology', *Investigations* IX, 29 (= *Schriften* VIII, 44).
4. We confine ourselves to listing only a few of Rahner's many publications on the subject of man. See first 'Man, iii: theological', *SM* III, 365-70. On man and freedom: *Gefahren des heutigen Katholizismus,* Einsiedeln 1950, esp. 9-30; *Free Speech in`the Church,* London 1960; 'Freedom in the Church', *Investigations* II, 89-107 (= Schriften II, 95-114); 'The Dignity and Freedom of Man', *Investigations* II, 235-64 (= *Schriften* II, 247-78); 'Theology of Freedom', *Investigations* VI, 178-96 (= *Schriften* VI, 215-37); 'The Theology of Power', *Investigations* IV, 391-409 (= *Schriften* IV, 485-508); and 'Institution and Freedom', *Investigations* XIII, 105-21 (= *Schriften* X, 115-32). On man in society and the world: 'Christianity and the New Man', *Investigations* V, 135-56 (= *Schriften* V, 159-82); 'Ideology and Christianity: Marxist Utopia and the Christian Future of Man', *Investigations* VI, 43-70 (= Schriften VI, 56-90); 'Christian Humanism, the Experiment with Man and the Problem of Genetic Manipulation'. *Investigations* IX, 187-252 (= *Schriften* VIII, 239-321); 'Theological Reflections on the Problem of Secularisation, Practical Theology and Social Work in the Church, and the Peace of God and the Peace of the World', *Investigations* X, 318-88 (= *Schriften* VIII, 637-707); and many others.
5. 'Anthropology', 40 (= 58).
6. 'Anthropology', 42 (= 60f).
7. See: 'Philosophy and Theology', *Investigations* VI, 71-81 (= Schriften VI, 91-103); 'Philosophy and Philosophizing in Theology', *Investigations* IX, 46-63 (= *Schriften* VIII, 66-87); and Fischer, *Der Mensch,* esp. 210-30.
8. 'Anthropology', 34 (= 50).
9. 'Anthropology', 34 (= 50f).
10. 'Anthropology', 35 (= 51).
11. 'Anthropology', 36 (= 51).
12. 'Anthropology', 37 (= 52): our italics.
13. 'Anthropology', 36 (= 53).
14. 'Anthropology', 36 (= 53).
15. 'Anthropology', 41 (= 60).
16. Bernard Lonergan's *Method in Theology* was published in 1971, in London. See: Lonergan, 'Functional Specialities in Theology', *Greg* 50 (1969), 485-505; and Rahner, 'Bermerkungen zu B.J.F. Lonergans Aufsatz "Functional Specialities in Theology"', *Greg* 51 (1970), 537-40. There is a good survey of this Rahner-Lonergan confrontation in P. Surlis, 'Rahner and Lonergan on Method in Theology', *ITQ* 38 (1971), 187-201 and 39 (1972), 23-42.
17. 'Methodology', *Investigations* XI, 72 (= *Schriften* IX, 83).
18. 'Methodology', 73 (= 84).
19. See 'Pluralism in Theology and the Unity of the Creed in the Church', *Investigations* XI, 3-25 (= *Schriften* IX, 11-35). See also G. Perini, 'Pluralismo

teologico e unita della fede: a proposito della tema di K. Rahner', *DC* 22 (1979), 135-89.

20. 'The Relationship between Theology and Contemporary Sciences', *Investigations* XIII, 95 (= *Schriften* X, 105).

21. 'Theology as Engaged in an Interdisciplinary Dialogue with the Sciences', *Investigations* XIII, 90 (= *Schriften* X, 99f).

22. *Foundations*, 9f (= *Grundkurs*, 21).

23. See H. Fries, 'Theologische Methode bei J.H. Newman und Karl Rahner', *Cath* 33 (1976), 159-70, esp. 131.

24. 'Methodology', 80f (= 91f).

25. 'Methodology', 81 (= 92).

26. 'Methodology', 83 (= 94).

27. P. Eicher, 'Wo der Mensch an das Geheimnis grenzt: Die mystagogische Strukturen der Theologie Karl Rahners' *ZKT* 89 (1967), 159-70, esp. 161 n 10.

28. 'Transcendental Theology', *SM* VI, 287-9.

29. 'Methodology', 85 (= 96).

30. 'Methodology', 87 (= 98).

31. 'Methodology', 88 (= 99): our italics.

32. We cannot avoid quoting here the German text: 'Es genügt für uns eigentlich die Einsicht, dass die Frage nach dem erkennenden Subjekt nicht einen regionalen Erkenntnisbereich unter vielen anderen gleichgeordneten meint, sondern eine *Wirklichkeit*, die jeder regionalen, die Gegenstände material aufteilenden Erkenntnis als die bedingung von deren Möglichkeit vorausliegt.' ('Methodology', *Schriften* IX, 101 [= *Investigations* XI, 89]: our italics.)

33. 'Methodology', *Investigations* XI, 89ff (= *Schriften* IX, 100ff). See also 'Transcendental', 288.

34. 'Methodology', 91 (= 103).

35. 'Methodology', 93 (= 105).

36. See *Zur Reform des Theologiestudiums*, Freiburg-im-Breisgau 1969, 56 n 42. See also *Foundations*, 4 (= 16).

37. 'Methodology', 99 (= 111f).

38. 'Methodology', 99 (= 111f).

39. 'Methodology', 100 (= 112).

40. 'Methodology', 103 (= 115).

41. 'Methodology', 111 (= 123).

42. 'On the Theology of the Incarnation', *Investigations* IV, 105-20 (= *Schriften* IV, 137-56).

43. 'Incarnation', 108 (= 140).

44. See section 6.4 of our first volume, *A Theologian in Search of a Philosophy*.

45. See Karl Barth's essay 'Rudolph Bultmann: An Attempt to Understand him', Kerygma and Myth II, ed. H.W. Bartsch and R.H. Fuller, London 1972, 83-132.

46. F. Gaboriau, *Le tournant théologique aujourd'hui selon Karl Rahner*, Paris 1968.

47. The opposition of these two theologians is sometimes overstated: see, for example, L. Roberts, 'The Collision of Rahner and Balthasar', *Continuum* 5 (1968), 753-7. Nonetheless, H.U. von Balthasar's early book *Cordula, oder*

der Ernsfall (Einsiedeln 1966) seems to have Rahner as its target, while in
his beautiful small book *Love Alone: the Way of Revelation* (London 1968:
German original *Glaubhaft ist nur Liebe*, Einsiedeln 1975[4]), about the
anthropological reduction of Christianity, Rahner's thought, though
unuttered, hovers in the background.

48. Fischer, *Der Mensch*, 212ff.
49. There is an obvious hesitation in Rahner's definition of transcendental
     theology. 'Methodology' (1969), states: 'transcendental theology is that
     theology which uses transcendental philosophy as its method' (85 [= 96];
     'Transcendental' (1975) states: 'This does not mean that transcendental
     theology is merely an application of a philosophy' (287), so that it 'cannot
     and does not try to be the whole of theology' (288). A certain caution is thus
     observable. See also G. Neuhaus, *Transcendentale Erfahrung als
     Geschichtsverlust*, Düsseldorf 1982, 41f.

Notes to Chapter 2

1. K.P. Fischer, *Der Mensch als Geheimnis*, Freiburg-im-Breisgau 1973.
2. Speck, *Karl Rahners theologische Anthropologie,* Munich 1967.
3. A. Tallon, 'Personal Becoming: Karl Rahner's Christian Anthropology',
    Thom 43 (1979), 7-177.
4. *Hominisation: the Evolutionary Origin of Man as a Theological Problem,* London
    and New York 19 (German original: *Das Problem der Hominisation,*
    Freiburg-im-Breisgau 1961).
5. 'Christology within an Evolutionary View of the World', *Investigations* V,
    157-92 (= *Schriften* V, 183-221). The ideas of *Hominisation* are anticipated by
    'The Unity of Spirit and Matter in the Christian Understanding of Faith',
    Investigations VI, 153-77 (= Schriften VI, 185-214). They are again summed
    up in 'Evolution, II: Theological', *SM* II, 289-97: see J. Doncell, 'Causality
    and Evolution: a Survey of some Neo-Scholastic Theories', *NS* 39 (1965),
    295-315; and H. Falk, 'Can Spirit Come from Matter?' *IPQ* 7 (1967), 541-
    55. For the relationship between evolution and Christology, see
    'Christology in the Setting of Modern Man's Understanding of himself
    and of his World', *Investigations* XI, 215-29 (= *Schriften* IX, 227-41). The
    relationship of Christology to anthropology is a recurring theme in
    Rahner's writing: see, for example: 'Current Problems of Christology',
    Investigations I, 165 (= *Schriften* I, 185f); 'Thoughts on the Possibility of Belief
    Today', *Investigations* V, 12ff (= *Schriften* V, 21ff); 'Incarnation', *SM* III,
    116ff; 'Transcendental Theology', *SM* VI, 289; the introduction to
    Christology in *Foundations*, 178-203 (= *Grundkurs*, 180-202); etc.
6. 'Christology', 177 (= 204): our italics.
7. See sections 3.2.3 and, in particular, 3.2.4 of our first volume, *A Theologian
    in Search of a Philosophy*. The way we here formulate this difficulty is due to
    Tallon: 'In hominisation we face the difficulty, how spirit can come from
    matter. The difficulty arises because we were earlier explaining how
    matter emanated from spirit. Now so flagrant a conflict, more than mildly
    irritating, provokes one to resist letting the author have it both ways.'
    ('Personal Becoming', 151).

8. It was a constant teaching of the Roman Catholic Church: (a) that the soul was God's creation out of nothing (*ex nihilo*); (b) that it does not develop, is not born, from the material contribution of parents (traducianism); and (c) that it does not develop from the sense-substratum, but is directly created by God (see Pius XII, *Humani generis*: 'animas enim a Deo creari catholica fides nos retinere iubet' [D-S, 3896]).

9. *Hominisation*, 56f (= *Problem*, 70f).

10. *Hominisation*, 58f (= 73).

11. 'Christology', 164 (= 190).

12. *Hominisation*, 57 (= 78).

13. 'Christology', 191 (= 164f).

14. Compare to this Tallon's account of *Hominisation* in 'Personal Becoming', 150-58. But note Tallon's almost monomaniac reading of Rahner's work, centered around the 'becoming of the person'. According to this view, Rahner's theory of evolution is the projection of his transcendental gnoseology (since being and knowing are the same). Tallon seems to accept this background, however, with the proviso that intersubjectivity, not single subjectivity, is the paradigm case for evolution. 'In other words, out of the experience of personal self-enactment through self-transcendence is to be derived a theory of *all cases* of becoming.' (155; see also 157).

15. 'Christology', 168 (= 195).

16. 'Christology', 171f (= 199f).

17. See section 5.2 of our first volume, together with the corresponding comments and questions in 5.3 (c) and 5.3 (d).

18. 'Concupiscentia', *Investigations* I, 347–82 (= *Schriften* I, 377–414). See also J.P. Kenny, 'The Problem of Concupiscence: A Recent Theory of Prof. K. Rahner', *ACR* 29 (1952), 290–304 and 30 (1953), 23–32.

19. 'Sünde', *LTK* IX, 1177–81; 'Original Sin', *SM* IV, 328–33, esp. 330; and 'Sin of Adam', *Investigations* XI, 257 (= *Schriften* IX, 269).

20. See Rahner's reference to this theory in 'Concupiscentia', 362 n 2 (= 293 n 1); and in 'Current Problems of Christology', *Investigations* I, 160 (= Schriften I, 180f).

21. 'Concupiscentia', 358f (= 388f).

22. 'Concupiscentia', 358f (= 388f); our italics.

23. 'Concupiscentia', 360 (= 391).

24. 'Concupiscentia', 360 (= 391).

25. 'Concupiscentia', 361 (= 392).

26. 'Concupiscentia', 362 (= 393): our italics.

27. 'Concupiscentia', 362 (= 393).

28. 'Concupiscentia', 362f n 2 (= 393, n 1).

29. 'Concupiscentia', 365 (= 395).

30. For 'the finite person itself is at the same time always nature . . . the finite person itself as a person is affected by the fate of his nature, since the possibilities of personal existence always rest essentially on the possibilities of nature.' ('Passion and Asceticism', *Investigations* III, 69f [= *Schriften* III, 86ff].)

31. 'Concupiscentia', 369 (= 401).

32. 'Concupiscentia', 365 (= 395).

33. 'Concupiscentia', 369 (= 400).
34. See the basically similar interpretation of Rahner's essay 'The Theology of Power', *Investigations* IV, 391–409 (= *Schriften* IV, 485–508): power and its use are something naturally given to mankind, as God's creature. It is a condition of the possibility for freedom itself, yet it can become the autonomous source of holiness or guilt, like concupiscence.
35. Tallon, 'Personal Becoming', 104ff: 'Rahner's approach . . . has now more clearly emerged as a "personalist" approach.' Yet he adds that, at this early stage, Rahner presented his thought in (what Tallon calls) in*tra*personal categories without advancing to an explicit in*ter*personal way of understanding. However, this seems to us rather a forced understanding of Rahner.
36. *On the Theology of Death*, 35 (= *Zur Theologie des Todes*, 26).
37. *Death*, 40f (= 31f).
38. *Death*, 21ff (= 15ff).
39. *Death*, 42 (= 33).
40. *Death*, 56 (= 45).
41. *Death*, 61f = 49f.
42. *Death*, 77f (= 63).
43. See, among other, 'Passion and Asceticism',*Investigations III*, 58-85 (= *Schriften III*, 73–104), esp. 73 (= 90): totally free self-determination (= person) and imposed total fate (= death of the finite suffering nature of the person) can become one only by the person's turning his total fate into a personal deed by freely saying 'yes' to it. Or, 75 (= 91): passion expresses the necessity of death in man taken as *nature* , whereas asceticism expresses the freedom of death in man taken as a *person*.
44. 'Guilt and its Remission', *Investigations* II, 265–81 (= *Schriften* II, 279–98), esp. 266 (= 282).
45. 'Guilt, 269f (= 284f: 'ein zeichenhaftes In-Erscheinung-Treten einer personalen Schuld').
46. 'Guilt', 276ff (= 290ff).
47. 'Guilt', 267 (= 283).
48. 'Guilt', 278 (= 293).
49. 'Guilt', 279 (= 294).
50. 'Guilt', 269f (= 284).
51. 'Guilt', 269f (= 284).
52. 'Guilt', 272 (= 287).
53. 'Guilt', 274f (= 289).
54. We borrow these terms from Tallon, 'Personal Becoming', 104ff. (See further note 35 above).
55. 'Theological Reflections on Monogenism', *Investigations* I, 229–96 (= *Schriften* I, 253–322).
56. German Idealism was almost obsessed by the idea of evil. Beginning with Kant's notion of radical evil in man, through Hegel's dialectics of lord and slave, to the late Schelling's existentialism, the necessity or inevitability of evil and sin was, so to speak, transcendentally deduced. See the brief summary of this trend in R. Schanne, *Südenfall und Erbsünde in der spekulativen Theologie,* diss. Frankfurt and Bern 1976. On the other hand, it

is a well-known fact that Luther identified original sin with the experience of concupiscence. This view was duly rejected by the Council of Trent (D-S, 1515).

57. See D-S, 3987: 'There are other conjectures about polygenism (as it is called) which leave the faithful no such freedom of debate. Christians cannot lend their support to a theory which involves the existence, after Adam's time, of some earthly race of men, truly so called, who were not descended ultimately from him, or else supposes that Adam was the name given to some group of our primordial ancestors. It does not appear how such views can be reconciled with the doctrine of original sin, as it is guaranteed to us by Scripture and tradition, and proposed to us by the Church. Original sin is the result of a sin committed, in actual historical fact, by an individual man named Adam, and it is a quality native to all of us, only because it has been handed down by descent from him.' (ET from *The Teaching of the Catholic Church*, ed. K. Rahner, H. Roos, and J. Neuner, Cork 1966.)

58. Compare Rahner's first (1954) article on this question, 'Theological Reflections on Monogenism' (see note 55 above), where we find a cautious defence of monogenism in the wake of *Humani Generis*, with his later (1967) 'Original Sin and Evolution' (*Conc* 3 [1967], 30–35) and with his remark under 'Monogenism' in *SM* IV, 106: 'The declaration in *Humani Generis* should not be regarded as the definitive position of the Church.' His still later (1970) article 'Erbsünde und Monogenismus', *Theologie der Erbsünde*, ed. K.H. Weger, Freiburg-im-Breisgau 1970, 176–223, avails itself of this freedom concerning the question.

59. 'Sin of Adam', 252 (= 264).

60. See the concept of protology in *LTK* VIII, 935ff and in *MS* II, esp. 417–20.

61. For the concept of etiology see *LTK* I, 1011–22 and *Hominisation*, 36f (= 38). The biblical story about the origins of mankind is no myth, but a historical etiology which arises from reasoning about man's historical situation.

62. See 'Original Sin', *SM* IV, 330.

63. 'Sin of Adam', 261 (= 273f).

64. 'Sin of Adam', 260f (= 273).

65. 'Sin of Adam', 262 (= 275).

66. 'Sin of Adam', 256 (= 266).

67. 'Sin of Adam', 253 (= 265).

68. *Foundations*, 97 (= *Grundkurs*, 104).

69. *Foundations*, 101 (= 108).

70. *Foundations*, 100 (= 107f).

71. *Foundations*, 104 (= 111).

72. *Foundations*, 105 (= 112).

73. *Foundations*, 105 (= 112).

74. *Foundations*, 105 (= 112).

75. *Foundations*, 39 (= 50).

76. *Foundations*, 41 (= 53).

77. *Foundations*, 107 (= 113f): our italics.

78. *Foundations*, 107 (= 113f).

79. *Foundations*, 109 (= 115).

80. *Foundations*, 109 (= 115).
81. See *Foundations*, 112 (= 118).
82. *Foundations*, 111 (= 117).
83. *Foundations*, 113 (= 119).
84. *Foundations*, 114 (= 120).
85. Jacques Monod, *Chance and Necessity: An Essay on the Natural Philosophy of Modern Biology*, London 1972.
86. F. Nietzsche, 'Unschuld des Werdens', *Erkenntnis, Natur, Mensch* (in *Nachlass in Auswahl* II, ed. Baeumler, Stuttgart, 69).
87. In suggesting this alternative hypothesis we do not intend to set one truth against another. Nor is it our purpose to lean over backwards to accommodate an almost materialistic view about man's origins. However, what leads us to prefer this latter is our overall view on creation hinted at or argued repeatedly on these pages (and in our first volume). Creation is much more a 'letting-be' than a 'forming', a 'making', of this universe by its Creator, who then in his personal care for the created is at the same time the source of providence and grace. But these realities are on another level – on the level of faith – and not simply the coming-to-be of our world. (See section 5.3 in our first volume, *A Theologian in Search of a Philosophy*.).
88. See E. Jüngel's fascinating study, 'Der Gott entsprechende Mensch', *Entsprechungen: Gott-Wahrheit-Mensch*, Munich 1980, 290–317 (esp. 295f).
89. 'Concupiscentia', 362 (= 393).
90. 'Concupiscentia', 369ff (= 400ff).
91. The term 'sin' (and not 'guilt') should, in our contemporary way of speaking, be reserved for an exclusively religious context.
92. It is virtually impossible to give a full survey of either favourable or critical studies of Rahner's theory of death. However, see in particular: R.W. Gleason, 'Toward a Theology of Death', *Tht* 23 (1957), 39–68; P. Glorieux, 'In hora mortis', *MSR* 6 (1949), 185–216; J. Pieper, *Tod und Unsterblichkeit*, Munich 1968; B.J. Callopy, 'Theology and the Darkness of Death', *TS* 39 (1978), 22–57; G. Greshake and G. Lohfink, *Naherwartung, Auferstehung und Unsterblichkeit*, Freiburg-im-Breisgau 1975, esp. 113–48; and K.P. Fischer, 'Der Tod: Treenung von Seele und Leib', *'Wagnis'-Theologie*, 311–38.
93. It's is F. Gaboriau who remarks: 'une première équivoque guette ici nos penseurs: ils confondent le mourant qui est un vivant, avec le mort qu'il n'est pas encore; ils jugent de la mort en elle-même à partir de l'apprehension qu'on a, suivant un degré variable de conscience, le moribond'. (Interview sur la mort avec K. Rahner, Paris 1967, 99.) It should be noted that in later articles Rahner preferred to speak of the *Sterbende* (e.g., in 'Ideas about a Theology of Death', *Investigations* XIII, 169–86 [= *Schriften* X, 181–99], esp. 179f [= 191f]).
94. See especially L. Boros, *The Moment of Truth*, London 1965. See also G. Greshake and G. Lohfink, *Naherwartung*; and K.P. Fischer, 'Der Tod'.
95. See, for example, 'Experience of the Spirit and Existential Commitment', *Investigations* XVI, 24–34 (= *Schriften* XII, 41–53), where Rahner speaks of the possibility of a total existential commitment as 'the free act of a human being in which he has ultimate control over himself.' To this a footnote is

added: 'This notion should not be understood in the sense of a hypothetical decision, as L. Boros proposes in *The Moment of Truth*.... The author has never supported this hypothesis and his conception is much broader. Nothing is stated here about the historical moment in which man actually takes a decision.' (24 n 2 [= 41 n 2].) See also his cautious statement in *MS* V, 466–72; and Fischer, 'Der Tod', 116 (Boros' hypothesis is a 'mystification of dying'!).

96. 'Because only then do we exist in a properly human manner, if we do die all through our life' (*Death* 93 [= 77]; from the epilogue on martyrdom). Or: 'Because death is permanently present in the whole of human life, biologically and existentially, death is the act of freedom' (*Death*, 93 [= 77]). Compare the more cautious tone elsewhere: 'But the dying man, who of his freedom possesses his own life, nevertheless inescapably confronts death with a demand that it must constitute the sum total of his life as an act of freedom and its claim to the absolute dignity of responsibility and of love belonging to it cannot give its assent to a mere empty draining away of life.' ('Ideas for a Theology of Death', 179f [= 192].)

97. F. Gaboriau, *Interview sur la mort*, 54: 'Or la mort est la négation de toutes les modalitées du vivant, y compris de sa substance; et par là force est bien de l'admettre, il n'y a pas d'autre définition, pas d'autre raison ultime au décès qui nous retire de ce monde, que le *non-esse*.'

98. E. Jüngel, *Tod*, Stuttgart 1971, 116: 'Es gibt eine Passivität, ohne die der Mensch nicht mehr menschlich wäre. Dazu gehört, dass man geboren wird ... Dazu gehört, dass man stirbt.' Yet, as he goes on, God the Creator is not inactive at these moments: 'Doch die göttliche Aktivität des *Beendens* Schliesst menschliche Beteiligung aus, weil hier menschilche Aktivität doch nur ein illegitimer Vorgriff wäre.'

99. G. Neuhaus, *Transzendentale Erfahrung als Geschichtsverlust?*, Düsseldorf 1982, esp. 33ff, 83ff, and 137ff.

Notes to Chapter III

1. See such basic studies as: A. Deneffe, 'Geschichte des Wortes "supernaturalis",' *ZKT* 46 (1922), 337–60; and Z. Alszeghy, 'La teologia del' ordine sopranaturale nella scolastica antica', *Greg* 31 (1950), 414–50.

2. It was, to my knowlege, Lonergan who first pointed out the theoretical status of the supernatural. See B. Lonergan, *Grace and Freedom: Operative Grace in the Thought of St Thomas Aquinas*, London 1971, 13–19 and *passim*.

3. J.A.T. Robinson, *Honest to God*, London 1963 (paperback edition), esp. 15ff and 29–32. (Note that Robinson's context is God's transcendence and immanence.)

4. 'Relationship', 298 (=324). 'Concerning the Relationship between Nature and Grace', *Investigations* I, 296–317 (= *Schriften* I, 322–46) is an expanded version of Rahner's first reaction to the *nouvelle théologie* as represented by D. Delahaye (*Orient* 14 [1950], 14ff). See also the good summary of extrinsicism in F. Greiner, *Die Menschlichkeit der Offenbarung*, Munich 1978, esp. 153ff; and see K.H. Weger, *Karl Rahner: An Introduction to his Theology*, London 1980, esp. 104ff; J.P. Kenny, 'Reflections on Human Nature and the Supernatural', *TS* 14 (1953), 280–87; and E.L.

Mascall, *The Openness of Being*, London 1971, esp. 233–45.

5. See J. Splett, 'Natur', *SM* IV, 171f.

6. 'alio vero modo est secundum naturam ipsius: inquantum scilicet *per naturam suam* est capax eius.' (*ST* III, q 9, a 3 ad 3: our italics.)

7. 'impossibile est naturale desiderium esse inane: natura enim nihil facit frustra.' (*SCG* III, c 48.) See also: P. Bastable, *Desire for God*, London 1947; O'Mahoney, *The Desire for God in the Philosophy of St Thomas Aquinas*, London 1929; and J. Alfaro, 'Desiderium Naturale', *LTK* III, 248ff.

8. *ST* I, q 2, a 1 ad 1; II/1, q 62, a 1 corpus; II/2, q 2, a 3 corpus; II/2, q 186, a 3 ad 4; *SCG* III, c 48; etc.

9. Aquinas, *de Veritate*, q 12, a 3 ad 18: 'potentia passiva ad recipiendum lumen propheticum'; *de Virtutibus in Comm*, q 1, a 10 ad 13: 'tota creatura est quaedam oboedientialis potentia'; etc. See also B. Stoeckle, *'Gratia supponit naturam': Geschichte und Analyse eines theologischen Axioms*, Rome 1962, esp. 237ff.

10. See P. Greiner, *Die Menschlichkeit*, 169f. The author's description of obediential potency as incapable of mediation is correct, although his interpretation of it as being 'contra naturam' is exaggerated.

11. On the origin of the expression 'natura pura', see H. de Lubac, *Surnaturel*, Paris 1948. De Lubac appears to attribute it to Cajetan (esp. on pp 113–23). See also the later and revised edition of the same work in ET: *The Mystery of the Supernatural*, London 1967. His view is corrected by J. Alfaro, *Lo Natural y lo Sobrenatural*, Madrid 1952.

12. See the good summary of this line of thought by G. Muschalek, *MS* II, 551ff; P. Smoulders, *SM* I, 135f; and F. Greiner, *Die Menschlichkeit*, 179.

13. H. Mühlen, 'Heilsgeschichtliche Gnadenlehre', *Bilanz der Theologie in 20. Jahrhundert*, Freiburg-im-Breisgau 1970, 148–92 (esp. 164f).

14. See the acts of the Council on the *Constitution 'Dei Filius'* (D-S, 3015: ET in *The Teaching of the Catholic Church*, Cork 1966, 35f). 'Haec est illa hominis elevatio quam . . . doctores catholici recte supernaturalem vocaverunt, ut quae naturae creatae tum exigentias transcendat, ideoque nec meritis nec naturali conditione . . . debita, gratiutum sit dinae largitatis beneficium.' (*Collectio Lacensis* VII, 557f.)

15. H. de Lubac, *Augustinianism and Modern Theology*, London, Dublin and Melbourne 1968, esp. 164–206.

16. 'contre une façon courante de les entendre . . . maintenons que le désire de Dieu est absolu. . . .' (de Lubac, *Surnaturel*, 483f.)

17. See *The Mystery of the Supernatural*, 217 (French original: *Le Mystère du Surnaturel*, Paris 1965, 209).

18. 'Others destroy the gratuitous character of the supernatural order by suggesting that it would be impossible for God to create rational beings without ordaining them for the Beatific Vision and calling them to it.' (ET in *The Teaching of the Catholic Church*, 411: D-S 3891.)

19. See in particular: C. Boyer, 'Nature pure et surnaturel dans le *Surnaturel* de P. de Lubac', *Greg* 28 (1947), 375–95; T. Deman, 'Tentative français pour un renouvellement de la théologie', *Revue de l'Université d'Ottawa* 1950, 129–67; R. Garrigou-Lagrange, 'La nouvelle théologie, où va-t-elle?', *Ang* 23 (1946), 126–45; L. Malevez, 'La gratuité du surnaturel',

NRT 75 (1953), 561-86 and 673-89; H.U. von Balthasar, *Karl Barth*, Cologne 1961, 278-335 (esp. 306ff).

20. See de Lubac, *Supernaturel*, 486-9; and H. Bouillard, 'L'intention fondamentale de M. Blondel et la théologie', *RSR* 36 (1949), 321-402.

21. On account of the tendency to this intrinsicism concerning the supernatural, Rahner could exclaim: 'Hier ist der Punkt wo wir gestehen müssen, dass die Ansicht de Lubacs uns immer nicht einleuchten will' (*Orient* 14 [1950], 14) – i.e., it may be correct, but it needs correction.

22. *Hearers*, 78-82 (= *Hörer*, 100-03).

23. Hearers, 60f (= 79f).

24. 'Potentia Oboedientialis', *SM* V, 65.

25. 'Relationship', 310 and 315 (= 336 and 342).

26. See the similar article 'Über das Verhältnis des Naturgesetzes zur übernatürlichen Gnadenordnung', *Orient* 20 (1956), 8-11. See also E.L. Mascall, *The Openness of Being*, 237f.

27. See in advance F.K. Mayr, *SM* II, 304f; and P. Eicher, *Die anthropologische Wende*, Freiburg-im-Breisgau 1970, 11-22 and 88f.

28. M. Heidegger, *Being and Time*, trans. J. Macquarrie, Oxford 1973, 12 (= *Sein und Zeit*, 33): 'Only the particular Dasein decides it existence, whether it does so by taking hold or by neglecting. The question of existence never gets straightened out except through existing itself. The understanding of oneself which leads *along this way* we call "existentiell".' Yet this existing has structures: 'The question about that structure aims at the analysis . . . of what constitutes existence. The context (*Zusammenhang*) of such structures we call "existentiality". Its analytic has the character of understanding which is not existentiell, but rather *existential*.'

29. 'Because Dasein's characters of Being are defined in terms of existentiality, we call then *existentialia*. These are to be sharply distinguished from what we call *categories* — characteristics of Being for entities whose character is not that of Dasein.' (*Being and Time*, 44 [=70].)

30. See, for example, the cited article in *Orient* 20 (1956), 9: the existential is 'eine dauernde, bleibende Verfasstheit einer endlichen Geistperson, die die Ermöglichung und ontologische Vorherbestimmung eines personalen Handelns ist (das also, was in der freien Tat an der Person ins Spiel kommt).' Similarly, Rahner lists as examples of existentials of human life: corporality, religiosity relatedness to God and Christ, 'to be a cultural being', 'to be at home'. In the same way Christ himself is an existential of human life (see, e.g., *Investigations* V, 191). Under the entry 'Culture' (in his *CTD*) he mentions finitude, threatenedness, sinfulness, ambiguity, openness for the incalculable, the need for redemption a being redeemed: all these are *existentials*.

31. 'Relationship', 311-17 (= 338-45).

32. K.H. Weger, *Karl Rahner*, 86.

33. Weger, *Karl Rahner*, 106f.

34. The systematic structure of Schleiermacher's whole *Christian Faith* could be summed up by the application of this principle: the supernatural becoming natural. See its theoretical foundation in paras. 10 and 13 on Revelation and Redemption; para 88, 4 (p 365) with regard to

Christology; para 117, 2 (p 537) and para 120 (p 553) with regard to the Church and election.

35. See Karl Barth, *Dogmatics in Outline*, London 1966, cc 8 and 9; and *Church Dogmatics* I/1, para 41. For Barth's notion of 'objective redemption' in general, see von Balthasar, *Karl Barth*, 131–48.

36. See J. Oman, *The Natural and the Supernatural*, Cambridge 1931; and *Grace and Personality*, Oxford 1917, esp. chap X.

37. See the good discussion of Rahner's supernatural existential in U. Kuhn, *Natur und Gnade? Untersuchungen zur deutschen katholischen Theologie der Gegenwart*, Berlin 1961, esp. 113–21 and 150–54.

38. See H.U. von Balthasar, *Karl Barth*, 310ff. See also F. Stoeckle, *Gratia supponit naturam'*, 532; 'dass dieses übernatürliche Existential einen recht zwielichtigen Eindruck hinterlässt; es sitzt gewissermassen *zwischen zwei Stühlen*: auf der einen Seite scheint es ... einen auch natürlichen Sachverhalt zu formulieren. Kann denn etwas wirklich 'innerste' Mitte des Menschen als Mensch sein, was im Grunde genommen doch auch fehlen kann, ohne dass dadurch der Mensch als Mensch in Frage gestellt wird.' (Our italics.)

39. See Maréchal's cautious formulations, according to which only a certain 'velleity' is attributed to this dynamism. (In the 1930 essay 'De naturali perfecta beatudinis desiderio', reprinted in *Mélanges Maréchal*, Brussels 1950: see esp. I, 327.)

40. Von Balthasar, *Karl Barth*, 132.

41. E. Gutwenger, 'Natur und Übernatur: Gedanken zu Balthasars Werk über die barthsche Theologie', *ZKT* 75 (1953), 82–97. See also von Balthasar's reply to Gutwenger, 'Der Bergriff der Natur in der Theologie', *ZKT* 75 (1953), 452–61; and Gutwenger's rejoinder, *ZKT* 75 (1953), 461–4 (the supernatural existential is an illegitimate 'Zwischenschaltung', p 462). See also L. Malevez, 'La gratuité du surnaturel', *NRT* 75 (1953), 561–86. De Lubac himself repeats a similar counter-argument in *Mélanges de Lubac* III, 136 n 1. J. Endres suggests that Rahner's theory leads to a certain *progressus ad infinitum* ('Menschliche Natur und übernatürliche Ordnung', *ZFPT* 4 [1957], 3–18). See also J. Motherway, 'Supernatural Existential', *CS* 4 (1965), 79–103 (esp. 96).

42. See F. Greiner, *Die Menschlichkeit*, 185–249 (esp. 197).

43. K.H. Weger, *Karl Rahner*, 168 n 29.

44. Weger, *Karl Rahner*, 88.

45. Weger, *Karl Rahner*, 88.

46. 'Nature and Grace', *Investigations* IV, 169f (=*Schriften* IV, 215).

47. See the adaptation of the Scotist view already in 'Nature', 176 (= 222), viz., that the incarnation of the Logos would have happened even if man had remained in his innocence.

48. See 'Nature', 179 (= 225).

49. 'Nature', 180f (= 228).

50. 'Nature', 180f (= 228).

51. See 'Methodology', *Investigations* XI, 100 (= *Schriften* IX, 112): 'For that which is initially and in the truest sense freely posited by God is precisely the enduring and *existential modality* of grace considered as the offering of

God's self-communication.' See also under 'Transcendental Theology', *SM* VI, 288.

52. 'The "Existential"', *SM* II, 306.
53. 'Existential', 306.
54. F. Greiner, *Die Menschlichkeit*, 186.
55. M. Theunissen, *Der Andere: Studien zur Sozialontologie der Gegenwart*, Berlin 1961: see especially the early part on Husserl and Heidegger. (We are indebted to Greiner for calling our attention to this valuable work.)
56. 'Existential', 306.
57. Reference will be made to this point in section 4.3. below.
58. 'Existential', 306.
59. This view not only comes to the fore in 'Nature', but will be all the more emphasized in his developing thought in Christology. (See our projected third volume, *The Concept of God and Jesus the Christ*.)
60. As we saw in section 3.2 above, the third chapter of *Foundations* gives a special emphasis to this line of thought: the possibility of guilt is organically connected with man's transcendence to the Absolute Mystery. Hence, in the first (theological) short formulation of faith: 'God . . . communicates himself in *forgiving* love to man . . . as man's own fulfilment.' (*Foundations*, 454 [*Grundkurs*, 435f].)
61. *Possibilia* refer to future instances, whilst *futuribilia* refer to instances dependent on free choice; however, these are never taken as *de facto* alternatives, i.e., as things that might have been, but never were. Of these God in his *scientia media* according to the Molinist sense is aware.
62. E. Gutwenger, 'Natur und Übernatur', 89.

Notes to Chapter 4

1. See F. Schupp, 'Zwei Reflexionsstufen: Bermerkungen zu Pluralismus, Probabilität, Theorie und Kritik in der Theologie', *ZKT* 93 (1971), 61–73, esp 68f; and J. Ratzinger, 'Vom Verstehen des Glaubens', *TR* 74 (1978), 176–186, esp. 178f. Schupp's article refers to Rahner's *Zur Reform des Theologiestudiums*, Freibrug-im-Breisgau 1969, and sees the difference between these two levels in a critical approach to systematic thought patterns. Ratzinger, on the other hand, exemplifies the first level of reflection by *Foundations* as an 'abschliessende Reflexion' *after* the main positions are firmly established. To go beyond that to a second level of reflection should in Rahner's case be 'eine Unmöglichkeit'—i.e., Rahner never reaches this second level.
2. 'Some Implications of the Scholastic Conception of Uncreated Grace', *Investigations* I, 315–46 (=*Schriften* I, 347–75) first appeared in *ZKT* 63 (1939), 137–57), and is obviously connected with Rahner's first teaching of the scholastic treatise on grace. For the technical background to this problem, see his bibliographical notes in 'Uncreated', 319 n 1, 320 n 1, 323 n 5, and 333 nn 1 and 2; and 'Grace', *SM* II, 421, where there are summarized bibliographies.
3. 'Grace', 418.
4. For a further discussion of 'quasi-formal' causality see especially: J. Auer, 'Zur Gnadentheologie Rahners', *TR* 60 (1964), 145–56; P. de Letter,

'Divine Quasi-Formal Causality', *ITQ* 30 (1963), 36–47; D. Gelpi, *Life and Light: A Guide to the Theology of Karl Rahner.* New York 1966, esp 47–53 (more on the side of Rahner's theory); W.J. Hill, 'Uncreated Grace: A Critique of Karl Rahner', *Thom* 26/27 (1963), 333–56; and H. Mühlen, *Bilanz der Theologie* III, 148–92.

5. See, by way of anticipation, his 'Disposition', *SM* II, 92f (section 2), which provides a later summary of his view. The foundation for this is doubtless his 1939 article.

6. See 'Uncreated', 333 (= 361).

7. The main Thomistic authority for Rahner is *De Veritate*, q 8, a 3 c: 'Lumen illud intelligibile, per quod intellectus creatus fit in *ultima dispositione* ut coniungatur essentiae divinae ut formae intelligibili non est naturale sed supra naturam.' See other supporting evidence in 'Uncreated', 333 n 2; and see also a good summary of critical reactions to Rahner's interpretation of Aquinas in van der Heijden, *Karl Rahner: Darstellung und Kritik,* Einsiedeln 1973, esp 9–121.

8. Note that the early Rahner definitely considers creation along the lines of efficient causality. But later he applies the same category with some hesitation: 'But usually the concept of creation is too primitive a fashion upon the idea of causality accessible to us in other ways.' ('The Incomprehensibility of God in St Thomas Aquinas', *Investigations* XVI, 244–54, esp. 249.)

9. Compare the original German of 'Uncreated' with the (to our mind) inadequate ET: 'Gott teilt sich selbst mit seinem eigenen Wesen in einer *formalen* Ursächilichkeit dem begnadeten Menschen mit, so dass diese Mitteilung nicht bloss die *Folge* einer effizienten Verursachung der geschaffenen Gnade ist.' (*Schriften* I, 362.) 'God communicates himself to the man to whom grace has been shown in the mode of formal causality.' (*Investigations* I, 334.) One wonders from where the ET's 'has been shown' has crept in.

10. 'The Concept of Mystery in Catholic Theology', *Investigations* IV, 67 (= *Schriften* IV, 91).

11. 'Uncreated', 343–6 (= 372–5).

12. 'Uncreated', 342 (= 371).

13. See 'Uncreated', 344f (= 374f).

14. See further literature about the question of indwelling in *SM* II, 421; H.P. Lyons, 'The Grace of Sonship', *ETL* 27 (1951), 438–66; and M.J. Donnelly, 'Sanctifying Grace and our Union with the Holy Trinity', *TS* 13 (1952), 33–58.

15. Rahner's lecture notes on grace have gone through a number of editions, and it would be well worth the while to study the development—albeit slight—of his thought through these various editions. Here we confine ourselves to the fifth edition (Innsbruck 1959–60) which would appear to come in the middle of this development.

16. A brief reminder: Banezian Thomism teaches that for each salutary act a divine initiative (*praemotio physica*) is required which is infallibly decided in God's predestining decree. Molinism, on the other hand, assumes that God knows the conditionally free acts of man (*per scientiam mediam*) and in

his predestining decree posits the individual in circumstances favouring his free choice for the infallibly better course of action. See 'Grace and Freedom', *SM II*, 424ff; and 'Grace, Systems of',*CTD*, 196f.

17. See 'Gratia', caput V, sectio 1/B under 'Disputatio scholastica de natura gratiae', which ends with the apparently Molinist thesis: 'Efficientiam gratiae Molinismus ope scientiae mediae recte explicat' (132), as prepared by the question whether or not man is in need of grace as a divine aid to arrive at salvation (caput II, sectio 1, 26).

18. Thus, for example, 'Gratia' Theses 22–3 simply repeat 'Uncreated' (195–225); caput VIII, sectio 2 introduces the topic of the formal object of man's engracement concerning the consciousness of grace (328–338).

19. See 'Gratia', caput II, sectio 1, 26–64.

20. 'As a result the systems of grace now have little importance in modern theology.' (*CTD*, 196f.)

21. See 'Freedom', 426: 'In the fundamental transcendental experience of man's orientation towards God as the incomprehensible mystery, both man's independence and his derivation from God are simultaneously given. . . . It culminates in the experience of the independent yet derivative character of freedom . . . i.e., total origin from God in every respect and independent freedom' go together harmoniously.

22. 'Questions of Controversial Theology on Justification', *Investigations* IV, 206f (= *Schriften* IV, 257),

23. See, for example: 'Membership of the Church' (1947), *Investigations* II, 1–88 (= *Schriften* II, 7–94); 'The Christian among Unbelieving Relations' (1954), *Investigations* III, 355–72 (= *Schriften III*, 419–48); 'Heilswille Gottes, Allgemeine' (1959), *LTK* V, 165ff; 'Christianity and the Non-Christian Religions' (1966), *Investigations* X, 52–9 (= *Schriften* VIII, 355–73); 'Anonymous and Explicit Faith' (1974), *Investigations* XVI, 52–9 (= *Schriften* XII, 76–84); 'The One Christ and the Universality of Salvation' (1974), *Investigations* XVI, 195–224 (= *Schriften* VIII, 251–83); and 'Über die Heilsbedeutung nicht christlichen Religionen' (1975), *Schriften* XIII, 341–50 (= *Investigations XVIII*, 288-95).

24. 'Salvific Will' *SM* V, 405–08.

25. 'Salvific Will', 408.

26. The quotations in the text here are from 'Order, III: Supernatural Order', *SM* IV, 297–300. This summary contribution can be regarded as a storehouse of Rahner's ideas concerning the supernatural. By its very nature as a lexicon article, it is not an argued discussion of the topic but rather a straightforward presentation.

27. 'Order', 298.

28. Hans Küng, *Justification: The Doctrine of Karl Barth and Catholic Reflections*, London and New York 1964. See also Rahner's 'Questions of Justification Today', *Grace and Freedom*, London 1969, esp. 95–100.

29. 'Justification', 204 (= 255).

30. 'Justification', 206 (= 257).

31. See Küng, *Justification,* 248f; and 'Justification', 205 (=256).

32. 'Justification', 206 (= 257).

33. 'Justification', 208 (= 260).

34. 'Justification', 210 (= 262).

35. 'Justification', 212 (= 264).

36. See 'The Order of Redemption within the Order of Creation', *The Christian Commitment*, London and New York 1963, 38-74 (originally in *Sendung und Gnade* I, Innsbruck 1959, 51-88). See in advance 'Christology within an Evolutionary View of the World', *Investigations* V, 157-92 (= *Schriften* V, 183-222).

37. 'Justification', 213f (= 265f): our italics, and our own translation for the last sentence.

38. See 'Justification', 217 (= 271).

39. 'Justification', 218 (= 271).

40. See 'Justification', 216 n 18 (= 269, n 18).

41. *Foundations*, 117 (= *Grundkurs*, 123).

42. 'Selbstmitteilung Gottes', *LTK* IX, 627ff.

43. 'Selbstmitteilung Gottes', 627.

44. *Foundations*, 116 (= 122): our italics.

45. *Foundations*, 117 (= 124).

46. *Foundations*, 120 (= 126); *et passim.*

47. *Foundations*, 119 (= 125).

48. *Foundations*, 119 (= 125).

49. *Foundations*, 120 (= 126): our italics.

50. *Foundations*, 120 (= 126).

51. *Foundations*, 123 (= 129).

52. *Foundations*, 123 (= 129).

53. *Foundations*, 123 (= 129).

54. L. Lallement, *Doctrine Spirituelle,* ed. F. Courcel, Paris 1959, 77: 'Nous avons dans notre coeur une vide que toutes les créatures ne saurayent remplir. Il ne peut être rempli que de Dieu.'

55. *Foundations*, 244 (= 130).

56. *Foundations*, 128 (= 139).

57. *Foundations*, 118 (= 124).

58. *Foundations*, 133 (= 138): 'Man never stands before the pure possibility of a previously completely natural freedom, but always before a freedom which has already been freely exercised.'

59. *Foundations*, 129 (= 135). Compare the almost completely parallel categories which Lonergan uses for describing religious experience: 'Being in love with God, as experienced, is being in love in an unrestricted fashion. All love is self-surrender, but being in love with God is being in love without limits or qualifications or conditions or reservations. Just as unrestricted questioning is our capacity for self-transcendence, so being in love in an unrestricted fashion is the proper fulfilment of that capacity. That fulfilment is not the product of our knowledge and choice. On the contrary, it dismantles the horizon in which the love of God will transvalue our values and the eyes of that love will transform our knowing ... This dynamic state is conscious, without being known [compare Rahner: *bewusst*, but not *gewusst*!], it is an experience of mystery.' (B. Lonergan, *Method in Theology*, London 1971, 106.) It is remarkable that authors writing on grace cannot do so without recourse to the analogy of human

love: they are usually, with few exceptions, celibates.

60. See section 4.4.5 below.
61. 'Justification', 127 (= 271).
62. See the lucid summary in the dissertation by J. Truetsch, *SS Trinitatis inhabitatio apud theologos recentiores,* Trent 1948, esp. 107–17.
63. We intend to discuss this topic with respect to Rahner's soteriology in a forthcoming volume.
64. 'Justification', 213 (= 265).
65. *Foundations,* 128 (= 135).
66. *Foundations,* 125f (=132).
67. See 'Justification', 213 (= 265).
68. *Foundations,* 130 (= 136).
69. *Foundations,* 127 (= 133).
70. See section 1.3.b above.
71. See J.B. Lotz 'Die transzendentale Methode, Wesen und Notwendigkeit', *ZKT* 101 (1979), 351–60 (esp. 357f). This article is a controversial review of A. Brunner's *Kant und die Wirklichkeit des Geistigen,* Munich 1978. The debate is about a personalist as opposed to an ontological approach to reality. Whereas Brunner sees our experience of supreme reality as 'personal und *ungegenständlich* [i.e., 'objectless']', Lotz wants to call our experience of an all-embracing Being 'übergegenständlich'. This we can only translate as: 'we can know being as object yet not as an object.' The same is also characteristic of Rahner.
72. See *Foundations,* 128 (= 134).
73. That Rahner in his ontologico-transcendental approach was unable to envisage a dialogal relationship was laid at his door in various forms. See, among others, E. Simons and K. Hecker, *Theologisches Verstehen: Philosophische Prolegomena zu einer theologischen Hermeneutik,* Düsseldorf 1970, esp. 224f. W.J. Hoye (*Die Verfinsterung des Geheimnisses,* Düsseldorf 1979, ep. 69f) comes to a similar conclusion, albeit from another point of view. We shall return to Hoye's book in a later context (our vol. III).
74. See van der Heijden, *Karl Rahner,* 11f, who sums up his main objection in a similar way: 'Es ist nicht ohne weiteres evident, dass Selbstmitteilung Gottes genau dasselbe besagt wie *Seins*-Mitteilung.'
75. See sections 1.3.a and 3.4.d above.
76. See 'Experience of Self and Experience of God', *Investigations* XIII, 125 (= *Schriften* X, 136f). See also 'The Concept of Mystery', *Investigations* IV, 53ff (= *Schriften* IV, 74ff).
77. See *Foundations,* 127 (= 133).
78. Rahner emphasizes that the supernatural order is a personal order, but adds significantly: 'That does not mean that the supernatural order can be reduced merely to a relation between God and man determined simply by the *abstract concept of personality.* For 'personal' and 'constituted by grace' are not identical concepts.' ('Order', 299: our italics.) The point which we are making here is that there is no such thing as a formal or 'abstract concept of personality': person is the very concreteness of a personal relationship.
79. See section 2.5.b. above.

80. See Aristotle, *Categories*, ed. J.L. Ackrill, Oxford 1963, chapter 7 (esp. 22). To be sure, Aristotle says that to the category of 'relation' there is attributed the *minimum* of being. The same category of 'relation' will gain another complexion in the strictly personalist thinking of a Buber, Ebner, or Rosenzweig.

Notes to Chapter 5

1. See our *A Theologian in Search of a Philosophy*, chapter 1 ('The Faith of Karl Rahner').
2. See *A Theologian*, chapter 6 ('Hearers of the Word').
3. *Hearers*, 66f (= *Hörer*[2], 86f).
4. *Hearers*, 66f (= 86).
5. *Hearers*, 71 (= 91).
6. 'For man has always been essentially a listener for a possible revelation from God. That is to say, if this moment of standing before God coincides with the moment of standing before a possible revelation of God, then some sort of revelation does in fact take place. God speaks or is silent. What man essentially hears is the speaking or silence of a free God.' (*Hearers*, 92 [= 115].) Briefly, one is a listener either to the speech or to the *silence* of God, 'because man's listening must reckon equally upon God's silence' (*Hearers*, 174 [= 213f]). Thus the word is always an unmerited grace for us, since 'perceiving the silence of God can also be an answer, made meaningful by listening, because man can become what he must be even through God's silence' (ibid.).
7. Here we prefer to quote the German text: 'Denn einmal ist mit dem Horchen kein tatsächliches Hören notwendig verbunden ... denn das Vernehmen des Schweigens Gottes ist *ebenso eine Antwort*, die das Horchen sinnvoll macht, weil durch das *abweisende Schweigen* Gottes der Mensch zu dem werden kann, was er allerdings notwendig sein muss: persönlicher, endlicher und geschichtlicher Geist *vor* dem persönlicher freien Gott. (*Hörer*[2], 213 [= *Hearers*, 175]: our italics.)
8. See, for example, *Hearers*, 11 n 11; 14 n 12; 20 n 3; 22 n 6; 157 n 4 (with an emphasis on historicality); 9 n 7; 10 n 8; (the supernatural existential); 22 n 6; 73 n 3; 111 n 1; 113 n 3; 116 n 5; 152 n 2; and 158 n 6 (with allusions to transcendental revelation).
9. *Hearers*, 10 n 8 (= 23 n 8).
10. *Hörer*[1] 90 n 1.
11. *Hearers*, 72 (= 91f).
12. See *Grace and Freedom*, London 1969, esp. 230ff (the chapter on the origin of freedom).
13. 'The Theology of Freedom', *Investigations* VI, 181 (= *Schriften* VI, 218).
14. 'History of the World and Salvation History', *Investigations* V, 102f (= *Schriften* V, 120f).
15. 'History', 104f (= 123f).
16. 'By virtue of the grace of Christ (as possibility and obligation), which is at least a constant offer, he [i.e., man the sinner] is always in a Christ-determined situation, whether he has accepted this grace or not.' ('Atheism and Implicit Christianity', *Investigations* IX, 146 [= *Schriften* VIII,

188].) And this is due to man's existent*ial* (but not existent*iell*) 'Christian' position, as based on the radical distinction 'between grace merely offered and grace existent*ielly* offered in faith and love.'

17. 'Revelation, B: Theological Integration', *SM* V, 349f.

18. The origin of this extended essay dates back to a period before the controversy about the *nouvelle théologie*, and was then slightly revised by Rahner: 'Ueber Visionen und verwandte Erscheinungen', *GL* 21 (1948), 179–213; and 'Les révélations privées: quelques remarques théologiques', *RAM* 25 (1949), 506–14.

19. *Visions and Prophecies*, 23f (= *Visionen und Prophezeihungen*, 24).

20. *Visions*, 26 (= 27).

21. *Visions*, 41f, 44f (= 41f, 44f).

22. *Visions*, 80f (= 80f).

23. 'Propheten (iii)', *LTK* VIII, 800.

24. 'Propheten', 800.

25. *Inspiration in the Bible*, London and New York 1961 (ET of *Ueber die Schriftsinspiration*, Freiburg-im-Breisgau 1958).

26. 'The works of the history of redemption are God's in some other higher way than human works of nature. In the latter, God deals with the world; in the former, he enacts his own history in the world. ' (*Inspiration*, 41 [= 49].)

27. *Inspiration*, 65 n 36 (= 70 n 38).

28. 'Integration', 348.

29. *Revelation and Tradition*, London and New York 1966, 13.

30. 'Integration', 348.

31. 'History', 103 (= 123).

32. 'History', 104 (= 124).

33. 'History', 105 (= 124).

34. 'History', 98 (= 116).

35. See 'History', 101 (= 120).

36. See 'History', 104 (= 123).

37. 'History', 105 (= 124). See also 'Prophecy', *SM* V, 110f: 'Transcendental history, being the history of God's universal self-communication in grace, is inconceivable without being consciously objectivated in words, a process which is necessarily the history and mediation of this transcendental revelation itself.'

38. 'History', 107 (= 126). It is important to see the text which follows what we have quoted: 'For the interpreting and revealing word of God which *constitutes* the official and special revelation — and salvation history, as distinct from general salvation — and revelation history, does not occur always and everywhere, but has its special place in time and space within history,' Thus Rahner requires a kind of 'condensation' of certain revelatory events which, as distinct from general salvation history, function as causing (constituting) as well as interpreting other salutary events of history.

39. 'History', 106 (= 125).

40. *Foundations*, 156f (= *Grundkurs*, 160f).

41. *Foundations*, 161 (= 165).

42. Rahner speaks of the Old Testament as 'the interpretation of history as the event of a *dialogical* partnership with God and as a prospective tendency towards an open future.' (*Foundations*, 167 [= 170].)
43. *Foundations,* 169 (= 172).
44. *Foundations,* 170 (= 173).
45. 'Faith, I: Way to Faith', *SM,* 311.
46. 'Faith', 311.
47. 'Faith', 311.
48. 'Faith', 310.
49. In these references we are following Rahner's 'Opportunities of Faith' in *Theses on the Problem of Revelation,* London 1974 (ET of *Chancen des Glaubens,* Freiburg-im-Breisgau 1970). Here (p 83) he adds an important note to the effect that the utterance of salvific words posits also the person who utters them: 'Salvation occurs where the whole person occurs, but it does not occur in the word alone.'
50. 'This entative divinization which is proffered to freedom, *even if it is not freely* accepted in faith, involves a transcendental divinization of man's *fundamental subjective disposition,* the ultimate horizon of man's knowledge and freedom, in the perspective of which he accomplishes his life.' ('Integration', 350: our italics.)
51. The word ... although and because it is a human word, can be word of God (and not only a word about God as produced by God), only if and because it is sustained even as *heard* (a necessary condition for it to be at all) by God himself as principle of hearing and so as heard is not reduced by the creaturely assumptions of human hearing to the powerlessness of a purely human word.' ('Opportunities', 83.) This principle in us, he adds, is the Holy Spirit indwelling man. It is in this sense that he will term man's coming-to-faith as a 'word-event' (*Wortgeschehen*), i.e., 'productive word and not merely the production of word'. (ibid.) In the terminology of Austen, Rahner seems to be speaking of 'performatives'.
52. 'The subjective disposition of the believer must be thought of as distinct from faith and yet as one with it, i.e., in the *a priori* capacity to believe ... *a priori* capacity for revelation ...' ('Integration', 352.)
53. 'Integration', 351: our italics. Compare this passage with its German original: *fides implicita* 'besagt im Grunde nichts anderes als dies, dass aller kategorial ausdrückliche Glaube als solcher ein Ergreifen des *Zeichens* ist, der darum dann wirklich Glaube ist, wenn er das Zeichen ergreift in dem Ergriffen-sein durch das unsagbare Geheimnis der Nähe des sich selbst vergebend mitteilenden Gottes.' (*SM* [German edition] III, 839.)
54. *Foundations,* 172 (= 175).
55. *Foundations,* 171 (= 174).
56. Foundations, 139 (= 144). Compare 'Opportunities', 84 'in this categorial manifestation [i.e., Jesus dead and risen] the word has a unique function and consequently a special nature ... [It] directs this world as a whole to its hoped-for, unexperienced future already breaking through in the risen Christ. But this can appear enduringly only in the *word of promise.*'
57. K. Rahner and W. Thüsing, *Christologie, systematisch und exegetisch,* Freiburg-im-Breisgau 1972, 38: 'In diesem Sinn kann man ruhig and muss

man sagen, dass Jesus in den Glauben seiner Jünger hinein aufersteht . . .'
(i.e., Christ is risen into the faith of his disciples). This whole paragraph is
repeated without alteration in *Grundkurs*, 268 (= *Foundations*, 263). The
same idea is expressed in 'Integration', 351: 'it would follow that the
theology of the act of faith and that of revelation-occurrence are to a large
extent identical. Fundamental theology is, therefore, entirely right from
the point of view of method if it deals with the *analysis fidei* within its own
sphere, on the condition that it does so where faith and the reception of
revelation can still be seen in their original unity. For the transcendental
side of the original reception of revelation and that of faith coincide.'

58. By 'Protestant orthodoxy' we mean the reaction to theological liberalism
within the churches of the Reformation. Its main representative is the so-
called dialectical theology headed by Karl Barth.

59. P. Eicher, *Offenbarung, Prinzip neuzeitlicher Theologie*, Munich 1977, esp.
347–421. In what follows we are in many ways indebted to Eicher's
analysis.

60. We quote here the German text: revelation is to be taken 'als eine Summe
von einzelnen, durch Gottes Autorität garantierten Sätzen über
Sachverhalte, die der menschlichen Erfahrung im Welthorizont von
diesem selbst her unzugänglich sind.' (*Hörer*[2], 187.)

61. See Eicher, *Offenbarung*, 389f, 381f, and 385.

62. See, for example, R. Garrigou-Lagrange, *De Revelatione*, Rome 1929[2], 539:
'credibilitas et iuditium speculativo-practicum credenditatis inveniuntur
non solum in his qui perveniunt ad fidem, sed etiam in his qui cum plena
advertentia committunt peccatum infidelitatis. E contra iuditium
practico-practicum credenditatis non invenitur nisi in his qui ad fidem
perveniunt, et per se requirit aliquod auxilium gratiae.' The author's
polemic is clearly directed against some exponents of contemporary
modernism. See, too, the account of G. Muschalek, *LTK* VIII, 654–7
('Praeambula fidei').

63. Concerning the history of apologetics in Protestant theology, see Avery
Dulles, 'A History of Apologetics', *Theological Resources*, London 1971, esp.
302ff (comparing Roman Catholic and Protestant approaches to
apologetics). For Barth, see 231f. See also H.H. Schrey, 'Apologetik und
Polemik, iii. Syst.-theologisch', *RGG* I, 485–9; and K.G. von Steck and
H.R. Müller-Schulte, 'Apologetik, ii', *TRE* III (1978 edition), 416–22 and
426–8 respectively (giving a short survey of the trends in contemporary
apologetics). Note that all these accounts qualify the statement that
apologetics is rejected *en bloc* by Protestant theology: the English-speaking
apologetes and the work of Paul Tillich are the best counter-examples.

64. This is valid for the first edition of *Hörer* (e.g., 94, 99, 118, etc.).

65. *Foundations*, 171 (= 174), as already quoted in section 5.3 above.

66. See Eicher's remark. 'Warum muss der Mensch, um Mensch zu sein, in
dieser Partikularität der Menschheitsgeschichte das freiheitlich sich
mitteilende Sein selbst vernehmen?' (*Offenbarung*, 283).

67. Read, for example, the tortuous text of 'Integration', 151f.

68. For a wider orientation, see A. Vidler and W. Knox, *The Modernist
Movement in the Roman Church*, Cambridge 1934; and B. Reardon, *Roman*

Catholic Modernism, London 1970, esp. 9–67 (his introduction to the selections). Note, however, that throughout his *Foundations* Rahner is aware of the modernistic danger. See, too, *Investigations* IX, 41f (= *Schriften* VIII, 60).

69. See *Visions.*
70. See *Inspiration.*
71. See Laberthoniere, *Essais de philosophie religieuse,* Paris 1930, esp. xxiv–xxix. See also the concise presentation by B. Reardon, *Liberalism and Tradition: Aspects of Catholic Thought in Nineteenth-Century France,* Cambridge 1975, esp. 243–8.
72. See G. Tyrrell, *External Religion: Its Use and Abuse,* London 1900, esp. 248.
73. *Foundations,* 149 (= 154).
74. See our discussion in section 6.4.a of vol. I: 'Man's striving toward a goal is the way he shares in history and shapes his destiny and is what we call *historicality,* whereas the actual realization of his objective is *historicity.* In this latter sense history is a factor, a coefficient not entirely in the control of our actions. We suffer it or we are challenged by it, we resign to it as inevitable or take it as ground for further action.' Our point is that the 'objectifications' mentioned belong to the first and not to the second category, at least according to Rahner's conception.
75. See H. Fries, *Die katholische Religionsphilosophie der Gegenwart,* Heidelberg 1948, esp. 258.
76. F. Brüngel, 'Erfahrung des Geistes: Rahners Modell der Auseinandersetzung mit Modernismus und Humanismus', *'Wagnis'-Theologie,* ???
77. J. Ratzinger, 'Vom Verstehen des Glaubens', *TR* 74 (1978), 176–86. See further our note 1 to chapter 4 above.
78. For this formulation we are indebted to Eicher, *Offenbarung.* 362.
79. See W. Pannenberg, 'Die Frage nach Gott', *Philosophische Theologie im Schatten des Nihilismus,* ed. J. Salaquard, Berlin 1971, summing up the recent attempts of dealing with revelation and faith in the question and answer scheme (esp. 119–27). See also His 'Weltgeschichte und Heilsgeschichte', *Probleme biblischer Theologie: G. von Rad Festschrift,* ed. H.W. Wolf, Munich 1971, 349–66, esp. 357 n 18. With reference to *Hearers,* Pannenberg uncovers an unwarranted leap from the absolute Being of God to God as free person: 'Mit diesem Sprung überspringt Rahners transzendentale Anthropologie die knonkrete Geshichte . . . um unmittelbar das Resultat dieser Geschichte als Bestandteil einer zeitlos allgemein zu denkenden Struktur des Menschseins zu verankern.'
80. F. Gaboriau, *Le tournant theologique aujord'hui selon K. Rahner,* Paris 1968, esp. 155ff. Compare, however, Gaboriau's work as criticized by P. Eicher, *Die anthropologische Wende,* Freiburg-im-Breisgau 1970, 93–8 and 413.
81. E. Simon, *Philosophie der Offenbarung: Auseinandersetzung mit K. Rahner,* Mainz 1966. Simon's basic dilemma concerning Rahner's view is this: 'Ist die Geistestranszendenz wesennotwendig Offenbarkeit Gottes, dann is *freie* Offenbarung nicht mehr möglich, weil Gott als Entsprechung der Transzendenz der Offenbarung seiner selbst immer schon schuldig wäre. Ist jedoch die Offenbarung Gottes nicht das Wesen der Geisttranszendenz,

dann ist der Mensch ursprünglich nicht auf Gott hingeordnet.' (43.) But see also B. Puntel's criticism of Simon's own personalistic solution (59ff) in his review of the work in *PJ* 76 (1968), 203–11.

82. W. Pannenberg, *Die Frage nach Gott*, 238: 'die Fraglichkeit des Menschen [Wird] erst von der Antwort [Gottes] her aufgedeckt . . . im christlichen Glauben lebt die menschliche Frage von einem *Widerfahrnis* göttlicher Antwort.'

83. P. Eicher, *Offenbarung*, 368, where he ends with the question: 'Feiert hier die *Apokalypse der deutschen Seele* den Triumph ihrer Selbstoffenbarung?' — a reference, no doubt, to von Balthasar's earlier work with the same title.

84. 'Faith between Rationality and Emotion', *Investigations* XVI, 60-68, esp. 70.

85. Concerning this *novum* character of Christian revelation, see J. Ratzinger, 'Heil und Geschichte', *WW* 25 (1970), 3–14. Ratzinger criticizes the concept of revelation in *Hearers*: 'Das eigentliche Problem liegt . . . in der Reduktion des Christlichen auf das Reflex-Werden des allgemein Gelebten. . . . Im Christentum tritt gar nicht mehr wirklich *von aussen her* etwas uns zu, was wir nur als *das Neue*, aus uns selbst nicht deduzierende empfangen können, sondern es wird nur gegenständlich, was immer schon Horizont unseres Denkens und Reflektierens ist.' (11.) In Ratzinger's conception, revelation is not the linear transcendence of reflection, but a 'von-sich-selbst-Weggenommenwerden'.

86. 'Faith between Rationality and Emotion', 70: 'Christian faith is not of an arbitrary sort, but rather the one in which human rationality, set free in its very roots for the direct presence of God, is mediated to itself.'

87. 'Faith between Rationality and Emotion', 72: 'The Christian message as it develops in revelation and faith may be *secondary*, but this does not mean that the explicit, moral obligation of faith becomes unnecessary.'

88. See section 6.4.a of our first volume.

89. It was often emphasized that undue insistence on the certainty of faith can, on the one hand, degenerate into an empty ritualism and sectarianism, or, on the other hand, can — from the imagined certainty of a youthful conviction — lead to a later sacrificing of the whole of one's faith. We are inclined rather to speak of a 'security' in faith — a word which might be rendered in German as 'Geborgenheit'.

90. See section 2.5. c above.

91. See 'History', 105 (= 124).

92. See section 5.2.2 above.

93. 'Faith between Rationality and Emotion', 65.

94. 'Faith between Rationality and Emotion', 65.

Notes to the Epilogue

1. *Foundations*, 39 (= *Grundkurs*, 50).

2. This indeed, in more detail, will be the central topic of our concluding volume IV.

Bibliography

Bibliography

Only works cited in the text and notes are included in this bibliography. Section A comprises works by Karl Rahner himself and Section B works by all other authorities.

The full titles of periodicals and certain other works, normally abbreviated in the bibliography here, are given in the Table of Abbreviations above.

A. *Works by Karl Rahner*

'Anonymous and Explicit Faith', *Investigations* XVI, 52–9 (= *Schriften* XII, 76–84).

'Atheism and Implicit Christianity', *Investigations* IX, 146 (= *Schriften* VII, 188).

'Bermerkungen zu B.J.F. Lonergans Aufsatz "Functional Specialities in Theology"', *Greg* 51 (1979), 537.40.

'Christian among Unbelieving Nations, The', *Investigations* III, 355–72 (= *Schriften* III, 419–48).

Christian Commitment, The, London and New York 1963 (ET of *Sendung und Gnade* I, q.v.).

'Christian Humanism, the Experiment with Man and Genetic Manipulation', *Investigations* IX, 187–252 (= *Schriften* VIII, 239–321).

'Christianity and the New Man', *Investigations* V, 135–56 (= *Schriften* V, 159–82).

'Christianity and the Non-Christian Religions', *Investigations* X, 52–9 (= *Schriften* VIII, 355–73).

Christologie, systematisch und exegetisch (with W. Thüsing), Freiburg-im-Breisgau 1972.

'Christology in the Setting of Modern Man's Understanding of himself and of his World', *Investigations* XI, 215–29 (= *Schriften* IX, 227–41).

'Christology within an Evolutionary View of the World', *Investigations* V, 157–92 (= *Schriften* V, 183–221).

'Concept of Mystery in Catholic Theology, The', *Investigations* IV, 36–73 (= *Schriften* IV, 51–99). Concerning the Relationship between Nature and Grace', *Investigations* I, 296–317 (= *Schriften* I, 322–46).

'Current Problems in Christology', *Investigations* I, 165ff (= *Schriften* I, 185ff).

De gratia Christi (polycopied lecture notes), Innsbruck 1959/60[5].

'Dignity and Freedom of Man, The', *Investigations* II, 235–64 (= *Schriften* II, 247–78).

'Disposition', *SM* II, 92f.

'Erbsünde und Monogenismus', *Theologie der Erbsünde*, ed. K.H. Weger, Freiburg-im-Breisgau 1970, 176–223.

'Evolution, II: Theological', *SM* II, 289–97.

' "Existential", The', *SM* II, 304–06.

'Experience of Self and Experience of God', *Investigations* XIII, 125ff (= *Schriften* X, 136ff).

'Experience of the Spirit and Existential Commitment', *Investigations* XVI, 24–34 (= *Schriften* XII, 41–53).

'Faith, I: Way to Faith', *SM* II, 310ff.

'Faith between Rationality and Emotion', *Investigations* XVI, 60–78 (= *Schriften* XII).

Foundations of Christian Faith, London and New York 1978 (ET of *Grundkurs des Glaubens: Einführung in den Begriff des Christentums*, q.v.).

'Freedom in the Church', *Investigations* II, 89–108 (= *Schriften* II, 95–114).

Free Speech in the Church, London 1969.

Gefahren des heutigen Katholizismus, Einsiedeln 1950.

'Grace', *SM* II, 415–24.

'Grace and Freedom', *SM* II, 424–7.

'Grace, Systems of', *CTD* 196f.

'Guilt and its Remission: the Borderland between Theology and Psychotherapy', *Investigations* II, 265–81 (= *Schriften* II, 279–98).

Grundkurs des Glaubens: Einführung in den Begriff des Christentums, Freiburg-im-Breisgau 1976 (ET: *Foundations of Christian Faith*, q.v.).

Hearers of the Word, trs. R. Walls, M. Richards, and P. Bourne, London, Sydney, and New York 1969 (ET of *Hörer des Wortes*[2], q.v.).

'Heilswille Gottes, Allgemeine', *LTK* V, 165ff.

'History of the World and Salvation History', *Investigations* V, 97–114 (= *Schriften* V, 115–36).

Hominisation: the Evolutionary Origin of Man as a Theological Problem, London and New York 1966 (ET of *Das Problem der Hominisation*, q.v.).

Hörers des Wortes, Munich 1940[1]; and (with J.B. Metz) Munich 1963[2] (ET *Hearers of the Word*, q.v.).

'Ideas about a Theology of Death', *Investigations* XIII, 169–80 (= *Schriften* X, 181–99).

'Ideology and Christianity: Marxist Utopia and the Christian Future of Man', *Investigations* VI, 43–70 (= *Schriften* VI, 56–90).

'Incarnation', *SM* III, 116ff.

Inspiration in the Bible, London and New York 1961 (ET of *Ueber die Schriftsinspiration*, q.v.).

'Institution and Freedom', *Investigations* XIII, 105–21 (= *Schriften* X, 115–32).

'Investigation of the Incomprehensibility of God in St Thomas Aquinas, An', *Investigations* XVI, 244–54 (= *Schriften*, XII, 306–19).

'Man, iii: theological', *SM* III, 365–70.

Meditations on Priestly Life, London and New York 1973.

'Membership of the Church', *Investigations* II, 1–88 (= *Schriften* II, 7–94).

'Monogenism', *SM* IV, 106.

'Nature and Grace', *Investigations* IV, 165–88 (= *Schriften* IV, 209–36).

Offenbarung und Ueberlieferung (with J. Ratzinger), Freiburg-im-Breisgau 19XX (ET *Revelation and Tradition*, q.v.).

On the Theology of Death, London and New York 1961 (ET of *Zur Theologie des Todes*, q.v.).

'On the Theology of the Incarnation', *Investigations* IV, 105–20 (= *Schriften* IV, 137–56).

'One Christ and the Universality of Salvation, The', *Investigations* XVI, 195–224 (= *Schriften* VIII, 251–83).

'Opportunities of Faith', *Theses on the Problem of Revelation*, London 1974 (ET of *Chancen des Glaubens*, Freiburg-im-Breisgau 1970).

'Order, iii: Supernatural Order', *SM* IV, 297–300.

'Original Sin', *SM* IV, 323–33.

'Original Sin and Evolution', *Conc* 3 (1967), 303–35.

'Passion and Asceticism', *Investigations* III, 69f (= Schriften III, 86f).

'Potentia oboedientialis', *SM* V, 65f.

'Philosophy and Philosophising in Theology', *Investigations* IX, 46–63 (= *Schriften* VIII, 66–87).

'Philosophy and Theology', *Investigations* VI, 71–81 (= *Schriften* VI, 71–81).

'Pluralism in Theology and the Unity of the Creed in the Church', *Investigations* XI, 3–25 (= *Schriften* IX, 11–35).

Problem der Hominisation, Das, Freiburg-im-Breisgau 1961 (ET *Hominisation*, q.v.).

'Prophecy', *SM* V, 110f.

'Propheten (iii)', *LTK* VIII, 800.

'Questions of Controversial Theology on Justification', *Investigations* IV, 189–225 (= *Schriften* IV, 237–71).

'Questions of Justification Today', *Grace and Freedom*, ed. B. Lonergan (?), London 1969.

'Reflections on Methodology in Theology', *Investigations* XI, 68–114 (= *Schriften* IX, 79–126).

'Relationship between Theology and the Contemporary Sciences, The', *Investigations* XIII, 95 (= *Schriften* X, 105).

Revelation and Tradition, London and New York 1966 (ET of *Offenbarung und Ueberlieferung*, q.v.).

'Revelation, B: Theological Integration', (*SM* V, 348–55 and 358f.

'revelations privess, Les: quelques remarques theologiques', *RAM* 25 (1949), 506–14.

Sacramentum Mundi (ed. with C. Ernst and K. Smyth), 6 vols., London and New York 1968–70.

'Salvific Will', *SM* V, 405–08.

Schriften für Theologie, Einsiedeln 1957ff, 20 vols. (ET *Theological Investigations*, q.v.).

'Selbstmitteilung Gottes', *LTK* IX, 627ff.

Sendung und Gnade I, Innsbruck 1959 (ET *The Christian Commitment*, q.v.).

'Sin of Adam', *Investigations* XI, 247–62 (= *Schriften* IX, 259–75).

'Some Implications of the Scholastic Concept of Uncreated Grace', *Investigations* I, 315–46 (= *Schriften* I, 347–75).

'Sünde', *LTK* IX, 1177–81.

Teaching of the Catholic Church, The, (ed. with H. Roos and J. Neuner), Cork 1966.

'Theological Concept of Concupiscentia, The', *Investigations* I, 347–82 (= *Schriften* I, 377–414).

'Theological Reflections on Monogenism', *Investigations* I, 229–96 (= *Schriften* I, 253–322).

Theological Investigations, London, Baltimore, and New York, 1961ff 20 vols. (ET of *Schriften für Theologie*, q.v.).

'Theological Reflections on the Problem of Secularisation, Practical Theology and Social Work in the Church, and the Peace of God and the Peace of the World', *Investigations* X, 318–88 (= *Schriften* VIII, 637–707).

'Theology and Anthropology', *Investigations* IX, 28–45 (= *Schriften* VIII, 43–65).

'Theology as Engaged in an Interdisciplinary Dialogue with the Sciences', *Investigations* XIII, 90 (= *Schriften* X, 99).

'Theology of Being, The', *Investigations* VI, 184 (= *Schriften* VI, 222).

'Theology of Freedom, The', *Investigations* VI, 178–96 (= *Schriften* VI, 215–37).

'Theology of Power, The', *Investigations* IV, 391–409 (= *Schriften* IV, 485–508).

'Thoughts on the Possibility of Belief Today', *Investigations* V, 12ff (= *Schriften* V, 21ff).

'Transcendental Theology', *SM* VI, 287-9.

'Über die Heilbedeutung nicht christlichen Religionen', *Schriften* XIII, 341-50.

Über die Schriftsinspiration, Freiburg-im-Breisgau 1958 (ET *Inspiration in the Bible*, q.v.).

'Über Visionen und verwandte Erscheinungen', *GL* 21 (1948), 179-213.

'Unity of Spirit and Matter in the Christian Understanding of Faith, The', *Investigations* VI, 153-77 (= *Schriften* VI, 185-214).

Visionen und Prophezeihungen, Freiburg-im-Breisgau 1960 (ET *Visions and Prophecies*, q.v.).

Visions and Prophecies, London and New York 1963 (ET of *Visionen und Prophezeihungen*, q.v.).

Zur Reform des Theologiestudiums, Freiburg-im-Breisgau 1969.

Zur Theolgie des Todes, Freiburg-im-Breisgau 1958 (ET *On the Theology of Death*, q.v.).

B. *Works by other authorities*

ALFARO, J., '*Desiderium naturale*', *LTK* III, 248ff.

—, *Lo Natural y lo Sobrenatural*, Madrid 1952.

ALSZEGHY, Z., 'La teologia del' ordine sopranaturale nella scolastica antica', *Greg* 31 (1950), 414-50.

AQUINAS, St Thomas, *Quaestiones disputatae de veritate*.

—, *Quaestiones disputatae de virtutibus in communi*.

—, *Summa contra Gentiles*.

—, *Summa theologiae*, XII (ET London 1968).

ARISTOTLE, *Categories*, ed. J.L. Ackrill, Oxford 1963.

AURER, J., 'Zur Gnadentheologie Rahner's, *TR* 60 (1964), 145-56.

BALTHASAR, H.U. von, *Cordula, oder der Ernsfall*, Einsideln 1966.

—, 'Begriff der Natur in der Theologie, Die', *ZKT* 75 (1953), 452-61.

—, *Karl Barth*, Cologne 1961.

—, *Love Alone: the Way of Revelation*, London and New York 1968.

BARTH, K., *Church Dogmatics*, Edinburgh 1960ff.

—, *Dogmatics in Outline*, London 1966.

—, 'Rudolf Bultmann: An Attempt to Understand him', *Kerygma and Myth* II, London 1972, 83–132.

—, *Schleiermacher Auswahl*, Munich 1968.

BASTABLE, P., *Desire for God*, London 1947.

BOROS, L., *The Moment of Truth*, London and New York 1965.

BOUILLARD, H., 'L'intention fondamentale de M. Blondel et la théologie', *RSR* 36 (1949), 321–402.

BOYER, C., 'Nature pure et surnaturel dans le *Surnaturel* de P. de Lubac', *Greg* 28 (1947), 375–95.

BRUENGEL, F., 'Erfahrung des Geistes: Rahners Modell der Auseinandersetzung mit Modernismus und Humanismus', *'Wagnis'-Theologie*, ed. H. Vorgrimler (q.v.).

BRUNNER, A., *Kant und die Wirklichkeit des Geistigen*, Munich 1978.

BRUNNER, E., *Die Mystik und das Wort: Der Gegensatz zwischen modernen Religionsauffassung und christlichen Glauben dargestellt an der Theologie von Schleiermacher*, Tübingen 1928.

CALLOPY, B.J., 'Theology and the Darkness of Death', *TS* 39 (1978), 22–57.

DEMAN, T., 'Tentative francais pour un renouvellement de la theologie', *Revue de l'Universite d'Ottawa* 1950, 129–67.

DENEFFE, A., 'Geschichte des Wortes "supernaturalis"', *ZKT* 42 (1922), 337–60.

DONCEEL, J., 'Causality and Evolution: a Survey of some Neoscholastic Theories', *NS* 39 (1967), 541–55.

DONNELLY, M.J., 'Sanctifying Grace and our Union with the Holy Trinity', *TS* 13 (1952), 33–58.

DULLES, A., 'A History of Apologetics', *Theological Resources*, London 1971, 302ff.

EICHER, P., *Die anthropologische Wende: K. Rahners philosophischer Weg vom Wesen des Menschen zur personalen Existenz*, Freiburg-im-Breisgau 1970.

—, *Offenbarung: Prinzip neuzeitlicher Theologie*, Munich 1977.

—, 'Wo der Mensche an das Geheimnis grenzt: Die mystagogische Struktur der Theologie Karl Rahners', *ZKT* 89 (1967), 159–70.

ENDRES, J., 'Menschliche Natur und übernatürliche Ordnung', *ZFPT* 4 (1957), 3–18.

FISCHER, K.P., *Der Mensch als Geheimnis: Die Anthropologie K. Rahners*, Freiburg-im-Breisgau 1974.

—, 'Der Tod: Trennung von Seele und Leib', *'Wagnis'-Theologie*, ed. H. Vorgrimler (q.v.), 311–38.

FRIES, H., *Die katholische Religionsphilosophie der Gegenwart*, Heidelberg 1948.

—, 'Theologische Methode bei J.H. Newman und Karl Rahner', *Cath* 33 1976), 159–70.

FUESSEL, K., 'Die Wahrheitsanspruch dogmatischer, Aussagen: Ein Beitrag zur theologischen Wissenschaftstheorie', *'Wagnis'-Theologie*, ed. H. Vorgrimler (q.v.), 199–212.

GABORIAU, F., *Interview sur la mort avec Karl Rahner*, Paris 1967.

—, *Le tournant théologique aujourd'hui selon Karl Rahner*, Paris 1968.

GARRIGOU-LAGRANGE, R., *De revelatione*, Rome 1929².

—, 'La nouvelle théologie, où va-t-elle?', *Ang* 23 (1946), 126–45.

GELPI, D., *Life and Light: A Guide to the Theology of Karl Rahner*, New York 1966.

GLEASON, R.W., 'Toward a Theology of Death', *Tht* 23 (1957) 39–68.

GLORIEUX, P., 'In hora mortis', *MSR* 6 (1949), 185–216.

GREINER, F., *Die Menschlichkeit der Offenbarung*, Munich 1978.

GRESHAKE, G., and G. Lohfink, *Naherwartung: Auferstehung und Unsterblichkeit*, Freiburg-im-Breisgau 1975.

GUTWENGER, E., 'Natur und Uebernatur: Gedanken zu Balthasars Wek über die bartsche Theologie' *ZKT* 75 (1953), 82–97 (and 452–61).

HEIDEGGER, M., *Being and Time*, trs. J. Macquarrie, Oxford 1975³ (ET of *Sein und Zeit*, Halle 1931³).

HEYDEN, G., van der, *Karl Rahner: Darstellung und Kritik*, Einsiedeln 1973.

HILL, W.J., 'Uncreated Grace: A Critique of Karl Rahner', *Thom* 26/27 (1963), 333–56.

HOYE, W.J., *Die Verfinsterung des Geheimnisses*, Düsseldorf 1979.

JUENGEL, E., 'Der Gott entsprechende Mensche', *Entsprechungen:*

Gott-Wahrheit-Mensche, Munich 1980, 290–317.

—, *Tod*, Stuttgart, 1971.

KENNY, J.P., 'The Problem of Concupiscence: A Recent Theory of Prof. K. Rahner', *ACR* 29 (1952), 290–304 and 30 (1953), 23–32.

—, 'Reflections on Human Nature and the Supernatural' *TS* 14 (1953), 280–87.

KUENG, H., *Justification: The Doctrine of Karl Barth and Catholic Reflections*, London and New York 1964.

KUHN, U., *Natur und Gnade?*, Berlin 1961.

LABERTHONNIERE, L., *Essais de philosophie religieuse*, Paris 1930.

LALLEMENT, L., *Doctrine spirituelle*, ed. F. Courcel, Paris 1959.

LETTER, P. de, 'Divine Quasi-Formal Causality', *ITQ* 30 (1963), 36–47.

LONERGAN, B., 'Functional Specialities in Theology', *Greg* 50 (1969), 485–505.

—, *Grace and Freedom*, London 1971.

—, *Method in Theology*, London 1972.

LOTZ, J.B., 'Die transzendentale Methode, Wesen und Notwendigkeit', *ZKT* 101 (1979), 351–60.

LUBAC, H. de, *Augustinianism and Modern Theology*, London, Dublin and Melbourne 1968.

—, *Mélanges de Lubac* III.

—, *The Mystery of the Supernatural*, London 1967 (ET of *Le Mystère du surnaturel*, Paris 1965²).

LYONS, H.P., 'The Grace of Sonship', *ETL* 27 (1951), 438–66.

MALEVEZ, L., 'Le gratuité du surnaturel', *NRT* 75 (1953), 561–86 and 673–89.

MARECHAL, ., 'De naturali perfectae beatudinis desiderio', reprinted in *Mélanges Maréchal*, Brussels 1950.

MASCALL, E.L., *The Openness of Being: Natural Theology Today*, London 1971.

MAYR, F.K., "The Existential", *SM* II, 304ff.

MONOD, J., *Chance and Necessity: An Essay on the Natural Philosophy of Modern Biology*, London 1972.

MOTHERWAY, J., 'Supernatural Existential', *CS* 4 (1965), 79–103.

MUEHLEN, H., 'Heilsgeschichtliche Gnadenlehre', *Bilanze der Theologie in 20. Jahrhundert*, Freiburg-im-Breisgau 1970, 148.92.

MUSCHALEK, G., *MS* II, 551ff.

NEUHAUS, G., *Transzendentale Erfahrung als Geschichtsverlust?*, Düsseldorf 1982.

NEWMAN, J.H., *On the Development of Christian Doctrine*.

NIEBUHR, R., *Schleiermacher on Christ and Religion*, London and New York 1964.

NIETZSCHE, F., 'Unschuld des Werdens', *Erkenntnis, Natur, Mensch* (in *Nachlass in Auswahl* II, ed Baeumler, Stuttgart 19XX).

O'MAHONEY, M., *The Desire for God in the Philosophy of St Thomas Aquinas*, London 1929.

OMAN, J., *The Natural and the Supernatural*, Cambridge 1931.

PANNENBER, W., 'Die Frage nach Gott', *Philosophische Theologie im Schatten des Nihilismus*, ed. J. Salaquard, Berlin 1971, 119–27.

—, 'Weltgeschichte und Heilsgeschichte', *Probleme biblischer Theologie: G. von Rad Festschrift*, ed. H.W. Wolf, Munich 1971, 349–66.

PERINI, G., 'Pluralismo teologico e unita della fede: a proposito della tema di K. Rahner', *DC* 22 (1979), 135–89.

PEUKERT, H., *Wissenschaftstheorie und fundamentale Theologie*, Düsseldorf 1976.

PIEPER, J., *Tod und Unsterblichkeit*, Munich 1968.

PIUS XII, Pope, *Humani generis* (in *AAS* 42 [1950], 561ff).

RATZINGER, J., 'Heil und Geschichte', *WW* 25 (1970), 3–14.

—, 'Vom Verstehen des Glaubens', *TR* 74 (1978), 176–86 (review of K. Rahner, Grundkurs des Glaubens [q.v.]).

REARDON, B., *Liberalism and Tradition: Aspects of Catholic Thought in Nineteenth-Century France*, Cambridge 1975.

—, *Roman Catholic Modernism*, London 1970.

ROBERTS, L., *The Achievement of Karl Rahner*, New York 1967.

—, 'The Collision of Rahner and Balthasar', *Continuum* 5 (1968), 753–7.

ROBINSON, J.A.T., *Honest to God*, London 1963².

RUPP, E., *Zur Kritik der transzendentalen und analytischen Wissenschaftstheorie*, Berlin 1972/Wiesbaden 1973.

SCHANNE, R., *Sündenfall und Erbsünde in der spekulativen Theologie*, Frankfurt and Bern 1976 (dissertation).

—, *The Christian Faith*, Edinburgh 1968².

SCHREY, H.H., 'Apologetik und Poelmik, ii. Syst.-theologisch', *RGG* I, 485-9.

SCHUPP, F., 'Zwei Reflexionsstufen: Bermerkungen zu Pluralismus, Probabilität, Theorie und Kritik in der Theologie', *ZKT* 93 (1971), 61-73.

SIMONS, E., *Philosophie der Offenbarung: Auseinandersetzung mit K. Rahner*, Stuttgart, Berlin and Mainz (?????) 1966.

—, and E. Hecker, *Theologisches Verstehen: Philosophische Prolegomena zu einer theologischen Hermeneutik*, Düsseldorf 19XX.

SMULDERS, P., 'Baianism', *SM* I, 135ff.

SPLETT, J., 'Natur' *SM* IV, 171f.

SPRECK, J., *Karl Rahners theologische Anthropologie*, Munich 1967.

STECK, K.G. von, and H.R. Müller-Schulte, 'Apologetik, ii', *TRE* 1978, XXX-XX.

STOECKLE, B., *'Gratia supponit naturam': Geschichte und Analyse eines theologischen Axioms*, Rome 1962.

SURLIS, P., 'Rahner and Lonergan on Method in Theology', *ITQ* 38 (1971), 187-201 and 39 (1972), 23-42.

TALLON, A., 'Personal Becoming: Karl Rahner's Christian Anthropology', *Thom* 43 (1979), 7-177.

THEUNISSEN, M., *Der Andere: Studien zur Sozialontologie der Gegenwart*, Berlin 1961.

TILLICH, P., *Systematic Theology*, London and Chicago 1953¹ and 1960².

TRUETSCH, J., *SS Trinitatis inhabitatio apud theologos recentiores*, Trent 1948.

TYRRELL, G., *External Religion: Its Use and Abuse*, London 1900.

VIDLER, A., and W. Knox, *The Modernist Movement in the Roman Church*, Cambridge 1934.

VORGRIMIER, H. (ed.), *Geist in Welt: Festgabe für Karl Rahner*, 2 vols., Freiburg-im-Breisgau 1969.

—, (ed.), *'Wagnis'-Theologie: Erfahrungen mit der Theologie K. Rahners*, Freiburg-im-Breisgau 1979.

WEGER, K.H., *Karl Rahner: An Introduction to his Theology*, London 1980.